The Kingdom of New Mexico

Its Colonization
and
The Story of El Rancho de las Golondrinas

The Kingdom of New Mexico

Its Colonization
and
The Story of El Rancho de las Golondrinas

Shirley Barnes

Sunstone Press
SANTA FE

© 2012 by Paulette D. Dubickas
All Rights Reserved.

No part of this book may be reproduced in any form or by any electronic or mechanical means including information storage and retrieval systems without permission in writing from the publisher, except by a reviewer who may quote brief passages in a review.

Sunstone books may be purchased for educational, business, or sales promotional use. For information please write: Special Markets Department, Sunstone Press, P.O. Box 2321, Santa Fe, New Mexico 87504-2321.

Book and Cover design › Vicki Ahl
Body typeface › Constantia
Printed on acid-free paper

Library of Congress Cataloging-in-Publication Data

Barnes, Shirley, 1927-
  The Kingdom of New Mexico : its colonization and the story of El Rancho de las Golondrinas / by Shirley Barnes.
       pages cm
  Includes bibliographical references and index.
  ISBN 978-0-86534-886-8 (softcover : alk. paper)
  1. New Mexico--History--To 1848. 2. Spain--Colonies--America. 3. Rancho de las Golondrinas (N.M.)--History. I. Title.
  F799.B35 2012
  972'.01--dc23
                                    2012024537

WWW.SUNSTONEPRESS.COM
SUNSTONE PRESS / POST OFFICE BOX 2321 / SANTA FE, NM 87504-2321 /USA
(505) 988-4418 / ORDERS ONLY (800) 243-5644 / FAX (505) 988-1025

To Benjamin Keen

Contents

Author's Note .. 9
Preface .. 10
Introduction .. 13

1 Forerunners in the Río Grande Valley .. 15

The Seven Cities of Cíbola / 15
The Francisco Vásquez de Coronado Entrada / 16
Ancestral Puebloans / 19
Indian Nomads / 21

2 The Reign of Juan de Oñate and the Two Majesties .. 23

The Oñate Entrada / 23
Oñate as Governor / 30
The Two Majesties / 36

3 Revolt and Re-conquest .. 40

Popé and the Expulsion / 40
The Vargas Entrada / 45

4 El Rancho de las Golondrinas .. 57

Miguel Vega y Coca, Progenitor / 57
A Paraje / 64
The Casa Mayor and Baca House / 71

5 Threats from the East .. 83

The Comanche / 83
Juan Bautista de Anza / 87
Trade Fairs and Cautivos / 90

6 Everyday Life in Ciénega Valley .. 96

Transformation in Isolation / 96
Land and Water / 99
Agriculture and Husbandry / 104

7 The Colonial Family in Transition .. 111

Honor and Marriage / 111
The Changing Role of Women / 113

8 Faith of their Fathers .. 117

Children of the Medieval Church / 117
The Penitentes / 129
Our Lady of Guadalupe / 140
The Art of the Santero / 142

9 The Emergence of New Mexican Society and Culture .. 145

Mexican Independence / 145
Law and Order / 147
Fashions / 152
Schools and Literacy / 153
Curanderas / 159

10 Doing Business on the Santa Fe Trail .. 166

El Camino Real de Tierra Adentro / 166
The Santa Fe Trail / 170
Trappers and Ciboleros / 178

11 Folkways of New Mexico .. 182

Oral Traditions / 182
Dichos and Proverbs / 186
Witchcraft / 187
Fiestas, Folk Dramas, and Morality Plays / 192

12 Rites of Passage .. 202

The Early Years / 202
The Sacrament of Marriage / 205
The End of Life / 209

13 The Day of the Yankee .. 211

The Republic of Texas / 211
The Mexican-American War / 212
The American Civil War / 220
Post American Civil War / 226

14 The Long and Painful Road to Statehood .. 229

Padre Martínez and Bishop Lamy / 229
Education and Statehood / 233
The Coming of the Railroad / 236
The Twentieth Century / 239
The Living History Museum / 240
Special Programming / 249
La Ciénega Valley and Emotional Ties / 252

Epilogue .. 257

Appendix I Provenance of Las Golondrinas Historic Buildings .. 263

Appendix II Motion Pictures Filmed at Las Golondrinas .. 267

Glossary .. 269

Bibliography .. 275

Index .. 283

Author's Note

Information unique to La Ciénega Valley and to El Rancho de las Golondrinas appears in a box in the text.

Most oral history anecdotes included were collected in 1991–1992 by Louann Jordan, the Curator of Exhibits, for the exhibit hall display, "La Ciénega: Biography of a Hispanic Community."

The Spanish accented forms, *Santa Fé* and *Río Grande,* are used for the Colonial period, and the Anglicized forms sans accents, *Santa Fe* and *Rio Grande,* are employed for the American Period.

Although museum founders, Yuri and Leonora Paloheimo, believed that Miguel Vega y Coca and his family played a primary role in the early days of El Rancho de las Golondrinas, their reasons for maintaining this belief are not clear. Most recent research into the matter has not been able to completely clarify the role of Vega y Coca's presence, but does indicate that at least some of what comprises today's Las Golondrinas was land owned by Vega y Coca. Over the years a number of families that were closely related actually owned portions of the land which is now the living history museum.

Preface

To visit El Rancho de las Golondrinas outside Santa Fe, New Mexico is to be transported back to a time long past where family, faith, and fortitude shaped all. As the premier living history museum of Spanish Colonial New Mexico, El Rancho de las Golondrinas brings back to life a fascinating and nearly forgotten world. Its historic buildings, collected artifacts and exhibits, interpretations, and live demonstrations provided by a staff of enthusiastic and well-trained docents help interpret the experiences of those who have gone before. All are invited to visit this ancient home of the Vega y Coca and Baca families, nestled in the vale of La Ciénega, and experience a moment of what once was, and is yet again.

The Kingdom of New Mexico, Its Colonization, and the Story of El Rancho de las Golondrinas began as a document born out of my interest as an amateur historian, an aficionado of the incredibly rich culture of New Mexico, and as a docent at Las Golondrinas. I assembled a personal resource center, and with the collections at the New Mexico State Records and Archives at my disposal, I have attempted to create a tool that encapsulates the history of the colonization and culture of New Mexico. The manuscript was intended to serve as an aid to interpret the museum's extensive Spanish colonial, Mexican, and United States Territorial experience, exhibits, and activities.

With the encouragement of the Las Golondrinas museum staff, I turned to Michael King, Louann Jordan, Lolly Martin, Julie Anna Lopez, Leroy Romero, Beatrice Maestas Sandoval, Julia Gomez, Charles Bennett, Nasario Garcia, PhD, Bill Baxter, PhD, and others for input. Librarians Faith Yoman of the New Mexico State Library, and Tomas Jaehn of the Fray Angélico Chávez Library, were most able in providing what information I requested. Douglas Peterson, an accomplished lay historian and native of New Mexico, not only participates in the Las Golondrinas docent training program, but was always available to supply germane information. Earl Porter, a foremost authority on tub mills, and a docent with planning and engineering know-how, provided background detail for many topics. Genealogical information was graciously shared by Henrietta Martínez Christmas. Indispensable to this effort was social historian Adrian Bustamante, PhD who shared his considerable expertise, both in content and form, and the late Benjamin Keen, PhD who was with me in spirit.

I have attempted to view what happened in the annals of colonial times with an historical perspective, not through the lens of today's mores. Any errors herein are mine, and all photographs are of my authorship taken at El Rancho de las Golondrinas and Alcalde, New Mexico.

After the re-conquest of New Mexico in 1692–1693, Spanish settlers were awarded grants to again occupy lands and villages abandoned during the Pueblo Revolt of 1680. Sometime early in the 18th century, the area now known as Las Golondrinas was deeded to Miguel Vega y Coca. He and his family were some of the earliest post-revolt settlers of the La Ciénega Valley.

The Vega y Coca Coat of Arms

In the year 2002, Manuel Gullon y de Oñate of Madrid, Spain, gifted El Rancho de las Golondrinas with a rendering of the Vega y Coca Coat of Arms. The left side has a gold field with "AVE MARIA GRATIA PLENA" (Hail Mary Full of Grace), spoken to Mary by the Archangel Gabriel when he announced to her that she had found favor with God and would conceive and bear a son, Jesus, and represents the Vega family of Santander in mountainous region of northern Spain. The right section of the shield represents the Coca family with a field of silver bearing a green pine tree and two red lions in combat. After the Muslims were expelled from Spain, the Coca family spread throughout Castile, Andalusia, the Canary Islands, and on to the Americas.

The shield is surmounted by a silver helmet topped with a black and gold twisted wreath along with the ostrich feather symbols used in Spanish heraldry.

Introduction

Historian Marc Simmons, an ardent supporter and academic contributor to El Rancho de las Golondrinas, said in his 1988 publication, *New Mexico: an Interpretive History*, "The high, dry country of New Mexico is the birthplace of America's tall tale." And so it is.

Since the days of Christopher Columbus, Spain had been the hegemonic power of the world with influence that circled the globe. From 1598 until Spain lost control of her lands in Latin America some 225 years later, the Spanish crown controlled all of Mexico. It was during this time that Spanish colonizers arrived intending to remain in the Río Grande River environs even though the territory was already occupied. Native Americans found their traditional homelands, ways of life, and economies severely disrupted, and the story of the colonization of New Mexico began.

By 1829, Spain lost control of her New World empires. Power shifted from Madrid, Spain to Mexico City, Mexico with the advent of Mexico's liberation in 1821. Mexico was now in control of an immense territory from the 42nd parallel from the Pacific Ocean eastward to headwaters of the Arkansas River in Colorado, and on to the boundary of the Louisiana Purchase. Anglo appetites for more territory, power, and wealth were not to be denied. With the mindset that the United States was fated to overspread the continent, she was destined to become a recognized political and social superpower. The 1846 Mexican-American War left Mexico with less than half of her territory. Through it all, Native Americans had little say in the matter, especially the nomadic tribes, although they caused much discord.

Regardless of the changing political landscape, New Mexico stayed a territorial province until 1912 statehood with her subsistence farming, livestock, and devotion to her Catholic faith. Her inhabitants were used to privations, were hardworking, pious, and remarkably resilient. Again, Marc Simmons, ". . . insecurity . . . bred in the New Mexicans both a deep sense of fatalism and a particular kind of inner toughness . . . and in sheer grit, tenacity, and fortitude, they had no peers."

A unique fusion of Indian, Hispanic, and Anglo societies evolved from this cultural mix to become today's New Mexico.

1

Forerunners in the Río Grande Valley

The Seven Cities of Cíbola—The Francisco Vásquez de Coronado
Entrada—Ancestral Puebloans—Indian Nomads

The Seven Cities of Cíbola

In the 1530s, the arrival of a mysterious group of strangers disrupted the lives of the great Indian communities living in northern Nueva España (New Spain), the early name for Mexico. Marcos de Niza, a friar of Spain's spiritual conquest of the Indies, as Spanish possessions in the New World were then known, was in search of pagan souls to convert to Spanish Catholicism. The friar came from Mexico City with his Indian retainers and Esteban (a.k.a. Estebanico and Estevan), a "black Arab" known in his native Morocco as al-Zemmouri.

While scouting ahead of the Niza party, Esteban and his party reached the Zuni pueblos in present-day western New Mexico. Legend says that upon entering the Zuni town of Hawikúh, Esteban demanded turquoise and took liberties with the women. The Spanish outsiders may also have been suspected of being the advance party of slave raiders. Esteban sent glowing accounts of the wealth of the people he met back to Marcos before angry Zuni inhabitants killed him and dismembered his body.

During the great drought of 1520–21, Portuguese overlords sold Moroccans, including Esteban, into Spanish slavery. As as result, the resourceful Christianized Moor, who had a facility for language dialects, found himself in servitude to Andrés Dorantes.

Esteban was one of four survivors of the 1527 ill-fated Pánfilo de Narváez expedition to Florida. Storms in the Caribbean and other disasters decimated the six hundred would-be colonizers. Only four were to survive. The tiny party walked from Galveston on the Gulf Coast to Caliacán, Northwest Mexico, a trek that took eight years. Other members of the party were Andrés Dorantes, Alonso del Castillo, and Cabeza de Vaca.

Alarmed by Esteban's fate, but encouraged by his report, Fray Marcos hastened on until he glimpsed from afar the walls of the golden, sun-bathed Hawikúh; fear kept him from entering the pueblo. On his return to Mexico City, capital of the kingdom of New Spain, Marcos de Niza told tales of having seen one of the Seven Cities of the mythical golden realm of Cíbola. It is possible that the Franciscan friar believed he saw one of the coveted seven cities. He had been present at the fall of the Incan empire and Atahualpa, its ill-fated ruler, and had seen Cuzco in mountainous Peru, a city laden with gold. His belief was in accordance with a popular legend that seven Spanish bishops fled the Moorish invasion after 711, and sailed to the west where they reached Antilia, known today as the Caribbean Antilles Islands. There each erected a wondrous city filled with many riches. Spanish explorers were particularly taken with the mystic number of seven, and an ancient map of 1482 recorded the name of each golden city. The tale of the Seven Cities of Cíbola grew with each telling. In the north, according to the imaginative Marcos, there was an abundance of gold and a civilized people who rode on strange beasts and wore woolen clothes. Surely here was the first of the fabulous seven golden cities, or so the Spanish wanted to believe.

The Francisco Vásquez de Coronado Entrada

The remarkable tale persuaded the first viceroy of Nueva España, Antonio de Mendoza, to send an *entrada* (formal entry, expedition) northward, under the command of Francisco Vásquez de Coronado. The year was 1540, and the young governor of the province of Nueva Galicia, southern Nayarit and northern Jalisco on the central Pacific coast, consumed by gold fever and recalling the exploits of Hernán Cortés in Mexico and Francisco Pizarro in Peru, was more than ready to believe stories of a mythical golden kingdom. Expeditions of conquest had to be financed by private money. Investing heavily in the enterprise with his own money and that of his wife, Coronado organized the first major *entrada* into New Mexico.

With Fray Marcos as his guide, Coronado set out with five friars, three hundred enlisted soldiers, many prospective settlers, and hundreds of Mexican Indians, the largest party ever to explore the territory. Beginning at Compostela in Nayarit, Coronado set out on the longest march of any conquistador in the 16th

Century, and led his entourage through what is now Eastern Arizona to arrive in New Mexico. When he saw the reality of Niza's "golden city" of Hawikúh, a small, crowded, dusty sandstone village, he was bitterly disappointed. The people of Hawikúh did not welcome the intruders, and Coronado had to take the first of the legendary golden cities by force. He then read to the non-Spanish speaking villagers the *requerimiento* (formal statement of conquest) that included threats of dire consequences should the Zuni people not surrender and accept Christianity.

Before Coronado and his party returned to Mexico, the conquistador traveled through two long and harsh winters pursuing the elusive dream of gold through what were to become the states of Arizona, New Mexico, and Colorado, Oklahoma, and Kansas. Coronado gave up the search and returned to Pueblo country with his entourage, much discouraged. However, he had too much invested in the expedition to return to Mexico without the glory and wealth that so far eluded him. When Coronado encountered Bigotes (Whiskers), an emissary from Cicuye (Pecos), dreams of wealth seduced him once again. Bigotes told of many villages along the Río Grande, and of the countless herds of buffalo that roamed the plains to the east. Upon gaining Coronado's trust, Bigotes acted as emissary and mediator, and became the conquistador's trusted aide throughout the summer when Coronado met with the headmen of the twelve Tigüex villages on the banks of the Río Grande. Bigotes was welcomed "in good order" according to Don Hernando de Alvarado.

Capitan Alvarado was dispatched by Coronado to explore north along the Río Grande River where he inspected the pueblos of Santo Domingo, now known as Kewa Pueblo, San Felipe, and Cochiti, and then preceded upriver through the Tewa Pueblos to Taos. He persuaded the Taoseños to welcome the party into their homes. Then Alvarado, with the Pecos scout, led the contingent through the Galisteo Valley to Cicuye where the party was again welcomed. It was at this time the plot thickened; Bigotes introduced to Coronado a crafty native from Kansas whom the Spanish named El Turco (the Turk). Turco claimed that Bigotes had a "golden bracelet" obtained from the rumored to be wealthy Indians of Quivira, one of the mythical Seven Cities of Cíbola. Alvarado, his gold fever re-kindled, attempted to force the Pecos scout to surrender the bracelet and disclose the location of the golden civilization. Bigotes knew nothing of the claims although he did have a bracelet in his possession. He found himself back in Coronado's camp in chains and set upon by war dogs.

The stage was set for the devastating Tigüex War. Before the conflict was over, there were a dozen Spanish dead along with some two hundred Tigüex warriors, more than thirty of whom were burned at the stake. Twelve villages were destroyed or severely damaged. Although morale was at an all time low, Coronado, who feared the legal consequences of his reckless behavior, was driven to explore farther. He dispatched García López de Cárdenas west through the Hopi region as far as the Grand Canyon, and Hernando de Alvarado east to Quivira. After a lengthy search through western Texas and Oklahoma, Alvarado found the Quivira natives were little more than friendly part-time buffalo hunters who cultivated maize and lived in thatched houses in the tall grass prairies of eastern Kansas. In early October 1541, Coronado informed his sovereign that stories of "gold and other very magnificent things" were no more than wild speculation. Disillusionment and a bitter winter in New Mexico found the discouraged company anxious to go home to Compostela. Francisco Vásquez de Coronado suffered a near fatal accident while horseback riding shortly before the expedition began its 1542 return to New Spain, and died in Mexico City in 1544 at the age of forty-four. The three Franciscan missionaries who remained in New Mexico to convert Indians to Christianity were martyred.

Scholar Fray Angélico Chávez observed, ". . . on the whole, the expedition of Francisco Vásquez Coronado . . . no matter what the human drawbacks in its operation and the fantastic dream which made it a failure from the start, remains one of the most colorful and imaginable feats of derring-do in the history of North America."

The crown, now aware of the brutalities committed by military conquests, commanded that only campaigns of pacification were to be permitted. At least four more expeditions traversed the upper Río Grande Valley looking for pagan souls to save and, incidentally, to keep an eye open for mineral wealth. The 1581 entrada of thirty men, under the leadership Fray Agustín Rodríguez and Francisco Sánchez Chamuscado, made it to Tigüex. One of the three Franciscan missionaries, Fray Juan de Santa María, accompanied by two native servants, started south from the Galisteo Basin intending to recount the disobedience of two soldiers and recruit more priests. He was martyred when local natives dropped a large boulder on him as he lay sleeping. The two priests who remained behind to missionize were killed as soon as the expeditionary party began its return to Mexico. The following year, Antonio de Espejo financed a small group to seek out the fate of the missionaries. Then in 1590, without authorization, Gaspar Castaño de Sosa penetrated deep into Puebloan territory. A detachment of Spanish soldiers returned 170 hopeful settlers to Mexico along with Sosa in shackles. In 1595, another small unauthorized party under the leadership of Antonio Gutiérrez de Humaña made its way as far north as present day San Ildefonso Pueblo.

White strangers returned to stay in 1598. Spanish Capitán General Adelantado Juan de Oñate y Salazar, with his contingent of 130 travel-weary families, seventy ambitious single men, eighty-three squealing wagons and carts, eleven Franciscan friars and lay brothers, and seven thousand cattle, all churning up the dust, was sent to colonize and establish Spanish supremacy. The Indians had dim memories of Coronado's disastrous intrusion, and probably had only faint notions of what Oñate's coming was to mean. They could not know that the event would change their lives forever.

Ancestral Puebloans

When Oñate arrived, the Indian societies inhabiting this harsh and lovely land represented two different ways of life, those who farmed, and those who were nomads. Pueblo Indians, descendants of the Ancestral Puebloans (formerly known by the pejorative term Anasazi) had moved from their ancient homes in the Four Corners region some three to four centuries earlier. They built easily defended village homes along the mighty Río Grande. Here farmers, speaking the Tiwan, Tewan, Towan, Tanoan, and Keresan languages, lived an essentially agrarian life. The Pueblos, so named by the Spanish because they lived in *pueblos* (towns), planted several varieties of corn, beans, squash, herbs, and *punche*, a native tobacco. They supplemented their diet with bighorn sheep, deer, and other game, large and small, and held community rabbit hunts to provide a regular supply of meat. Storerooms were kept well stocked to save against lean times. The weather could be capricious; one year might see floods and another witness crops wither and blow away, so the Indians sought to gain some control of the natural cycle by means of ancient ceremonies. The Pueblos made pottery and wove baskets of plant fibers, and using native cotton, wove blankets, *mantas* (shawls), and other clothing. They raised wild turkeys in pens, incorporating the feathers or strips of rabbit skin into blankets to insulate against the cold. They mined turquoise in the Cerrillos Hills, traded it far and wide, and made handsome jewelry, some of it mosaic using local jet along with coral and mother-of-pearl imported from Mexico.

Pueblo Indian eagle dance

Long before the arrival of Spanish conquistadors into today's New Mexico, Indian people made their homes in villages in the well-watered valley of La Ciénega. One such pueblo inhabited by Keresan peoples, bore the Tanoan name of Tziguma (Lone Cottonwood Tree). The village was mentioned in the records of Don Juan de Oñate's colonizing enterprise, and entered the Franciscan mission system in the 1630s. It figured prominently during the Pueblo Revolt of 1680. The ruin of ancient La Ciénega Pueblo, also known as La Ciénega de Carbajal, is on a bluff southwest of Las Golondrinas. It is located on private property and not open to the public.

Some two miles to the north of Las Golondrinas is the abandoned Cieneguilla Pueblo, occupied between 1350 and 1600 with its five hundred rooms. The cliffs above contain 4,400 petroglyphs pecked into the basalt rock by Keres and Tano Indians as they watched over their pueblo and fields below.

Petroglyphs at La Cieneguilla Pueblo

Indian Nomads

About the time (1519–1521) that Hernán Cortés and his warrior band entered and conquered the wealthy Aztec capital of Tenochtitlan in the Valley of Mexico, the Pueblos acquired neighbors. These newcomers, the Navajo (Diné) and the Apache (Indé), speaking Athabascan tongues, arrived in the Southwest from 1400 to 1525 A.D. They were nomads who had wandered vast distances from northwestern Canada over centuries, often using travois-equipped dogs to help transport loads. The Navajo began to farm upon their arrival, thus earning their name *nava* for a field under cultivation, and *hu* for between mountains or at the mouth of a canyon. Fray Alonso de Benavides confirmed this fact, saying in 1630 that the word *nabaju* meant "great cultivated fields." The Navajo, like the Pueblo peoples, led a rich ceremonial life. Their scrappy mobile cousins, the Apache surrounded the sedentary Pueblo Indians. To the southeast lived the Jumano, a Tompiro-speaking Pueblo Indian trading group known by Cabeza de Vaca as "People of the Cows (buffalo)." By the mid-eighteenth century, several branches of the Apache, the Chiricahua, Mescalero, Lipan and Jicarilla, moved into the south and the east. The Ute (Nuutsiu) pitched their teepees in the north and made their living by hunting and raiding the Pueblos, their southern neighbors. But as long as the nomads had to travel everywhere on foot, with dogs as their only pack animals, their ability to inflict mischief or damage upon their sedentary neighbors was limited. These were the folk who lived in this strange and haunting land when Don Juan de Oñate arrived.

2

The Reign of Juan de Oñate and the Two Majesties

The Oñate Entrada—Oñate as Governor—The Church—The Civil Authorities

The Oñate Entrada

Juan de Oñate y Salazar, commander of the *entrada* of 1598 and the last conquistador, was born into a wealthy Zacatecas family that had made its fortune in silver. The Oñates were Basques from the cool, wet Pyrenees of northern Spain. Even the name of Oñate is said to mean "at the bottom of the mountain pass," and the dwellers of the Basque region were noted for being handsome, proud, hardy, stubborn, and self-reliant. The Oñate family displayed the firm resolve of the Basques as it sought to carve out a place for itself in New Spain. Juan was the second son of Count Cristóbal de Oñate, former governor of Nueva Galicia, and one of the discoverers of the rich Zacatecas mines on the exposed outcrop of greenish rock called La Bufa. From his estate in Pánuco, five miles north of the city of Zacatecas, *Conde* (Count) Cristóbal de Oñate ruled like a benevolent feudal lord. At age 45, Oñate married Catalina de Salazar y de la Cadena in a grand and colorful ceremony. Few details of Doña Catalina's life are known other than she was born in Granada in Andalusia some thirty years earlier. The union produced seven children, five boys, and two girls.

By the time the elder Oñate died, he had made and lost fortunes. The sources of his wealth included vast mining interests, *encomiendas* (grants of Indian labor and tribute) stock ranches, farms, and a sugar refinery. Cristóbal's neglect of the paper work of his estate, along with his generosity to others, and his penchant for employing dishonest overseers, contributed to the decrease of his finances. At his death he was reported to be near insolvency. However, many of his mines were good producers, and the title to these mines passed first to his widow, Doña Catalina, and then to his son, Juan. By age thirty, Juan de Oñate was a man of means in his own right. The Oñate family resided much of the year in Mexico City, where Juan acquired an education and the social graces befitting his rank. As might be expected, Juan de Oñate married well, taking for wife Isabel de Toloso Cortés Moctezuma, granddaughter of Hernán Cortés, conqueror of New Spain, and his Indian mistress Isabel Moctezuma.

The new silver boomtown of San Luis Potosí, one hundred miles southeast of Zacatecas and named for the incredibly rich strike in Peru, required someone of high social rank to administer its affairs. Frontiersman and soldier Miguel Caldera had discovered the bonanza, but as a commoner, was ineligible to develop the mines and the new city. Viceroy Luis de Velasco appointed Juan de Oñate as *alcalde mayor* (governor), and ordered him to give Caldera the major role in the planning and distribution of land to the many fortune hunters swarming into the city. Oñate registered valuable tracts in his own family's name and that of his relatives, the Zaldivar clan. Juan de Zaldivar, a nephew of Cristóbal de Oñate, served as a junior officer in Coronado's army. Juan and Vicente, nephews of Juan de Zaldivar, would ride with Juan de Oñate in 1598.

In 1583, the Spanish crown issued a decree charging the viceroy of New Spain to appoint as governor of New Mexico a wealthy and capable colonist willing to dedicate his energies and fortunes to the settlement of the distant colony. The king's directive signaled a revival of interest in New Mexico. Accounts of the Antonio de Espejo expedition recorded finding mineral wealth, influenced Oñate to follow his trail two decades later. In the excitement aroused by reports of another possible bonanza, Spain's resolve to allow explorations only for missionary purposes was forgotten.

From among the rich and powerful that hoped for the New Mexican contract, two leading contenders emerged. One was Juan de Oñate, now 43, who dreamed of matching the exploits of Cortés and Pizarro by discovering a new golden kingdom in the northern reaches of New Spain. The other was the capricious and grasping Juan Lomas y Colmenares who sought power and grants second only to those of Christopher Columbus himself. Meanwhile, a new contender, Francisco de Urdiñola, appeared on the scene, but was soon embroiled in a scandal choreographed by rival Colmenares. Urdiñola was absolved of guilt, but too late for him to be a candidate.

Before the dust settled, it fell to the viceroy to sort through many appeals, applications, and intrigues among contenders for command of the expedition. The astute Velasco eventually named Oñate as his choice. He knew the life stories of the pioneering Oñates and their success in prospecting and extracting precious minerals. In September 1595, Oñate entered into a contract with the crown to equip an expedition at his own expense. He was to feed and arm the soldier-colonists and their families on the journey to distant New Mexico. In addition to bringing *pobladores* (colonists) to New Mexico, Oñate agreed to take with him sowing wheat, corn, farm equipment, jerked beef, and goods to trade with the Indians, all on pack animals and in freight wagons. On the hoof came cattle, sheep, goats, mares, donkeys, mules, swine, and any other domestic animals that could be herded, led, driven, carted, or ridden.

In return, Oñate received the right to make grants of land and Indian tribute, create a royal treasury, build *presidios* (garrisons), establish governmental districts, name officials, and exploit any minerals. In addition, he was to receive a generous salary and the titles of "governor, captain general, *caudillo* (leader), discoverer, and pacifier." (The title of *caudillo* was granted in by King Philip in his Ordinances of 1573 that proclaimed conquest was out and pacification was in.) These were truly handsome terms, rarely granted to a *criollo* (a person of Spanish blood born in the New World) like Oñate. The *peninsulares* (persons born in Spain) were proud of their superior status, but as many disappointed Spanish conquistadors and colonists soon discovered, it had no cash value.

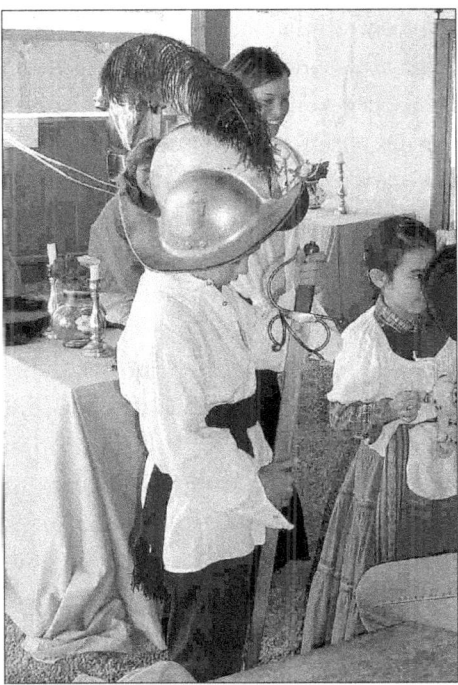

Young conquistador suits up

Oñate was also named *adelantado* (governor, captain general), a title granted by the crown in exchange for an initial exploration, and vested him with supreme authority over New Mexican civil and criminal jurisdiction. Velasco supplied Oñate with a suitable silken standard, decorated with a coat of arms and religious symbols that would serve as the personal emblem of Oñate and badge of his authority. (The relic is now in display at the New Mexican History Museum in Santa Fe.) Franciscan friars, agents of Spain's "spiritual conquest," would accompany him at the crown's expense.

Before Oñate could leave, the Count of Monterrey was appointed to replace Viceroy Velasco, and the count proceeded to review Oñate's contract. He struck out the provision that made Oñate responsible only to Spain's Council of the Indies in Spain, the supreme legislative and judicial body of the Spanish empire in New Spain. This meant, in effect, that Monterrey would bar any efforts by the ambitious Oñate to elevate New Mexico into a separate viceroyalty with himself as viceroy. Before leaving Mexico City, Monterrey appointed one of his trusted guards, Lope de Ulloa, to accompany Oñate and his party from Zacatecas to Santa Bárbara on the central plateau in Nueva Viscaya (southern Chihuahua). There in Santa Bárbara at the edge of the frontier of New Spain, Ulloa was to determine whether Oñate had met the requirements of his contract. Upon careful inspection of the troops, supplies, and armaments, he found all to be in order, and found no grounds to abort the Oñate *entrada*.

Enter Juan de Frías Salazar, another viceregal inspector and a military man who fought for the crown in Flanders, and made a fortune in mining. Impossible demands levied by Salazar resulted in a panicked horseback ride by Captain Gaspar Pérez de Villagrá to Juan Guerra de Resa, Oñate's uncle, to request aid. Rosa and his wife agreed to "sacrifice their entire fortune if need be" to underwrite the bond that Salazar had demanded which would guarantee any shortfalls he found in his review. This inspection meant another delay of Oñate's arrival in New Mexico. The endless impediments of the last five years caused many colonists to defect, and created a great drain on Oñate's funds. After innumerable setbacks and delays, the party set out for New Mexico in late January, 1598.

In point of size and financial commitment, Oñate's expedition was inferior to that of Vásquez Coronado's in 1540. Oñate's entourage of some five hundred people included eight Franciscan friars and two Franciscan lay brothers, an unknown number of wives and children, as well as personal servants, packers, herders and drivers, and Oñate's own Chichimec and black slaves. The ages of male colonists ranged from sixteen to sixty, one hundred twenty-nine of them of fighting age. With the train came seven thousand head of stock and eighty-three supply wagons. Each family was allotted a stipend in pesos to buy whatever they needed to immigrate to distant New Mexico. Many of the ancillary party were *mestizos,* offspring of Indian and Spanish parents, blacks, mulattos, and undoubtedly some *conversos* (converted Jews or descendants of such) who hid their status on pain of death.

Spanish society was exceedingly class-conscious; plebeians who came to the Indies often falsely claimed to be *hidalgos* (minor noblemen) or at least dreamed of becoming such. The title would exempt its bearers from performing artisan or other manual labor, and from paying taxes. Oñate's colonists would be reluctant to put hands to a plow or shoulders to the wheel while awaiting their *hidalgo* status. The ambitious colonist came to find gold, or to be granted an *encomienda*, not to till the soil like a peasant. Oñate promised his colonists that after five years of residence, a suitable accumulation of property, and exemplary service to the colony, they would be made *hidalgos*; the governor was unable to fulfill this pledge.

As the caravan of colonists with their wagons, ox-carts, and livestock, lumbered along, the expedition stretched for two miles. The party took the risky trail northward across Los Médanos, a section of the harsh Chihuahuan desert with great dunes of sand. The company suffered immense thirst, and was reported by Villagrá to have been saved only after prayers to God by a downpour that came to be known as the "Miraculous Shower." On Holy Thursday, Oñate ordered a halt at the Río Sacramento, a small stream in northern Chihuahua named by Oñate in honor of the occasion, in order to celebrate the Feast of the Blessed Sacrament, and constructed a small chapel. That evening, the men assembled to kneel, weep, pray for their sins, and beg forgiveness from the Almighty. The women and children soon joined them. Soldiers whipped their backs with scourges until "the camp ran crimson with their blood," a penitential practice for atonement of sins. Gaspar Pérez de Villagrá, poet and Oñate's official historian, a confidant, and a tough soldier to boot, recorded all these events in verse. Villagrá was Oñate's publicist, and was not above embellishing the conquistador's image. His epic history was the first publication about any region in today's United States to find its way into print.

Some months after the Oñate expedition put behind them the disparagements of Juan de Frías Salazar, the exhausted party reached the Río Grande where it had a brief respite from its hardships. Then the company traveled upstream until it found a suitable ford to cross the Río Grande at present day San Elizario, Texas. Oñate called a halt, and the joyful party witnessed their leader, dressed in full armor, proclaim with much pomp and circumstance Spain's formal possession of New Mexico. It must have been one of Oñate's proudest moments. "I claim these lands without limitations," he declared, "including the mountains, the rivers, valleys, meadows, pastures, and waters . . . pueblos, cities, towns, castles . . . in the name of the King." Oñate ordered a chapel be built to hold the party, and on April 30, 1598, he oversaw a celebration, the earliest recorded date of any thanksgiving by Europeans in the New World. A solemn high Mass and a sermon were followed by a performance of the play, *Los Moros y Los Cristianos*, the first ever put on by Europeans in New Mexico. The drama depicts the defeat of the Moors in Spain, implying the inevitable triumph of the Spanish and their religion. This ancient pantomime no doubt was meant to terrify and edify the Indian, and to lift the morale of his troops.

It can be argued that Juan de Oñate was a colonizer, not a conquistador, whose goal was not to conquer and exploit the native peoples, but to establish a peaceful Spanish colony prepared to thrive and defend itself.

The date Oñate set foot on the land that was to become the United States and founded his colony is 1598, nine years before the British established Jamestown, and twenty-two years before the Mayflower Pilgrims disembarked at Plymouth Rock.

The trek north resumed after the ordeal of passing through the Jornada del Muerto (Dead Man's March) in southern New Mexico, the wide, flat ninety mile expanse with no grazing or firewood, and most devastating of all, no water. Rough topography forced the party up and away from the Río Grande. Governor Oñate's *entrada* passed by San Felipe Pueblo and arrived at the Pueblo of Kewa where he spoke to the assembled Indians. In the ceremony that native leaders scarcely understood, they swore allegiance to the Spanish king and his Catholic faith. On July 11, Oñate's party reached the confluence of the Chama and Río Grande Rivers and the Tewa Pueblo twin villages, Okeh on the east bank and Yunge on the west of the Río Grande. He grandly proclaimed, "I take jurisdiction, from the edge of the mountains to the stones and sand in the rivers, and leaves of the trees . . . of the lands of the Río del Norte." Then he staged the ancient *Los Moros y Los Cristianos* open-air folk drama performed yet today at Ohkay Owingeh Pueblo (San Juan Pueblo) at Christmas. Oñate gave Yunge Pueblo the new name of San Gabriel del Yunge Oweenge, and proclaimed it the capital of his colony.

Initially the inhabitants received their Spanish visitors with gifts of food and welcomed them to their homes. The colonists needed more shelter and stores, so Oñate soon forced the residents to move out of their Yungue quarters which were then occupied by the newcomers, and designated the pueblo the capital of New Mexico. San Gabriel became the terminus for *El Camino Real de Tierra Adentro*, some twelve hundred hard miles from Zacatecas. In truth, the now famous trail was prehistoric in origin, much of its path having been used earlier by native peoples.

In the early optimism that he was about to create a new and brilliant center of Hispanic civilization, Oñate had months before stocked his supply train, not only with seeds and cuttings, tools and domestic equipment, armaments, iron horseshoes, nails, medicines and religious articles, but with elegant clothing for wear in festivals and fancy dress balls. How out of place these luxuries proved to be! Velvet suits with lace cuffs and fluted collars, silk dresses, embroidered mantillas, elegant tortoise shell combs and dancing slippers, and footwear of fine-tooled leather from Cordoba, Spain. Oñate's own inventory listed hundreds of pairs of shoes and boots. Within a generation, the colonists put away their finery and were wearing course cloth and *gamuza* (buckskin) not unlike that of their Pueblo neighbors.

The friendly attitude of the natives soon soured as the reality of the Spanish presence became clear. Before long Oñate had put into place the *encomienda* system that required the heads of Indian households to pay annual tribute in corn and *mantas* to their Spanish *encomenderos*. In return, the *encomenderos* were to look after the spiritual and physical welfare of their Indians. Such was the theory. In practice, the *encomiendas* became a system that allowed the unbridled exploitation of the natives as *encomenderos* had the right to extract tribute, and exploit natural resources.

In the absence of the gold or silver mines feverishly sought by the Spanish, agriculture and stock raising remained the only profitable economic activities. Most colonists had come north not to farm, but to become rich quickly and gain the status of *hidalgo*. Farming was not a virtue of members of the Castilian aristocracy. As a result, the *repartimiento* (labor system) was introduced that forced the Pueblos to farm Spanish fields and care for Spanish livestock. Employers were to supply workers daily rations and pay a trifling wage. But the *repartimiento*, like the *encomienda*, was subject to many abuses. Masters often failed to pay wages, held Indians in servitude beyond the contracted period, pulled Pueblo farmers from their own fields at harvest time, and abused Indian women.

Oñate as Governor

Oñate's actions as governor reflected the autocratic spirit of the age. Without consulting Pueblo elders, he appointed governors, *aguaciles* (sheriffs), *mayordomos* (irrigation ditch bosses), *regidores* (councilmen), and *fiscales* (church wardens) in each of the Pueblo villages. He earned a reputation as an exploiter and abuser of the Indians along with some of his colonists. In a clash at the Keresan pueblo of Ácoma, warriors killed Oñate's nephew, Juan de Zaldivar, and a dozen soldiers. Under the influence of Ácoman chief Zutucapán, the Indians intended to ambush and assassinate Oñate himself. Coronado's men had pronounced the fortified rock impregnable and "the greatest stronghold in the world." The Ácomans lived high atop their 361 foot sandstone mesa for their own defense because they had many enemies amongst their neighbors.

An atrocity of Oñate's that occured in the year 1599 still resonates in New Mexico today. Oñate sent the brother of the slain Spanish commander Zaldivar to exact revenge and bring Ácoma to heel. In the ensuing battle, Ácoma was captured and several hundred Indians were killed with but one Spanish casualty. Not content with this chastisement, Oñate brutally punished the Ácomans who surrendered. All males over the age of twenty-five were condemned to have *puntas de pies* (toes, not foot) amputated and to give twenty years of personal service; younger males were to give a like twenty years of servitude. Many Ácomans fled their bondage and returned to their 12th century home. One must note that historians are still questioning the degree of the punishment meted out to the Ácomans.

Sixty girls were sent to Mexico to be distributed to convents for religious training. Two visitors from Hopi reportedly had their right hands cut off and were then sent home to warn others of the cost of defying Spanish power. The

Ácoma chastisement, legal in the instance of a "just war," was so severe that no other pueblo community rose in revolt. Some Spanish, and at least one Indian who took part in the battle, claimed to have seen the warrior, San Santiago (St. James, the Apostle) fighting on the side of the Christians. Legend had long ago held that Santiago aided Ferdinand and Isabella in the final battle to expel the Moors from Spain. Villagrá, Oñate's chronicler, described the saint's appearance in New Mexico. "He was mounted on a white steed. He had a long white beard, a bald-head, and carried a flaming sword in his right hand. When he assailed [the Indians] they say he swept them before him like a whirlwind. This warrior was accompanied by a maiden of most wondrous beauty. . ." identified by Villagrá as the Holy Mother.

The people of Ácoma have never forgiven the Spanish for what happened there. In a symbolic act during the 1998 Cuatrocentenario, the 400th anniversary of Oñate's arrival, anonymous parties severed the right foot from the twelve-foot bronze equestrian statue of Juan de Oñate at the Oñate Monument and Visitors Center in Alcalde north of Española. The political symbolism of the act was clear to all.

Juan de Oñate equestrian statue, Alcalde New Mexico

The same toughness that Oñate displayed in dealing with the Ácoma affair was reflected in his insistence that successful conversion of the Pueblos to Catholicism required striking fear into the hearts of the Indians by the display of Spanish military force. He argued, " . . . should they lose fear it would inevitably follow . . . that the teaching of the holy gospel would be hindered . . . which I am under obligation to prevent." He reasoned that a powerful show of military force joined with a carefully calculated display of Franciscan compassion would serve to impress potential converts and allow the friars to work unhindered. He believed the Indians should "love and fear us."

Meanwhile the colony stagnated. New settlers, some seventy-three in all, arrived in 1600 only to be disillusioned with conditions and prospects in the colony. Colonists were contracted to remain in New Mexico, to carry passports, and to obtain permission to move. They were disappointed that they had not found the wealth they had been promised. After all, they had come to make a fortune, not to till bean patches, dig irrigation ditches, or slaughter livestock. Then in 1601, while Oñate was away on an expedition to the Great Plains in search of silver and/or other riches, more than half of his colonists illegally fled the province and made their way south to Nueva Galicia. The defectors, who escaped being followed and killed, returned to Mexico in pitiful condition. Their reports of the land's poverty caused policy makers in Mexico City and Madrid, Spain to question the wisdom and cost of trying to maintain the colony. However, abandonment would mean the loss of an important base for further expansion to North America, and of a buffer against attack on the rich mining country in northern Mexico. There was also the fate of the Indians who converted to Christianity to consider. Arguments for and against abandonment raged on.

Cristóbal Vaca [Baca] was a captain who came to reinforce the Oñate colony, and he and his family did not abandon San Gabriel when most of the colonists deserted. He was critical of friars who lead the movement to desert the colony. In 1603, Cristóbal returned to Mexico City with an escort under his command, and brought four new Franciscans from Mexico City into the colony.

The names of Cristóbal Vaca's descendants fill the annals of the history of New Mexico. The Vaca name was derived from a title given by the crown to a Spanish hero in 1212. King Alfonso VIII awarded the name Cabeza de Vaca and a coat of arms to a shepherd who is said to have marked a secret passage through the mountains above Seville with the skull of a cow. Invading through the corridor, the Spanish forces surprised the overlord Moors to emerge victorious in the Battle of Las Navas de Tolosa. The name Cabeza de Vaca literally translates to "head of a cow." By the seventeenth century, "Baca" came into common usage, and C'de Baca is the name used today throughout the La Ciénega Valley. The Baca family is wide-spread throughout New Mexico.

Defections, Indian raids, and intrigues continued to plague Oñate, and his credibility rapidly declined as he became more and more autocratic in an effort to maintain control. In 1606 Apache and Navajo turned hostile and attacked San Gabriel del Yunge itself. Another expedition to the Gulf of California, led by Vicente de Zaldivar, produced poor results, and probably contributed to Oñate's decision to resign. The pressures of his colonial project at last caught up with the resolute Captain General Oñate y Salazar. He decided to release San Gabriel colonists from their obligation to remain, and then tendered his resignation. In his letter of resignation, he wrote the viceroy, "Finding myself helpless in every respect, because I have used up on this expedition my estate and the resources of my relatives and friends, amounting to more than six hundred thousand pesos, I have no other recourse . . . than to renounce my office." The document was dated August 24, 1607. Oñate did not know that in the interim Phillip III's order for his recall had been sent and received in Mexico City.

Accused by his enemies of cruelty, immorality and false reporting while governor, Oñate stood trial before the *audiencia* (council of magistrates created by the crown) for his alleged crimes. He was found guilty of twelve charges that included the unjust execution of two Indians, unnecessary force in subduing the Ácoma Pueblo, and the execution of deserters; he was acquitted of seventeen other charges including adultery. He was stripped of his titles, fined, and exiled from New Mexico to Zacatecas in Mexico. Subsequent appeals brought a reversal of the sentence, but he was not restored to office. The conquistador left New Mexico in disgrace, never to return.

Following his wife's death in Pánuco, Mexico, Juan de Oñate spent his final years trying to clear his name and record. His Basque stubbornness made intolerable the disgrace he had suffered. He returned to Spain and pressed his case before the Council of the Indies and the crown for many years. Since most qualified mine inspectors were serving in the New World, he was appointed to the unsalaried position of mining inspector for all of Spain. In 1625, after the publication of a report with recommendations for mining reforms that won Oñate a personal audience with the king, he was appointed to the prestigious Military Order of Santiago. He collapsed and died in 1626 while examining a flooded mine. His will set aside part of what was left of his vast estate to build a chapel in the Jesuit Colegio Imperial in Madrid, Spain. There he and his descendants are interred under the Oñate coat of arms.

A memento of one of Juan de Oñate's expeditions through New Mexico is found today in El Morro National Monument in western New Mexico. It was carved by the governor into a sandstone cliff upon his return from his last journey in search of the South Sea (Pacific Ocean). Oñate had hoped to find pearl fisheries and a good harbor where ships might anchor to supply his needy colonists. An entry on Inscription Rock in the monument reads, "The Adelantado Don Juan de Oñate passed by here on his return from his search for the South Sea on the sixteenth of April 1605."

After Oñate was found guilty in 1608 of twelve charges, and Viceroy Louis de Velasco accepted Oñate's resignation in time to spare him the humiliation of learning he had been removed. Cristóbal Oñate, the eighteen-year-old son of Juan de Oñate, had reached manhood without a formal education, for none was available in New Mexico. He was well trained and experienced in art of war having lead forays against the Apache in his mid-teens, and later commanded the punitive force against Apache and Navajo attackers of San Gabriel. Little else is known of young Cristóbal other than the fact that the San Gabriel *cabildo* (town council) appointed him to carry on briefly as interim governor after Oñate resigned, and that he married, sired a son, and died at age twenty-two.

Bernardino de Ceballos served briefly as the second governor. In 1610, Velasco appointed Pedro de Peralta, Knight of the Order of Santiago, the third governor and captain general of the province of New Mexico. He was charged with founding La Villa de Santa Fé with orders to "maintain and enhance the prestige of the Spanish among the natives."

One has to look long and hard to find a street of two nondescript blocks named after New Mexico's first governor, Oñate. A major thoroughfare in Santa Fe today, Paseo de Peralta is named for New Mexico's third governor. The statue installed in his honor credits Peralta as being responsible for the founding of La

Villa de Santa Fé, the Royal City of the Holy Faith. Royal ordinance stipulated the layout of any colonial town in New Spain. A grid system of rectangular blocks and straight streets was required, and a central plaza was to be twice as long as it was wide. Intent was to require the Spanish to live in towns that were easy to defend. Self-sufficient colonists frequently ignored the stipulations as they preferred to live near their irrigated *milpas* (crop fields). Such independence put colonists at risk for subsequent raids by marauding Indians.

Royal policy forbade colonists to locate in close proximity to Indian villages, and San Gabriel had encroached on the homes and fields of Ohkay Owingeh Pueblo. The site chosen for the first capital of New Mexico was illegal from the start. By 1607, San Gabriel colonists had begun to move south twenty miles to an abandoned Tano pueblo site in a valley watered by a tributary of the Río Grande. Renamed Santa Fé (Holy Faith) in 1608 or earlier, the former pueblo became the seat of government. The exact date for the founding of Santa Fé has long been debated as all manuscripts recording its history were thought to have been destroyed during the Pueblo Revolt of 1680.

Scholar Thomas Chávez, then director of the Palace of the Governors, followed a lead by New Mexican historian France V. Scholes published in 1944, and located the manuscript by Captain Juan de Montoya at an antiquities dealer, Maggs Brothers of London. Published in 1785 by his descendents who wanted *hidalguía* (upper-class status), Montoya is said to have reported, ". . . and having protected [or waited] for a year [at San Gabriel], while he [Juan de Oñate] went to give notice to the Viceroy of the status of things in this land and having made a plaza [in 1608] at Santa Fé." The State of New Mexico purchased the manuscript, and it is now in the collection of the Palace of the Governors.

Following crown instructions, Governor Pedro de Peralta began construction of the new capital city of Santa Fé with its *presidio* (military headquarters) in the late spring of 1610. The *adobe* village bore the grand title of La Villa Real de Santa Fé de San Francisco de Asis. Historian Marc Simmons suggests that the capital might have been named in honor of the royal campsite near Granada from which Ferdinand and Isabella launched their final assault to rid Spain of its Moorish overlords.

The Two Majesties

Spain ruled its American empire with the aid of two hierarchies of officials, one civil, and the other religious. They served the same royal master, the crown, but viceroys and archbishops, governors and bishops often disputed over issues of privilege, jurisdiction, and policy. Their disagreements sometimes sparked confrontations and even large-scale violence. Researcher Charles Gibson wrote, "Few viceroys in Spanish America were able consistently to remain on cordial terms with the high-ranking churchmen of their viceroyalties." Fearing an excessive concentration of power in its servants, Spain built a system of checks and balances into the government of the Indies.

The humble northern province of New Spain did not escape the problem of church-state conflict. Indeed, its fragile economy and small Indian tributary population tended to sharpen the antagonism between the many greedy governors and sometimes imperious friars who competed for the right to control and exploit resources. The Franciscans often used the instrument of the Inquisition as a political weapon. The resulting struggle between the "Two Majesties" almost tore the struggling colony asunder.

No more than four hundred Indian conversions had been accomplished in New Mexico in eleven years of Oñate rule. Viceroy Velasco pondered whether he should terminate colonization efforts in New Mexico. When the Council of the Indies recommended abandonment, the Franciscan Order became alarmed. We do not know what urgent call to action was given, but during the summer of 1608, the friars reported seven thousand Pueblo conversions. News of the sudden success pleased the king who decreed that New Mexico should become a royal colony with all future expenses met by the royal treasury. New Mexico was transformed into a missionary field.

Caught between the Two Majesties were the native peoples. On one side were the governors, often puffed up with self-importance, and backed by the soldiery of their garrisons. These squeezed private gain from the impoverished province. On the other were friars in their missions, supplied by the crown once every three to six years imported by pack animals, oxen and mule-drawn wagon trains from Chihuahua via El Camino Real de Tierra Adentro. Since New Mexico, unlike the central and southern regions of New Spain, was not a wealthy mining or agricultural area, but a fertile field to save pagan soles. This provided an excuse for the heavy-handed authority of many friars.

> In 1662, Francisco Anaya de Almazán II the elder, alcalde ordinario of Santa Fé, a prominent New Mexican captain of the military and citizen of Ciénega Valley, died after the trauma of witnessing his son, Cristóbal, arrested by the Inquisition and taken for trial in Mexico City. Governor Diego Dionisio de Peñalosa confiscated the tributes of his encomiendas in the Salinas Pueblo missions region, Picurís, and La Ciénega. A self-important Cristóbal returned from his three year imprisonment after being ordered by his inquisitors to renounce his errors.

Franciscan friars were assigned to each pueblo, and they soon put the natives to work building the massive churches that glorified their God. The friars, who were expected to protect the religious and material interests of the natives, used Indian labor for the building of their massive churches, believing grand edifices would better serve God and the community's spiritual needs. It would be a mistake to assume that Christianized Indians were made to supply labor, for many willingly consented.

The clergy, who were not professional architects, employed the materials used by the Indians because they had to use the resources at hand, albeit technology to form *adobe* (sundried bricks) came with them to New Spain. The use of Spanish hand tools, along with their elementary skills in blacksmithing, enabled the clergy to build the huge interiors they thought necessary. The Franciscans imported rich church furnishings, fine priestly vestments, and chalices, statues, and paintings. Music, they found, was a most effective instrument converting the Indians to Catholicism and Spanish rule. The friars used plainsong as part of the mission liturgy, and Indians were taught to play violins, bassoons, trumpets, and the snare drums used by the military. A portable organ arrived at the church at Senecú about 1630. During the seven decades following the founding of Santa Fé, some 250 friars of the Franciscan Order lived and worked among the Pueblos to spread the "True Faith."

A torrent of charges of scandal and mistreatment of the natives by governors and missionaries, each accusing the other, flowed to the viceroys in Mexico City. Governors were charged with using the privilege of *repartimiento* to press gangs of Pueblo Indians to weave and sew in miserable conditions in their own Palace of the Governors. Possibly the worst of the lot was Governor Luís de Rosas, an unrepentant enemy of the clergy, who, in 1638, used the justification of "just war" to press Apache captives into his textile *obraje* (workshop). He wrested labor and commodities from the Pueblos by threatening to restrict their religious practices. Indians were forced to search the mountains for piñon nuts, and to carry bags of salt from the saline ponds in the south end of the Estancia Basin east of the Manzano Mountains to Santa Fé. Salt was in great demand as a food preservative, for curing animal hides, and as a necessary nutritional supplement for humans and animals. Rosas was subjected to the customary *residencia,* a judicial review of a governor's tenure while in office. As a result, the Santa Fé *cabildo* had the ex-governor arrested and his properties impounded. He was murdered in 1642.

The estancia (small ranch) of Diego Márquez at Los Cerrillos was established about 1630, the date determined by the use of Dendrochronology (tree ring dating). Marquéz and seven others were beheaded in 1643 after being convicted of having been involved in the 1642 murder of ex-governor Luís de Rosas. (The old village of Los Cerrillos, located by Alamo Creek, should not be confused with the modern railroad town.)

Ana Baca, the widow of Francisco López de Aragon, lived at her "estancia del Alamo," circa 1661, according to Fray Angélico Chávez. She was rebuked by Governor Mendizábal for her devotion of the Franciscans.

The missionary fathers sought total independence from the civil power. They had their own ecclesiastical capital at Kewa Pueblo where the *custos,* head of the Franciscan Order in New Mexico and representative of the Inquisition, resided. The *custos* assumed large powers. He granted and withheld sacraments, initiated ecclesiastical investigations into the lives of parishioners, and excommunicated persons he determined to be enemies of the Church. Those accused of heresy were sent to stand trial before the Inquisition in Mexico City.

The *custos* ordered natives to be instructed in catechism, music, weaving, painting, carpentry and, of all things, Latin! He imposed new and unfamiliar European categories of labor upon the Indians, and the slightest dereliction brought severe punishment. Indians regarded the chastisement of head shaving and the resulting loss of hair as a colossal affront. The shame associated with shorn hair was enough to cause many to flee to the mountains, and others to take their own lives.

The friars viewed Pueblo Indian refusal to give up their beloved deities and their persistence in dancing, singing, handling rattlesnakes, sprinkling sacred cornmeal, and wearing masks as evidence of devil worship and idolatry. The Indians were willing to accept the Christian God and to incorporate the saints into the ranks of *kachinas* (beneficent spirits), but the padres would have none of it. The friars launched attack after attack on the old traditions, condemned native priests as sorcerers, and punished them severely. Their *kivas* (ceremonial chambers) were desecrated, and holy objects destroyed and burned. The religion of the Pueblos went underground.

After 1650, climatic conditions deteriorated markedly, and the province found itself in the throes of a severe drought. Between 1665 and 1668, no crops were harvested and hundreds of Indians perished. The Pueblos blamed the Spanish friars for causing this misfortune by abolishing the rainmaking ceremonies. Famine hit the colonists equally hard even though they expropriated the few staples that remained. The ancient trade network that sustained native people in times of famine had been shattered.

To add to these woes, Indians succumbed to the diseases of smallpox, whooping cough, influenza, measles, and cholera brought by the Spanish, diseases to which they had no acquired immunity. Diseases spread ahead of the European intruders. At the time of Oñate, there may have been as many as forty thousand Indians in the Rió Grande and Pecos valleys, a decrease of some 20 percent since the days of Coronado. In 1640, smallpox killed 10 percent of the Pueblo population. Other epidemics in the 1660s continued to thin their numbers to fifteen thousand in the upper Río Grande and Pecos River drainages. Colonists were devastated by disease as well. By the late 1670s, the Spanish crown was forced to send fifty Spanish convicts to New Mexico in an attempt to increase numbers in the colony.

In an arbitrary move in 1675, Governor Juan Francisco Treviño dispatched soldiers to arrest forty-seven alleged Indian sorcerers and teachers of idolatry. The Spanish hanged three, a fourth hanged himself. All the others were whipped and imprisoned, but later released by Governor Treviño. The Spanish would come to rue the day, for one of the abused was the San Juan medicine man, Popé.

It was against this background of brutal repression and smoldering Indian anger that the Pueblo Revolt of 1680 exploded.

# 3

Revolt and Re-conquest

Popé and the Expulsion—The Vargas Entrada

Popé and the Expulsion

Popé, the talented leader of the Pueblo Revolt of 1680, spun a web of conspiracy. The medicine man burned with rage at his disgrace by the hands of the Spanish governor. Popé possessed considerable organizational skill as well as an ability to rouse Pueblo passions. He tolerated no opposition to his leadership, and put Nicolás Bua, his brother-in-law, to death when he discovered Bua planned to reveal the conspiracy to Governor Antonio de Otermín. Other angry leaders from the Picurís and Kewa Pueblos soon joined him to form a confederacy, an institution not characteristic of the Pueblos. Pueblo peoples had traditionally been at odds with one another, often times engaging in out-and-out war. One account, obtained by Otermín from Indian captives after the revolt, assigns to Popé an associate named Naranjo, a mixed blood who was "very tall, black, and had very large yellow eyes." This *teniente* (lieutenant) posed as the deity Po-he-yemo of Taos, and claimed to possess extraordinary powers. Three spirits, Caudi, Tilini, and Tleume, from the underworld regularly visited Naranjo in a Taos kiva and told him what he must do. These spirits emerged from the netherworld after receiving many prayers and offerings. They told Po-he-yemo that they were departing for the underground lake of Copala, and would remain until all the Spanish were gone. If we may credit this account, leaving aside its more radical elements, then Naranjo, not Popé, was the ideologue of the revolt.

The spirits instructed Po-he-yemo how to defeat the Spanish, giving him the knotted cords that he was to distribute to the Pueblos. Two messengers bearing supplies of knotted cords told each Pueblo leader that a message from Po-he-yemo, "the father of all the Indians, their great captain, who had been such since the world was inundated," had arrived from the north and commanded them to rebel. They should destroy any pueblo that refused to join the revolt and kill its people. The Pueblos joining the revolt were to untie one knot from the cord presented to them as a sign of obedience, and then continue to undo the remaining knots one each day until the last was untied, the signal for the revolt to begin.

Popé and his fellow plotters seemed unconcerned that Pueblo secrecy had been breached since Pueblo leaders of San Marcos and La Ciénega had informed Governor Antonio de Otermín that an uprising was imminent. By the time Governor Otermín in Santa Fé received news of the revolt from the valley of Santa Cruz to the north and from the *estancias* of Los Cerrillos to the south, it was too late to avert disaster. Most of the Pueblos joined the attack that resulted in a rampant slaughter of the colonists. Otermín hastened to bring his people and their livestock into the Palace of the Governors' compound, but dispersed settlers and missionaries were unprepared. They were caught by surprise on August 10, 1680, the day of vengeance. The Indians slew twenty-one of the province's forty friars, and defiled their places of worship as the Spanish had done to their kivas in their pueblos. Bodies of men, women, and children lay strewn on the trails where they fled and fell.

Escaping the carnage, Cieneguilla encomendero Francisco Anaya de Almazán was in Santa Cruz de la Cañada, twenty-five miles north of Santa Fé, when the revolt erupted. His party of five fought their way to Santa Fé, where it joined forces with Otermín and others defenders of the Palace of the Governors. Anaya's wife and children were taken by Indians. The Cieneguilla grant was made to Francisco Anaya de Almazán prior to 1680. Anaya accompanied Diego de Vargas on the 1692 expedition to reclaim the territory of New Mexico. In 1693 at El Paso, Vargas reconfirmed Anaya's Cieneguilla grant.

The Indians laid siege to the Palace for nine days. By now some Pueblo Indians, mounted on pillaged Spanish horses, were well-armed with captured firearms and swords taken from the enemy. After the water supply for the Palace of the Governors was diverted by the Indians, Governor Otermín fled with his soldiers, the old and infirm, women, children, and the wounded. Some Indians, notably from Isleta, fled south with the Spanish. The Indians won their war and allowed the governor and what remained of his colony to stagger south unmolested to El Paso del Norte, modern-day Juarez. Descendants of the refugees from Isleta Pueblo reside today in the Mesilla Valley south of Las Cruces. (Their descendants retain traces of the Tiwa language and Pueblo ceremonialism, and recently organized themselves into the Tortugas Indian Confraternity.)

Some fifteen thousand sedentary Indians and 2,800 Spanish inhabited the territory before the revolt began. Since many of the baptismal and burial records kept by the missions as well as the accounts housed in the Palace of the Governors were destroyed, the pre-revolt population figures are open to question. Twenty-one friars and 380 colonists lost their lives. Surviving friars mourned the thousands of Indian Christian souls lost to Satan.

The survivors who reached Salineta just north of El Paso del Norte numbered 1,946 women and children, and 155 men considered capable of bearing arms. Indian servants and members of the Piro Pueblo made up the majority of the refugee band. Two survivors of the flight south were Doña Josefa López Sambrano de Grijalva and the beloved Marian symbol of La Conquistadora, brought to New Mexico in 1626 by Fray Alonso de Benavides. Josefa had been chosen to carry the small wooden statue to safety, most likely in an ox-cart. La Conquistadora was also revered as Nuestra Señora de la Asunción, Nuestra Señora del Rosario, and Nuestra Señora de los Remedios.

It was at the time of the 1680 Pueblo Revolt that a pre-revolt hacienda, known as LA 20000 in the New Mexico registry of archaeological sites, was destroyed and abandoned. No doubt the inhabitants of the ancient Diego Márquez estancia fled when warned by La Ciénega Pueblo that an uprising was imminent. What remains of the ancient estancia lies less than two miles south of the museum at Las Golondrinas, and was deeded to the El Rancho de las Golondrinas Charitable Trust in 1991.

Alonzo Catiti of Kewa Pueblo, Diego's half-breed son, was an implacable leader of the Pueblo Revolt of 1680.

Margarita, daughter of Diego Márquez, mistress of Governor Juan Manso de Contreras, bore him two children. The governor arranged for a bogus baptism and a fake funeral performed by Fray Miguel Sacristan of Santa Fé. The governor intended to have his illegitimate son taken to Mexico to be reared as a Manso. The Inquisition considered the act as sacrilege, and Fray Miguel committed suicide.

Upon the viceroy's January 1681 order, expelled Governor Otermín attempted a foray to reclaim the lost province. On November 5 of that year, the governor set out with a company of 146 soldiers and 112 Pueblo auxiliaries, plus a small contingent of friars. Only twenty-five military were fully mounted and equipped, the others had to rely on what weapons and shields they could carry on foot. Otermín found each Pueblo mission abandoned and each *estancia* pillaged. By 1682, increasing animosity directed at the Spanish forced Otermín to return to El Paso. No other Amerindian society ever accomplished the feat of casting out its European colonial masters. Spanish authority in New Mexico ceased to exist.

Popé, in supreme command, issued orders; the Indians must throw off all Christian influence. They were instructed to wash away the taint of baptism in the river using the suds of crushed *amole* root. Couples married in Christian ceremonies were to marry again, adhering to native custom. Every vestige of the Spanish presence was to be destroyed. But Popé's edicts fell short of reality. During the four generations since Oñate's *entrada*, a slow transformation of New Mexican society had taken place. The vast gulf that initially separated Spanish and the Pueblos had diminished, and a considerable amount of acculturation had taken place. Prior to European contact, only dogs and turkeys had been domesticated. After the Spanish arrived, Pueblos became accustomed to *bueys* (oxen), *caballos* (horses), *burros* (donkeys) sheep, pigs, chickens, new vegetables, grains and fruits, iron tools, and a new God who joined the pantheon of their old familiar divinities. Some had even squirreled away Christian religious objects as a hedge against the day the Spanish might return. They could not bring themselves to give up all things Spanish and revert wholeheartedly to the old ways. There would be no return to the past. The Navajo, who were semi-nomadic, farmed, developed a taste for mutton, found the fleece of the *churro* (breed of sheep) indispensible to their economy, and grew Spanish fruits, much to their delight.

Over time old inter-tribal feuds between the Pueblos and their nomadic neighbors resurfaced. The Apache had ever been a tough adversary, and their possession of the Spanish horse after 1600 made them even more formidable. The Pueblos, it seemed, had more in common with the Spanish than with their warring neighbors. In fact, they had created a defensive co-dependency. The Pueblo confederacy fell apart. The arbitrary Popé, who had established himself as strong-man in the Palace of the Governors, found his influence dwindling, and was deposed by Luis Tupatú. Popé was dead by the time Diego de Vargas arrived. The fate of his mysterious lieutenant Naranjo-Po-he-yemo is unknown.

Yucca provides amole soap suds

Diego de Vargas specialist John L. Kessell, University of New Mexico professor emeritus and author, has chosen to classify the Pueblo Revolt of 1680 as one of three stages of a wider historical period he calls the Pueblo-Spanish War. He maintains that the first chapter covers the events that lead up to the revolt, the second encompasses the time when the Pueblos successfully expelled all Spanish, and the third is what happened after the re-conquest.

The Vargas Entrada

The revolt of the pueblos sent shock waves back to the mother country. Following the crown's directive, the viceroy appointed a member of Spanish nobility, Don Diego de Vargas Zapata y Lujan Ponce de León, as governor to reclaim the lost province of some fourteen thousand people and twenty-two pueblos. Before assuming his office as governor of Nuevo México, Vargas twice held the position of *alcalde mayor* in Mexico, first in the district of Teutila in north-central Oaxaca, and again in the mineral-rich region of Tlalpujahua northwest of Mexico City. Vargas received reports that the unity of New Mexico's pueblos was disintegrating, and envisioned a second entrada, a *reconquista* (re-conquest) like that which freed Spain from the infidel Moors.

Don Diego de Vargas, *reconquistador* (re-conqueror), was born into one of the oldest and most outstanding Spanish noble families. "*Los Vargas son gavilanes*" (those Vargases are hawks) a Spanish poet had sung. For six centuries Diego's ancestors had won praise as warrior-knights, bishops, counselors to kings, and friends of saints. In 1083, three Vargas brothers fought to liberate Madrid from the Moors. In the twelfth century, Ivan de Vargas was a witness to the miracles of San Ysidro Labrador (Saint Isidore the Farmer) while Ysidro was tilling Vargas lands at Torrelaguna. The laborer became the patron saint of the city of Madrid, Spain, of agriculture, and of El Rancho de las Golondrinas. In the next century, a Vargas gave Francis of Assisi land for a Franciscan convent near Madrid, Spain. Four Vargas generations, including Diego's father, brothers, and a son, were knights of the prestigious military Order of Santiago.

When Vargas made a will in the summer of 1672, he described himself as the legal and sole heir of Alonso de Vargas, and had four witnesses provide proof of his identity. They concurred that he was "a young man of medium stature, straight hair, and broad face, who lisps somewhat and cannot pronounce certain words." Despite his speech defects, he was a self-assured, ambitious, and fearless young man. He had refined tastes and dressed in style. He ordered tailored suits for each season, wore fancy hats, silk stockings and gloves, required linen be provided for underwear, handkerchiefs, and bedding, and owned twenty-two pairs of shoes including some for dancing. He is also known to have frequented bullfights and the theater.

His expensive tastes may lead one to believe that Don Diego had unlimited funds. But like many members of his class in the seventeenth century, a time known in Spanish history as the *decadencia* (decadence), a period of economic, political, and military decline, Vargas was burdened with many debts and unprofitable properties. He once referred to his entailed estates as "my miserable *mayorazgos*." An entailed estate ensured that assets of a noble family would remain forever vested in a fixed line of descendants, and would pass intact from one heir to the next. The Vargas estates were in constant need of repair, were heavily mortgaged, and their debt service was becoming intolerable. Professor John Kessell, the editor of the six volume set of *The Don Diego de Vargas* journals, captured Don Diego's plight from the time the aristocrat assumed his inheritance at the age of eighteen in a piquant phrase, "Don Diego was, without question, a noble and landed Spanish gentleman. But the roof leaked."

As Spain's fortunes declined, nobles and commoners alike took the sea road to the Indies. The age of great conquests was gone, but a post in the royal bureaucracy offered regular employment, and the hope of achieving wealth at the expense of Indians and lower class subjects. Since officials usually paid for their appointments, their major concern was to squeeze enough from their subjects to pay their debts, and still make a profit from their employment. The crown routinely sold offices as well as titles in order to relieve its desperate financial crisis.

When young Vargas sailed for New Spain in 1673, he was following the example of his father who left Spain to serve as *alcalde mayor* of a district in the Mexican province of Chiapas. He left behind his young wife, Beatriz, and five children born in the first five years of their marriage. She died suddenly in 1674. Widower at age thirty, the homesick Vargas never returned to Spain despite his expressions of nostalgia for the homeland.

All but one of Diego de Vargas' children, cavalry officer Juan Manuel de Vargas, never saw him again. Evidently his responsibilities in New Mexico kept him from returning to Madrid, Spain and marrying another woman of his own rank as he wished to do. But he was not denied female companionship. His Mexican lover, Nicolasa Rincón, bore him three natural (illegitimate) children, two sons and a daughter. Little is known of Nicolasa.

In late summer of 1692, Vargas led a force of two hundred, some soldiers drawn from the El Paso *presidio* plus Indian auxiliaries, and a contingent of chaplains and colonists, a number of whom carried Nuestra Señora de los Remedios, the same revered Marian relic that accompanied the colonists when they fled south during the Revolt. All were back in El Paso del Norte in time for Christmas. After the Vargas return in 1693, she came to be known as La Conquistadora, Our Lady of Conquest.

Francisco Lucero Godoy and his first wife, Josefa López Sambrano de Grijalva, lived in La Ciénega. In 1680, the Godoys, along with their eleven children and eight servants, escaped to El Paso del Norte during the Pueblo Revolt. Josefa is credited with fleeing with the revered bulto of La Conquistadora and then returning with the sacred image during the re-conquest. Francisco came back with Vargas as an alférez (ensign) in 1692. In 1695 Francisco, now a widower, married his second wife, Catalina de Espíndola, thirty-five years his junior. At age fifteen, she was younger than most of her step-children.

At the 350-year anniversary of the founding of Santa Fé in 1960, Pope John XXIII ordered a papal coronation of the *bulto* (statue of sacred person, most often carved of wood) of La Conquistadora. Archbishop Robert Sanchez renamed the icon Our Lady of Peace because Indians considered her former name to symbolize cultural dominance. Even so La Conquistadora remains her enduring name, and she resides today in the Our Lady Chapel in the Cathedral Basilica of St. Francis of Assisi in Santa Fe.

Passing abandoned pueblos en route, Vargas and his party reached Santa Fé four weeks later in September 1692. It found the Palace of the Governors converted into a fortified multistory pueblo surrounded by a defensive wall, and occupied by some one thousand defiant Indians. Addressing the startled natives, Vargas delivered a conciliatory speech, assuring them that he would pardon all if they left peacefully and again became loyal subjects of the Spanish king. After a tense interlude during which Vargas cut off their water supply and threatened a siege, the Indians accepted his terms and Vargas entered the Indian stronghold. With the Indians gathered around, Don Diego performed the ritual act of possession. His 1692 encampment was where Rosario Chapel now stands, "a musket shot distance away" from the Palace of the Governors.

Three Franciscan priests then absolved the Indians of apostasy and celebrated the first Mass held in New Mexico in twelve years. Vargas presented the Tupatú brothers of Picurís Pueblo, leaders of the 1680 revolt, with cups of hot chocolate, a Hispanic delicacy. The highly prized luxury was sometimes used as a ceremonial drink to honor an unwritten agreement. Two days later,

122 children born since the Spanish departed, were baptized with Vargas serving as godfather to many. Luis and Lorenzo Tupatú became allies of Vargas and received full pardons for their roles in the revolt.

Vargas then set about appraising the region, its land, pastures, water supply and wood, and found the only satisfactory place to re-establish LaVilla de Santa Fé was the locality of the former Palace of the Governors, now an Indian pueblo. During the next four weeks, the governor toured the northern pueblos and at each performed the ritual acts of possession. It was during this expedition that the governor's party left its inscription at El Morro near Zuni Pueblo, "Here was General Don Diego de Vargas, who conquered all New Mexico for our Holy Faith and for the Royal Crown at his own expense, in the year 1692." Returning to Santa Fé on October 16, he wrote the Conde de Galve, Viceroy of New Spain, recording his triumph of peaceful re-conquest, but cautioning that an additional one hundred *presidio* soldiers and five hundred colonizing families were needed to make his victory permanent.

Armoured presidio personnel re-enactors

News of Vargas' feat, achieved "without blood and sword," caused celebration in Mexico City. The viceroy commissioned Carlos Sigüenza de Góngora, New Spain's leading intellectual, to write an account that would commemorate Vargas's exploit Sigüenza y Góngora complied, writing the thirty-six page essay published in *El Mercuio Volante* in Mexico City in 1693, that claimed Vargas had recovered a whole kingdom "without wasting a single ounce of powder or unsheathing a sword and . . . without having cost the royal treasury a single *maravedí.*"

Never one to hide his light under a blanket, Vargas had affirmed his stringent economy and financial self-sacrifice in letters to the viceroy and the king. In a letter to Charles II, who had cautioned Vargas that his entrada must be made "with the greatest economy possible," he informed the monarch that he had made the peaceful re-conquest of New Mexico, "achieving what his predecessors in this office, with great cost, were unable to achieve." Vargas coupled his lavish self-praise with requests for suitable rewards for his great services. In a letter from Zacatecas (May, 1693), he asked the king for the noble title of marquis, and requested an appointment to the governorship of Guatemala, the Philippines, Chile, or the Río de la Plata. Professor John Kessell's careful examination of the finances of Vargas' 1692 expedition into New Mexico contradicts the claims of extraordinary fiscal self-sacrifice. Kessell notes that although the crown had long held that expeditions of discovery and conquest must be self-financed, it had substantially subsidized Vargas' 1692 campaign.

> Vargas felt abajo (lower) La Ciénega was unacceptable for presidial relocation because of shade cast by the mountains and mesas and the rays of the sun penetrated only at mid-day. He found heavy frosts and ice, thick fog and mists and the discomforts of the "extremely" cold climate unsatisfactory. In contrast, Governor Vargas concluded that the territory of El Alamo de San José in arriba (upper) La Ciénega was choice . . . "because the terrain and soil are of dry, fine gravel, and well drained, and where the sun shines from the time it comes up. It has the benefit of breezes from all directions." Vargas chose the site as a commons for pasturage for horses and mules of the presidio and of the settlers. Las Golondrinas lies immediately to the south of the abandoned hacienda of El Alamo.

The reconquistador returned to El Paso del Norte by Christmas, 1692 and in the late fall of 1693, Vargas was back in New Mexico with one hundred soldiers, a new contingent of seventy colonists and eighteen friars. No doubt some *conversos* were among those recruited to re-colonization. Vargas would advance under the protection of La Conquistadora. She was carried in a portable shrine to motivate and protect Vargas's soldiers as they were reclaiming La Villa de Santa Fé from the pagan Indians. His departure from El Paso del Norte at the onset of winter could be regarded as foolhardy. His late arrival was because Vargas had to first stabilize the El Paso area before continuing up the Río Grande. He found the situation had greatly deteriorated in his absence, and the dream of a peaceful re-conquest proved an illusion. The Indians entrenched in the Pueblo established in the Palace of the Governors refused to leave as they had agreed to do, and the bitter winter of 1693 brought illness and death to twenty-two colonists camped outside its walls.

After two weeks of failed negotiations, Vargas abandoned diplomacy in favor of war, storming and capturing the Indian stronghold after two days of battle. He executed seventy Indians on charges of treason and apostasy. Another four hundred men, women, and children who surrendered were distributed among the colonists and soldiers and given sentences of ten years of servitude. Widespread unrest continued, but divisions within the Pueblos helped to avert a revolt on the scale of the 1680 uprising. The wish for access to Spanish materiel moved some Indians to accept the return of Spanish rule who would help to repel attacks by the nomads. Others rejected Spanish domination and fled to live with the Navajo, the Apache, and the Hopi who refused to accept Spanish overlords. Vargas' relative moderation helped to consolidate his power; he did not make the mistake of burning kivas and destroying sacred objects as his predecessors had done.

On 21 July of 1695, Vargas recorded, "The reverend missionary fathers who have followed me on the preceding campaigns as the chaplains of the army accompanied me accepting the work and danger. With the military leaders and officers present, I commanded and ordered them to go on to the hacienda of El Alamo, and after arriving there, follow the royal standard and me."

"From that outpost at about four in the afternoon, I went on to the abandoned pueblo of Cieneguilla, where I ordered the company to halt to spend the night. In that outpost I told the military leaders and officers of my decision to go make offensive war against the nation of the Jémez rebels and the Keres, their allies from Kewa Pueblo, who have done so much to provoke it. Although it was very good to use the present time for the war because the river had prevented us from doing so before."

—Don Diego de Vargas Zapata Luján Ponce de León.

In June, 1696 after months of growing tension and complaint by friars of the insolence of their charges and their threats of another revolt, many Pueblos rose in a new effort to rid themselves of the Spanish. Five missionaries and twenty-one settlers lost their lives. Only Vargas' steely determination, the courage of his *presidio* soldiers and settlers, support of some Pueblo allies, the onset of winter, and another drought that dampened Indian militancy, kept the rebellious Pueblos from repeating their 1680 successes. Never again would the Río Grande Pueblos rise up against their Spanish overlords. Only the Hopi, far to the west, retained their autonomy.

Diego de Vargas recorded in his campaign journal that in July 17-19, 1696 that Adjutant Juan Ruiz "left his men-at arms to guard the horses at the abandoned hacienda of El Alamo. . . . After Vargas sorted out the pack and saddle mules, he ordered Juan de Archuleta to remain with the men and horses until the next day waiting for orders that Juan Ruiz would bring."

Understandably, most colonists who fled New Mexico in 1680 and re-established themselves in El Paso and elsewhere were not keen to return. But Vargas needed people with many skills to hold reclaimed lands, and so he turned to other means to entice colonists northward. Families of modest means were offered opportunities to obtain honor and status, and the privileges and favors granted. Mostly it was settlers recruited in Mexico City by Fray Francisco Farfán and Captain Cristóbal Velasco, one an Augustinian priest and the other an ex-convict, who accepted the challenge of re-establishing the colony in New Mexico. Fray Farfán deserves credit for seeing the recruits safely along the journey to Santa Fé.

The few New Mexicans returned to New Mexico in 1693 expected to resume their prewar properties, but most were disappointed. Vargas did not restore the large *encomiendas* to the elite, and a more egalitarian society emerged. The need to defend the colony took precedence over evangelism; military spending grew, and the colony became more secular. Vargas established a land distribution system with grants that secured some Pueblo lands, private grants to individuals as rewards for service, and large grants that were awarded to communities for common use.

Antônio Jorge of El Alamo escaped the Pueblo Revolt in 1680 with his mother and two sisters. He returned with Vargas as a captain in 1692.

There were four Bacas in the colony at the time of the Pueblo Revolt in 1680, Cristóbal, Ignacio, José, and Manuel. They returned to New Mexico in 1693. Manuel Baca was the father of Diego Manuel Baca who married María Vega y Coca in 1719.

In 1701, Bernabé Jorge received the sum of 200 pesos "common currency" from Miguel García for a grant given him in the name of His Majesty by Vargas. Also in 1701, Joseph Castellanos transferred title of the old pueblo site of La Ciénega to Miguel García de la Riba. In 1714–1716, Andres Montoya purchased La Cieneguilla land from Juana and Joachin Anaya de Almazán that had been awarded to Francisco, their father. In 1717, Diego Arias Quiros registered a virgin mineral vein five leagues from La Ciénega.

In the journals of Juan Diego de Vargas we first meet the family that established the *estancia* known as Las Golondrinas. The list of colonists compiled by recruiter Fray Francisco Farfán totaled 235 persons in sixty-six families recruited in Mexico City dated 1-3 September, 1693.

In the Mexico City Vargas/Farfán muster roles of 1693, we find the following:

Miguel de la Vega y Coca, son of Cristóbal de la Vega, native of Mexico City, sixteen years old, sound body, aquiline face, fair, small eyes.

Manuela de Medina, wife of the aforesaid, daughter of Alonso native of Mexico City, sixteen years old, a small slightly wide nose.

Josefa de Cabrera, widow of Alonso de Medina, mother of Manuela, native of Mexico City, thirty years old, aquiline face, large eyes, and a pointed nose.

On 1 September 1693, this family received from the hand of the lord treasurer, to José de Urrutia, 300 pesos, which the government has arranged for them to be given as financial assistance in order to supply themselves with what is necessary for the trip.

Miguel and Manuela were married in late August by Fray Francisco

Farfán, the colonist's recruiter, and the marriage recorded in the marriage book for españoles (Spaniards) of the Cathedral of Mexico.

Vargas could reasonably have expected the Spanish crown to be grateful for the successful completion of his mission. But his repeated appeals for a promotion to serve anywhere but in this "miserable kingdom of New Mexico . . . last on earth and remote beyond compare" were ignored. In 1697 Vargas was disagreeably surprised by the arrival in Santa Fé of his successor, Pedro Rodríguez Cubero. Vargas, who regarded Cubero, in Professor Kessell's words, a "vile usurper," vainly attempted to keep him from taking office, resorting, it was later alleged, to "intimidation, threats, and disobedience." Cubero proceeded, in proper legal form, to conduct a *residencia*.

The inquiry did not result in charges of misconduct against Vargas, but it encouraged the Santa Fé *cabildo*, which had no love for the ex-governor, to file its own criminal complaint against him. Vargas was charged, among other misdeeds, with misuse of royal funds, unfair distribution of booty and supplies, and failure to heed warnings from friars that the Pueblos were preparing to revolt again. Accordingly, Cubero placed Vargas under house arrest and ordered his property, including two black slaves, confiscated and sold at public auction to cover the costs of his trial. Vargas spent three years confined in Santa Fé, and three more defending himself in Mexico City.

While there, Diego de Vargas encountered his only surviving son, Juan Manuel de Vargas, whom he had not seen in twenty-seven years. The aristocratic Vargas had commented that the Indies was a fine place for storekeepers, but not for aspiring noblemen like his son. Viceroys, he recalled, were inundated with requests for posts, but doled out few. As a result, the Indies were already populated with nobles who had suffered humiliating rejections. A year later, Vargas cried out in anguish upon learning that his beloved son, "the idol of my affection," died on his voyage home during a disastrous sea-land battle in 1702. In his final years, the aging Vargas mourned his losses, longed to return to his homeland, sent hugs and kisses to grandchildren he had never seen, and continued his struggle to escape from "this damned kingdom, which I cannot leave, trapped by my debts."

Vindication finally came to the harassed ex-governor. At hearings held in Mexico City in 1703, he was exonerated of all charges, and his accusers were ordered to pay court costs. Vargas could now again assume the office of governor to which he had been reappointed in 1699, succeeding Pedro Rodríguez Cubero.

The year before, acting on the recommendation of the Council of the Indies, the king had granted Vargas the title of marquis, and an *encomienda* with an annual value of four-thousand pesos, to be collected from the Indians of New Mexico. But his wish for an appointment to some more attractive part of the Indies, enabling him to escape from the wilderness of New Mexico, remained unfulfilled.

> Because Spanish law forbad colonists settle within the four square leagues guaranteed the Pueblos, Vargas no doubt intended to encourage colonists to populate the lands once occupied and then abandoned by Puebloans so that the Keresan Indians would not be tempted to return and potentially set up conflict. La Ciénega Pueblo was granted to Bernabé Jorge before 1701; he promptly sold it in January, 1702 to Miguel Garcia for 200 pesos.
>
> Juan Garcia de la Riva purchased the abandoned site of Pueblo of La Ciénega from his father in 1704. The deed is the first reference to a place called Las Golondrinas named for the swallows that were drawn to the *ciénega*.

Golondrina feeds her chicks

In September 1693, Vargas granted the old pueblo of La Cieneguilla to Francisco Anaya de Almazán, the younger.

Alonso (a.k.a. Alphonso) Rael de Aguilar was with Diego de Vargas, along with the Romeros and Moras, when New Mexico was reclaimed for the Spanish crown, and for which Rael de Aguilar received land known as the Cerrillos Grant from Vargas. When his family moved to La Cieneguilla is not known.

In 1704, Captain Don Diego de Vargas ordered fifty soldiers and officers on an "offensive war, with fire and sword," against Apache who had committed thefts of cattle and sheep at nearby Cieneguilla.

During a career crowded with responsibilities and anxieties, Vargas found time to maintain correspondence with his family back in Spain and to share its joys and sorrows. "My heart will rejoice," he wrote at the pending birth of the first of four grandchildren by his daughter Isabel María, and "I send lots of kisses and give my blessing." He then requested portraits of the family and of Juan Manuel on whom he doted, his only surviving son and heir to his estates. The eldest son, Francisco Ivan, had died earlier.

Death came to Don Diego de Vargas in Bernalillo, New Mexico. He had been campaigning against Apache raiders in the middle Río Grande Valley when he fell ill of typhus or dysentery, and was carried to Bernalillo by his men. He died eight days later on the afternoon on April 8, 1704 at sixty years of age. Vargas requested Mass be celebrated in the church at Bernalillo, and that his bed be used as his bier. He further requested that, "In the same bed, let my body be borne to the church of the villa of Santa Fé and buried there in the main chapel . . . let it be buried according to military honors and privileges of a titled nobleman of Castile."

Vargas recognized his natural children in his will and freed his black slave, who had served him since 1691, on condition that he accompanies his two sons by Nicolasa Rincón back to Mexico City. Don Diego had hoped to be buried in the Vargas chapel in Torrelaguna (Madrid) with others of his family. However, in his will he requested to be buried "in the main chapel beneath the platform where the priest stands," most likely in reference to the La Parroquia (parish church) of Santa Fé. There is no reliable record as to where the church stood in 1704, and the governor's bones may have been transferred to a new parroquia that stood on the site of the present-day the Cathedral Basilica of St. Francis of Assisi. No one knows where he lies as no document or monument marks his grave. Eight years after Vargas died, Lieutenant Governor Páez Hurtado was instrumental in the drafting the 1712 Proclamation that established the first Fiesta de Santa Fé. The decree called for a mass, vespers, and a sermon.

Juan Páez Hurtado, the leader accused, but not convicted of fraud during the second expedition to recolonize New Mexico in 1693, the Acting Governor of New Mexico from 1704 to 1705, founder of the Santa Fe Fiesta in 1712, and Governor from 1716–1717, was an early owner of lands in La Ciénega Valley.

The loss of Franciscans during the 1680 Revolt sobered the religious, and they assumed a more liberal approach to the Pueblos and their religious practices. The 18th century brought dramatic change in Pueblo-Spanish relations. Mutual toleration and cooperation attained a level unimagined before. Spanish became the *lingua franca* (primary language) of the region, enabling communication between tribes that previously spoke only their many native tongues.

Pressures by the Navajo and Apache tribes drove Pueblo warriors to join colonial militia in campaigns against raiders. Recognizing the value of cooperation, and wishing to avoid a recurrence of previous tensions, colonial officials' moderated their demands on their Pueblo vassals. The *encomienda* system disappeared and tribute requirements were greatly reduced. As missionary zeal declined due to the liberalism of the European Enlightenment, Pueblo attempts to preserve traditional ways and beliefs went largely unchallenged. They were able to retain religious practices and cultural traits that disappeared forever in other regions of New Spain. A colorful new hybrid society was in the making.

Despite the slaughters and other transgressions committed by the Spanish conquistadors and colonists, New Mexico illustrates the fact that the natives they exploited, often unmercifully, survived Spanish contact, and retained much of their culture and historic lands. If we compare their fate with that of other native peoples conquered by the British on the Atlantic seaboard, the vanished Penobscot, Seneca, Pequot, and others too numerous to mention, the contrast speaks favorable of Spanish colonial policy and practice.

4

El Rancho de las Golondrinas

Miguel Vega y Coca, Progenitor—The Casa Mayor and Baca Houses

Miguel Vega y Coca, Progenitor

Miguel Vega y Coca responded to the second call to enlist as a colonist to settle in New Mexico, but he lacked a wife. Procurador Fray Francisco Farfán required all who signed the manifest to be wedded, so sixteen year old Miguel quickly married María Manuela de Medina. The ceremony, performed by Fray Farfán on July 29, 1693 was witnessed by Captain Cristóbal de Velasco and Captain Agustín de Coca. In late August, 1693 their union was duly recorded in the marriage book for the Cathedral in Mexico City.

Among the enlistees who signed up with Vega y Coca were persons whose skills were needed for the re-colonization of New Mexico. Recruited were citizens with useful trades, stonecutters, carpenters, weavers, millers, shoemakers, iron workers, farriers, and other craftsmen. Each family received 300 pesos for travel expenses and provisions for the 456 *leguas* trip, or twelve hundred miles, enough aid to sustain them for nine months until they were able to plant and harvest crops. (One Spanish league equals 2.6305 miles or 5000 *varas*.) Transport was provided in mule drawn *carros* (carts), sixteen persons to a conveyance. Colonists who met the terms of their contracts were hopeful they would be granted the rank of *hidalgo*. Some used the honorific "don" and "doña" before their names, a significant designation in a society where class status was important.

After a grueling journey of nine months, it was on June 22, 1694 that Miguel Vega y Coca, his wife, and companions saw the country on the western approach of the Sierra Madre Mountains, now known as the Sangre de Cristos, that was to become their home. Here the story of El Rancho de las Golondrinas and its first family began.

> By rare good fortune Las Golondrinas has been held in trust for us, so to speak, since the day when colonist Miguel Vega y Coca was recruited at age 16 in 1693 by Fray Francisco Farfán and Captain Cristóbal Velasco to join the efforts of Don Diego de Vargas to re-colonize New Mexico after the Pueblo Revolt.
>
> Miguel Vega y Coca came to New Mexico as a youth in search of prosperity. In due course he acquired the estancia and other properties, and held important civil and military posts that brought him honor and the honorific title of "don."

Miguel Vega y Coca and his young wife, María Manuela Medina, settled in the community of Santa Cruz in 1695, but were dissatisfied and requested permission to move. María died two years later. Esquibel & Colligan, authors of *The Colonization of New Mexico,* recorded "no known issue" from this union. But there is reason to believe that there was a son, Juan Coca, and possibly a second son born to Miguel and María Manuela Medina. On April 13, 1699 Miguel married María Ygnacia Montoya in Santa Fé. It was sometime later in the 1700s when Miguel, a seasoned military man with a burgeoning family, acquired the rights by "royal purchase" to the site of what was to become Las Golondrinas *estancia* near the village of La Ciénega. Under the Spanish legal system, Las Leyes de las Indias (Laws of the Indies), any sale of real property was a royal purchase because the crown owned all. The transactions were traditionally consummated by throwing a handful of soil into the air with shouts of "Long Live the King."

Esquibel and Colligan credit Vega y Coca and his second wife with having eight daughters and one son, Antonio José Laso de la Vega y Vique, who may have been born to a mistress; it appears that Antonio also had a brother, Miguel de la Vega of Valle de San Buenaventura, Chihuahua who became a priest and baptized some of Antonio's children.

All of Miguel's daughters found suitable husbands, no easy feat in the days when a dowry was needed to marry off a daughter. The two eldest, María and Apalonia, married two brothers of Bernalillo, Diego Manuel, and Cristóbal Baca. Feliciana, Vega y Coca's third daughter, married Bernardo de Bustamante y Tagle, Lieutenant Governor of New Mexico and head of the military from 1722 to 1731. Her will stipulated 800 Masses, a remarkable number, be performed at her death in 1762 in the parish of her birth, Santa Fé. The fourth daughter,

Francisca de la Vega y Coca married Manuel Lopez, also known as Tenorio de Alba, a soldier of the royal garrison of the Villa de Santa Fé. Manuel appeared before the Reverend Father to ask "for the better service of God and to save my soul," permission to contract marriage with Francisca de la Vega y Coca. The couple had lived in concubinage, a common practice of the time. Leonarda became the spouse of Toribio Alejandro Ortiz of the wealthy Ortiz family, and Isabel became the wife of Miguel de Alire. Records for two daughters, Marcelina Antonia de la Vega y Coca and Margarita, are incomplete.

The Miguel Vega y Coca daughters and their husbands were credited by Myra Ellen Jenkins, former New Mexico State Historian, as having been among the original post-Revolt settlers of La Ciénega. La Ciénega was also known as San José del Guicú and Cañada de Guicú.

After Miguel Vega y Coca settled in Santa Cruz de la Cañada, he was recorded as having received a livestock distribution in Santa Fé in 1697. His allotment listed thirteen sheep, one cow, and one bull.

In 1714, Miguel received one of six shares in the Nuestra Señora de los Reyes Linares mine from his compadre (ritual co-parent, godfather), Captain Sebastián de Vargas, in the San Lázaro Mountains. There is no evidence that the mine was successful.

In 1715 Miguel Vega y Coca became an alférez during military campaigns against the Apache and the Utes.

On July 20, 1716, Vega y Coca was ordered by Governor Felix Martínez to recruit ten militia men and to provide two mules and four horses to serve in a campaign against Apache raiders who were preying on Cieneguilla livestock.

At the same time, Captain Diego Manuel Baca, Miguel's son-in-law, was ordered by Governor Martínez to supply twenty men from Cochití, ten from Kewa Pueblo, and twenty from San Felipe Pueblo to make war on the Moqui (Hopi) west of the Río Grande.

In 1719, Miguel stated that he had been in the military for twenty-five years, and in 1725 was elected alcalde of Santa Fé.

On April 17, 1727, Don Miguel and Doña Maria sold a house and land in Santa Fé to move to Taos where he assumed the office of alcalde. There they remained until about 1731 when Miguel and his wife returned to La Ciénega to settle on their ranch. They then purchased land known as San Miguel de la Cruz between Kewa Pueblo and Jémez.

When María Josefa and Apolonia Vega y Coca married the two Baca Brothers in Bernalillo in 1719, the Baca line became firmly established at La Ciénega Valley and Las Golondrinas. The nuptials took place on August 14, a double wedding ceremony. No doubt the marriages had been arranged. Diego Manuel, who married María Josefa, held substantial assets. His will records, "I declare that at the time that I entered into matrimony there was given to my said wife a dowry of a ranch which consists of a house and cultivable lands for the purposes of planting wheat. The lands for planting wheat are as much tilled lands to cover three Spanish bushels of seed, and corn other lands, and a *fanega* of seed, about one bushel, and a little more contiguous to the lands of my Sir Father, of my said wife. . ." (A *fanega* also can be interpreted as one and nine-tenths acres of land.) His estate included, along with his home and its contents, three yoke of oxen fully equipped, six mules, six tame horses, three milk cows, a year old bull, two axes, an adze and pitchfork, a bow for projecting arrows and a sword, his saddle, and various personal items. Baca then recorded other sundry items and the names of many individuals who owed him money. He concluded with an account of the debts he owed to seven other individuals. The first known record of the site of the Vega y Coca *estancia* appeared in the 1727 will of his son-in-law, Diego Manuel Baca.

Cristóbal Baca, who wed Apolonia Vega y Coca, stated in his will: "I declare that at the time of my marriage with said Doña Apolonia, her parents gave her dower lands where I lived named after Jesús, María y José, on which I built this house of my residence, and other lands, as well as another tract which I added and bought from Andres Montoya, immediately adjoining these." Both brothers directed that ". . . if God deigns to take me from this present life . . ." that their remains be shrouded with the habit of St. Francis, and the interments take place in the church in the Villa de Santa Fé. Cristóbal Baca's will listed his livestock, 450 head of sheep, eleven mares, a stallion and the season's colts, four mules, a cow and a bull, plus itemized farm implements and tools, spurs, textiles, saddles, clothing, a suit of armor of white serge, and a wheelwright's cart plus innumerable other items. The sum of the estate totaled 3,553 pesos. In the end, he ordered that one hundred masses be said for his soul. Christóbal also declared ". . . to have an illegitimate son called José Antonio, and in my will he gets a share of property equal to that of my other children."

While it seems that through time the *rancho* properties remained in the Vega y Coca/Baca/Pino family hands, continuity can only be suggested. The

Bacas, along with the Montoyas, were some of the earliest settlers in Valley. Diego de Montoya was the son of Bartolomé Montoya, an Oñate colonist. The frequency with which these family names appear in documents implies consanguinity. Juan Esteban Baca, son of Diego Manuel Baca and María Josefa Vega y Coca, owned Las Golondrinas property as recorded in La Ciénega Census of 1790.

It has been believed the first building in the Vega y Coca *estancia*, a large stone and *adobe*-mortared structure, was constructed sometime after 1710, about the time Miguel Vega y Coca is thought to have acquired the property. But that date is subject to question. Was it Miguel de la Vega y Coca or Diego Manuel Baca who married his daughter, María Vega y Coca in 1719, or others of a later date who began to build? Researchers have been unable to find documents relevant to the Vega y Coca property "royal purchase" or the building of the Las Golondrinas complex itself. Myra Ellen Jenkins, author of the "Application for Registration, New Mexico State Register of Cultural Properties," declared that "Las Golondrinas was the home of María Vega y Coca and her husband, Diego Manuel Baca, son of Manuel Baca, who had lived in Bernalillo before the Pueblo Revolt." Esquibel and Colligan recorded, "Don Miguel's lands have included the land at Las Golondrinas in the original grant made to him. If so, this would explain how Diego Manuel Baca, husband of María de la Vega, came into possession of the land and whose *rancho* was inhabited continually by Baca descendants until the twentieth century."

> Scholar Donna Pierce, former Curator of Collections, holds that the area known as El Rancho de las Golondrinas was deeded to Miguel Vega y Coca in the year 1703.

The cavernous stone and *adobe* dwelling, La Salón y Capilla, was most likely occupied by the early families as a home and a livestock barn. The adjacent La Cocina con Fogón de Pastor appears to have been part of the original building. The rest of the fortress-like complex is assumed to have been built to provide more living quarters, work space, and for defense. The aged Salón and Capilla building has been in use in one capacity or another since that day when the Vega y Coca/Baca families purportedly began its construction in the early eighteenth century. It is now in use as La Capilla and La Sala de Fundadores (Colonial New Mexico Historical Founder's Room). The Capilla demonstrates the role of the Catholic tradition so important to New Mexico's colonial people. The Las Golondrinas Sala is used for display and interpretative purposes. Overall, what we see demonstrated today at El Rancho de las Golondrinas is an interpretation of Hispanic colonial life.

Capilla and barn

In 1730, Miguel and María temporarily returned to their ranch at Las Golondrinas, and subsequently purchased land from Captain Diego Aria de Quiros who acquired, through a royal grant, the parcel between Kewa Pueblo and Jemez Pueblos. Then in 1731, Vega y Coca and his wife moved to Taos where Miguel held terms as *Alcalde Mayor* of Taos and Picurís. It was in 1736 that a criminal case was filed against Captain Miguel Vega y Coca for having wounded Miguel Fernández in an altercation over irrigation water. We do not know the outcome of this affair, but it does not seem to have damaged the reputation of Vega y Coca who came to be referred to by one and all as "Old Miguel." At the ripe old age of seventy-three, he and his wife appeared in the 1750 census of with several members of their household. Don Miguel wrote his will in 1751, but unfortunately it has not survived; a final disposition of the property was executed in 1760. During Don Miguel's career, he was a respected man of honor and nobility, had acquired property, held civil and military positions, and arranged marriages with suitable dowries for his many daughters into prominent and aristocratic Santa Fé families.

The 1750 census of the paraje community of El Alamo had been resettled in 1730. It had been owned by pre-Pueblo Revolt Baca family members. The census listed a population of 39 families that totaled 622 persons. El Alamo remains in the historic record, but only its unexcavated mound is to be found today.

Don Miguel Vega y Coca left his farmlands and house in La Ciénega Valley to his many petitioners. Although the will has not survived, documents executed by his heirs track the distribution of Don Miguel's estate. On May 7, 1760 the Alcalde Mayor of Santa Fé certified the distribution of his considerable lands totaling 1841 *varas* along Ciénega Creek, and the dwelling of . . . the deceased Coca . . . in accordance with reason and justice. In order to be equitable, the *Alcalde Mayor* measured the four allotments of land himself using a rope of fifty *varas*. (One *vara* equals 2.8 feet.) Primary claimants on the settlement date were Miguel Tenorio, Cristóbal Martín, Miguel de Alire, and Toribio Ortiz.

By this time, the house, suffering from neglect, had deteriorated. From its remnants, a living room was granted to Miguel de Alire, Miguel Tenorio was given a bedroom and a *portal* (covered doorway). Cristóbal Martín received three windowless rooms "in bad condition," and Torbino Ortiz was awarded a kitchen and a store-room All were to be granted easements to their awarded properties.

Genealogical records of the Miguel Vega y Coca family show:
María Josefa—ABT 1700–1748.
Married Diego Manuel Baca—August 14, 1719
Apolonia—1701–1734.
Married Cristóbal Baca—August 14, 1719.
Francisca—ABT 1705–1760.
Married Manuel López (Tenorio de Alba)—July 13, 1721.
Leonarda—ABT 1706?
Married Toribio Alejandro Ortiz—June 14, 1735.
Isabel—ABT 1708–1752.
Married Miguel de Alire—May 18, 1728.
Feliciana—ABT 1710–1762.
Married Bernardo Bustamante y Tagle—June 17, 1733.
Marcelina Antonia—ABT 1712–?
Married Manuel Ortiz—November 6, 1735.
Margarita—ABT 1714–?
Married Juan Tenorio de Alba—October 23, 1728.
Antonio José Laso—ABT 1718–? (Mother unknown)
Married Micaela Lopez—ABT 1739.
Miguel—ABT 1719–? (Mother unknown)
Juan de Coca—ABT 1720–1777 (Possible son)
Married Margarita Bustamante—May 6, 1741.

A Paraje

The site of Las Golondrinas was ideal for an *estancia* and for a *paraje* on El Camino Real de Tierra Adentro. It was reported that the grass was chest high and the water sweet. In addition to having the requisites of timber, water, and forage for a choice campsite, the *estancia* had the advantage of being just one day's travel from Santa Fé.

Special guests may have been given shelter within the walled *estancia*. Others camped below on La Ciénega Grande as was the custom. Villagers selected well-drained sites not suitable for crops to lay foundations for homes of uncut stone mortared with mud up to about eighteen inches above the ground. The rock foundation hindered the capillary action of ground water. Above the foundation, wall construction was of *adobe* brick held in place with mud mortar. Bricks were formed of sifted clay with binders of straw, wild grass, hair from animal hides, or sand mixed with water until a dough-like material was produced. The raw *adobe* was packed into wooden molds that shaped bricks of approximately 10 x 14 x 4 inches, then blocks were freed from their forms to air-dry for two days. Bricks were then turned on end side-by-side and dehydrated for about a month. A finished brick weighed about 35 pounds. The bricks were then laid up to form walls, joined with an *adobe* mortar, and the exteriors and interiors were dressed with slurry of straw and *adobe*. The exterior surfaces required much annual maintenance.

Putting finishing touches on adobe model

Adobe construction has ancient roots. Archaeologists found *adobe* that dated to four thousand years ago in the Ocre site in southern Spain. The Spanish brought to the New World the tradition of construction using *adobe* bricks that were formed by hand in wooden molds. Both Pueblo Indians and Hispanics used *adobe* construction, but with notable differences. The Indians primarily used puddle *adobe*, a primitive wall construction that eroded easily. Caliche (calcium carbonate) was the only hardener used. Bands of *adobe* mud laid up by hand 15 to 20 inches high were dried and cured before other layers were added, a very time consuming job.

After the *adobe* building was raised to a height of eight to ten feet using bricks, the roof was installed. *Vigas* (log beams) of six to ten inches in diameter and up to twenty feet long served as beams, and were laid across the span in two to three foot intervals. Logs for use as *vigas* had to be cut and hauled long distances from the Sangre de Cristo Mountains. Across the span of *vigas*, *latias* (small dressed poles) were placed, sometimes in a herringbone pattern. At times *rajas* (split cedar strips) were used for the same purpose. Above the *vigas* and *latias*, several courses of grasses, straw, and dirt were installed, and sometimes brush and wood chips were mixed within. The depth of the roof was about eighteen inches, and before long it sprouted a stand of weeds and grasses. Although a building might be of any length, the span of the *vigas* dictated the width of the structure. *Vigas* were installed with their thicker ends placed on the same wall so as to create a gentle slope for drainage. Within a century after construction, it was necessary to replace the *vigas* that rotted away. The interior was dark, as windows were small and set deep within the walls, admitting little light. Window openings were covered with sheets of mica or selenite (transparent crystallized gypsum), or sometimes animal skins, scraped thin, oiled and stretched, and hung over windows and doors admitting little light. Imported panes of glass were so prized that they were used mostly for display purposes, never in a window.

In an attempt to reflect light and brighten the interior of the room, walls were often painted with a whitewash of *yeso*. Gypsum rock was baked for three days, crushed into a powder, and mixed with wheat flour and water to be applied with a sheepskin pad. No doubt the gypsum was collected from deposits west of the Cerrillos Hills near Peña Blanca or Galisteo Creek below La Bajada. A trade item, *tierra amarilla* (yellow clay), laced with flakes of mica, could be mixed with water and applied to the lower walls as a wainscot or *resguardo* (safeguard).

It was sometimes applied using a stencil and daub to create patterns that suggested wallpaper designs. When colored crepe paper became available, many housewives used its dye to color the ornamentation. Larger windows were provided with shutters swung on wooden pivots or leather hinges, and were barred with peeled saplings anchored in the *adobe* wall. Wooden doors were equipped with pintles that allowed them to swing freely, a technology used in ancient Egypt and Mesopotamia. Door openings reached to a height of about five feet, and raised sills were installed to control drafts. Corner bell-shaped fireplaces of *adobe* brick were installed, and *adobe* flues extended above the roofline to protect the ceiling from overheating. No andirons were needed in the *fogón* (fireplace) because the firewood was not stacked. Piñon firewood, standing upright in the firebox to resemble a tepee, used less fuel. The walls behind the *fogón* retained the warmth. Tamped earth floors had a gentle irregularity and were covered with pieces of *jerga* (woven wool rug) or un-tanned cow hides. A well-to-do villager took pride in having an ox-blood floor, achieved by soaking the tamped earth floor with animal blood, a strong cohesive. A glaze of *yeso* was then applied. The result was a warm red-brown surface, tough and springy, that buffed to a dull shine.

Ranch animals captivate children

A look at Las Golondrinas' Casa Mayor shows it served both as a shelter and a fortress. A necessary component of the complex was a *torreón defensivo* (watchtower). The Las Golondrinas Placita *torreón* is a representation of how one might have been designed, and how it was used. The many *torreones* were of necessity large because the colonists needed not only to have weapons close at hand, but to provide security against raiders. At the first sight of approaching marauders, a lookout posted on the upper level would sound an alarm to alert those working in the fields, giving them time to scurry back to the compound and prepare to defend themselves. Mounted Indian attackers struck with a swift deadly force. No doubt a horse was kept saddled and ready at the *torreón* in the event one was needed to ride for help. Bows, arrows, and lances were the principal defensive weapons. Firearms were scarce, often in poor repair, and ammunition in short supply. Farsighted colonists dug camouflaged pits where individuals would hide if there was no time to flee back to safety. Sometimes the Indians sighted were not part of a war party at all, but a band come to trade. Archaeological evidence recently uncovered at Las Golondrinas indicates that the original *torreón* most likely stood to the west overlooking La Ciénega Valley, not as depicted in the Casa Mayor today. The site is recorded as LA127373 in the New Mexico registry of archaeological sites

Torreón Defensivo looks over the Camino Real

Lookouts in the fields guarded against pilferers be they human, four-footed, or winged. Raccoons and birds took a frightful toll on grain, orchard fruit, and fields of vegetables. When human marauders struck, *pastores* ordered dogs to scatter their flocks; they hoped to be able to recover a number after the danger had passed. The most dangerous raiders were the Indian nomads for whom pillaging was a part of life. They often struck in the fall when lambs and kids had put on a summer's growth. Navajos boasted that they would leave enough sheep so as not to dishearten the farmers.

One can imagine the excitement of the dwellers at Las Golondrinas when a caravan arrived from Mexico. First, the "singing" of the *carretas* (carts) was heard long before they came into sight. The cumbersome iron-tired spring-less wagons, whose wheels and wooden axles with little lubrication, sounded a high-pitched squeal that was heard from far away. Axels and wheel hubs were greased with lard or tallow mixed with roasted green pine tar if lubricated at all. Soon a lookout in the *torreón* would sight the weary newcomers eager to rest, replenish their supplies, exchange news, and engage in festivities. *Carretas* used for long transport were larger and equipped with metal tires. Those that hauled freight over long distances were most often drawn by mules. The domestic *carretas* standing today by the *puertón* (large door) of the Las Golondrinas *zaguán* look as though they have just arrived from the fields. The tongue of the *carreta* was fastened to a crossbar that in turn was strapped to the horns of a team of oxen.

Descendants of the early families, that of Francisco de Anaya Almazán, Bernabé Jorge, Andres Montoya, Miguel Vega y Coca, Diego Manuel Baca and others, take pride in tracing their roots back to these hearty folk who arrived as members of the re-colonization efforts of Don Diego de Vargas.

Some might look back to Alonzo Varela Jaramillo when he and his wife, Catalina Pérez de Bustillo, settled their estancia in 1632. Francisco Lopez de Aragon, whose wife had ties to the estancia and paraje of El Alamo, escorted wagon trains over El Camino Real de Tierra Adentro in 1640 and again in 1646.

Another notable family came into the mix when Feliciana Vega y Coca married peninsular Bernardo de Bustamante y Tagle, Lieutenant Governor of New Mexico from 1722 to 1731. Their daughter, Josefa, was instrumental in re-establishing the Santa Fe Fiesta and the Confraternity of La Conquistadora. She donated vestments to the military chapel of Our Lady of Light along with painting and gifts to the church at Pojoaque. A recent Las Golondrinas reunion of the extended Bustamante family was attended by 150 persons.

Carretas and the Golondrinas Placita

The colonists living in this remote area were effectively cut off from the motherland, and were starved for news as well as for entertainment and gossip. Information and rumor from Mexico City was already six months old when it arrived with the travelers. Reports of events in Spain were at least a year old before they reached the *estancia*. It took at least two years to receive a reply to a letter posted to Spain. Visitors were warmly welcomed and then wished Godspeed and sent on their way, but often not before a *baile* or *fandango* (dance) was held in the *placita*. When a priest arrived at the *estancia* to perform his services, a *fiesta* (feast and entertainment) inevitably followed. Here was the occasion to dress in whatever finery had survived the arduous journey from deep Mexico and the ravages of time.

The Casa Mayor and Baca House

Recorded in the 1975 Application for Registration to the New Mexico State Register of Colonial Properties submitted by historian Marc Simmons, we find: The original Rancho de las Golondrinas compound consisted of a fortified dwelling built around a *placita*, with two *zaguanes* (covered entrances) and a defensive *torreón*. This complex has been reconstructed on the original foundation under the guidance of the Baca family to whom the ranch belonged for 200 years.

Golondrinas placita, noria and hornos

From the early period, only the barn survived. Its center section of stone possibly dates from the 18th century. *Adobe* extensions on each end were added later, one of which served for a time as a dwelling. Outside the main complex, a house was built for Manuel de Baca, (son of José Francisco Baca y Terrus) in 1835.

Manuel de Baca Casa

The entrance to the Las Golondrinas *placita* is a massive wooden *puertón* (large door) that, when closed, prevented unwanted intruders from entering. The smaller *puerta de zambullo* (pedestrian door) restricted entry to one person at a time, allowing easy defense against forced entry. To enter is to be transported back to the time when the Vega y Coca/Baca families lived, prayed, worked, raised families, and trusted in their God. The original *placita* structure of stone, thought to be the Vega y Coca/Baca home and barn, now houses a museum exhibit of a traditional *capilla* of the 1790s. The *placita* itself is surrounded by twelve rooms. Using historical records of the period, the museum staff has staged the rooms with spartan traditional furnishings in ways they may have been used. The first room a visitor enters after leaving the Las Golondrinas Capilla is a kitchen with a shepherd's fireplace and bed, La Cocina con Fogón de Pastor. This typical 18th century kitchen has an architectural feature to be found in many colonial homes. The Fogón de Pastor is in the corner, and is vented up through the corner chimney. It was installed under a shelf, long enough for a *cama* (bed) that extends over the cooking area. La Cama del Pastor, on the shelf high above the dirt floor over the *fogón*, collects the heat from the cooking fire beneath. As a result, the bed pallet was cozy during the cold winter and early spring weather. It is said that the farmer occasionally used the warm bed to nurse frail animals born in the bitter early springtime weather until they were strong enough to be returned to their mothers. The breeding of animals was timed so they would drop their young early, allowing the newborns to mature by fall.

To the left of the fireplace is a wood-frame fleece-lined *cuna* (cradle) suspended from the *vigas*. Nearby is a *mano y metate* (grind-stones) used to prepare corn meal for the family, a technique employed by all New World native civilizations. Minute grains of sand entered the meal, and it was claimed that, "Everyone swallows a *metate* and four *manos*" in the course of a lifetime. A tiny window is covered with selenite, and another is fitted with peeled sapling poles installed upright and close together. If the cooking fire did not emit enough light after sunset, the *araña* (spider) chandelier, suspended from the ceiling on a pulley, allowed the occupant to lower the crossbars so the hand-dipped mutton tallow candles could be lit. A large hollowed-out cottonwood log stored grain. Poles suspended from the *vigas* provided the means to hang herbs and medicinal plants, and the occasional *manta* (blanket). A *banco de pared* (adobe bench) against an outer wall provided seating. The *jerga de lana* (woolen rugs) are typical floor coverings, and were woven by the museum's weavers.

In the center of the *placita* one finds the *noria* (water well) and two *hornos* (beehive outdoor shaped ovens), essential for every household. Next to *zaguan* entrance are the Alcoba de Huespedes (guest bedroom) and the Cuarto de Recibo (living room). The *patrón* (master of the *estancia*) no doubt proudly furnished and decorated the guest room, for he received many important travelers as they passed through the *paraje* on El Camino Real de Tierra Adentro. One such guest to stay the night in 1780 was the military genius, Juan Bautista de Anza, the new *criollo* governor of New Mexico.

El Cuarto de Recibo in the Las Golondrinas complex gives us a look into the home of the *patrón* and his wife. The cozy, inviting atmosphere of the home's interior made the welcoming Spanish phrase, "*mi casa es su casa*," most appropriate. A fireplace once filled the room with pungent piñon wood smoke. The simple furnishings installed by the museum staff, a *ccja de madera* (wooden chest), a *petaquilla de piel* (leather chest), and a *silleta* (chair), faithfully recreates the setting of a guest room. The family altar, lovingly tended by the women, stood along one wall where members of the household would have worshipped daily. Religious art is displayed throughout the dwellings in the *paraje*. The *bancos de pared* provided the only seating aside from a wooden bench or chair. Relatively little furniture was to be found in homes of the elite as well as the impoverished. Another *fogón de esquina* (kitchen fireplace) was installed for cooking, heat, and light.

Juan Bautista de Anza visit re-enactors

Many rooms served multiple purposes, food preparation, dining, visiting, and as the sleeping quarters. It is difficult to estimate the number of people who lived the year round at Las Golondrinas; an estimate is from twenty to fifty persons. This number included the extended family, its servants and field hands.

Upon leaving the family living quarters, the visitor finds a Zaguán al Torreón, the entrance to the *placita's* watch tower. (As discussed earlier, the original *torreón* sat on a hill to the southwest apart from the Casa Mayor.) Here, weapons and other supplies would be stored against a threat of attack; included were machetes, bows and arrows, lances, swords, crossbows, a few guns, and where ammunition would be stockpiled. Lives depended on being well prepared and vigilant. Tradition holds that youths were often assigned the responsibility of serving as lookouts in the tower because they had better vision. Next to the *torreón* are an Alcoba de Dormir (bedroom) and a Dispensa (store room). Today, spinning wheels are on view in the *alcoba de dormir*. This technology was not readily available in the early days of the *paraje*. They became obtainable from traders after the opening of the Santa Fe Trail. A noteworthy display in the *paraje* is that of the Talleres de Tejer (weaving workrooms).

The museum has an ongoing weaving program where skilled spinners and weavers use replica period *telars* (looms) to weave the *jerga* on display throughout the museum. On the walls are skeins of yarn that have been spun from the fleece of the museum's flock of *churro* sheep, and dyed with traditional colorants.

Churro ram with four horns

First, the wool is shorn early in the spring before warm weather shedding, and then the wool is picked clean and carded. The women card the wool into fluffy bundles of parallel woolen strands using combs of stiff leather set with teeth of fine wire, hence the term "carding." A *malacate* (spindle), a smooth, straight stick thrust through a whorl (wooden disk), serves to spin the wool into yarn. With her elevated hand, the spinner catches the wool fibers from the carded bundles to the yarn on the malacate as it is spun by rolling the shaft against the weaver's thigh. The yarn is then looped into skeins and washed in warm water using mild suds made from crushed *amole* root swished in water, a soap favored by the Pueblo Indians.

It is necessary to use a mordant to open the pores of the fibers so they will accept dyes. The weaving program at Las Golondrinas is faithful to the technology of the past with the exception of the use of juniper ashes, salt, and human urine to set dyes. Alum alone is now employed. One marvels at the subtle shifts in hues from one dyed skein to another as subsequent dye baths lessen the saturation of color. The range of hues and shades are a feast for the eye. The fine colors the visitor sees exhibited at Las Golondrinas were dyed in the converted summer kitchen, the Tapeste de Teñir (Dye Shed), next to the Ratón Schoolhouse.

Of particular note is the wide range of hues of the much preferred cochineal red produced by a dye made from cochineal insects. After the Santa Fe Trail opened, American traders introduced commercial aniline dyes that lightened the intense labor required to gather and brew the herbal dyes used by early weavers. The new dyes also provided a wide range of bright colors previously unavailable. Two trade items became indispensible to New Mexican traditional weavers, cochineal and indigo. All others were available to the colonists from the natural world at hand. The red cochineal colorant is made from the female scale insect (*Dactylopius coccus*) that feeds on the *nopal* (prickly pear) cactus, and was found chiefly in the state of Oaxaca, Mexico. In a bit of industrial espionage, the tiny beetle-like insects were spirited out of the country and cultured elsewhere. This highly prized red is used today in dyes, cosmetic products, and as food coloring. Indigo is a blue vegetal dye obtained from a semi-tropical plant originally grown in India, exported to the Americas, and now grown in the southeastern United States. Its preparation is complex; leaves were fermented to a smelly, thick paste, dehydrated, and pressed into blocks which were later ground into a powder and put into an alkaline solution. Wool dipped into the green, slimy, odorous solution oxidized to blue when exposed to air.

Tapeste de Teñir with skeins of newly dyed yarn

The villager's *telar* (foot loom) employed a horizontal or low-warp design. Made entirely of wood, the earliest looms used two log rollers fastened to a frame. *Tela* (warp threads) were strung through *lisos* (heddles) attached to the rear roller, and wound onto the front roller as weaving progressed. *Lisos* of knotted string loops were fastened to upright oblong wooden frames. Ropes attached to the uprights were fastened to a pair of foot treadles that alternately raised selected warp strings when depressed. *Lanzaderas* (shuttles), flat sticks with end notches around which weft yarn was wound, were thrust through the raised warp. A *peine* (comb beater) of stout cord loops on a narrow wooden frame, captured the warp threads, and served to force the weft down with a firm stroke. In later years, metal wires replaced the heddle and beater strings.

Weaver in Taller de Tejer

Usually Hispanic men operated foot looms while women prepared the yarns. Looms of two sizes were used, the larger measuring four to five feet in width to weave the full width of a blanket. The narrower loom was the width of half a blanket or for a serape panel, and the worker sewed two matched pattern pieces together. *Jerga,* the quintessential all-purpose woolen textile, was woven and used by all in the home for floor coverings and bedding, and as a trade item.

Another textile product, New Mexican embroidered *colcha*, is especially notable. *Colcha* literally means bedspread or coverlet. Altar cloths and coverlets are among the finest examples of *colcha*. A museum quality wall hanging, displaying symbols unique to Las Golondrinas, and created by the museum's weavers, is on display in the museum's *capilla*. *Colcha* embroidery uses woolen yarn, dyed in delicate, harmonizing colors, and stitched to a plain, loosely woven cotton or woolen *sabanilla,* an all-purpose backing. *Churro* wool yarn results in the use of coarse stitches that fill the larger design elements. Solid areas of color requires the thread remain on top to hide the *sabanilla* fabric, thus conserving the labor-intensive dyed yarns as none was wasted on the back of the piece. Chintz, a floral printed cloth imported from India, provided inspiration for many *colcha* patterns. Stylized flowers, with winding stems and fanciful details found in chintz floral elements, influenced the designs created by the *colcheras* (embroiders).

New Mexican Hispanic colonial families typically had few personal effects; this was true of the families in La Ciénega Valley. Andres Montoya of Cieneguilla was better off than most, and recorded amongst his household goods one chest for chocolate with its key, one old cloak of *dieciocheno* with its warp of 1,800 threads, a new great coat lined with blue flannel, goods for some trousers, a black hat with a black band, and a wool mattress. This was in addition to his recorded tracts of agricultural land, livestock, and farm equipment. The 1727 will of Diego Manuel Baca of Las Golondrinas, who preceded his father-in-law, "Old Miguel," in death, itemized his estate. It included, along with his lands and home, personal property of a sword, a saddle, spurs, two bridles, and saddle blankets. Baca was buried under the high altar of the *parroquia* in Santa Fé. Diego's brother, Cristobal Baca, husband of Apalonia Vega y Coca, listed two copper candlesticks, five pewter plates and four silver spoons in the inventory of his estate.

Typical home furnishings were *armarios* (armoires) and *trasteros* (cupboards) used for clothing, dishes and foodstuffs, and *cajas* (boxes) that stored food and clothing. Chests, using dovetail or mortise and tendon joinery, were the most common items of furniture. *Alcenas* (wall cupboards) were sometimes installed, *nichos* (niches) served to display *santos* and other precious items, and there were but few chairs or wooden seats. Tables were used for display of prized objects. *Jerga* or an animal hide was spread on the floor where family members would work, eat, or receive guests. Families slept on the floor of packed earth using *jerga* and animal hides for warmth. Mattresses were stuffed with straw, grasses, or wool if available. During the day, pallets were rolled up and placed on the wall *bancos* to serve as seating.

Today a perceptive visitor grasps how times have changed. Constructed a century after Diego Manuel Baca and María Vega y Coca established the Casa Mayor, the Casa de Manuel de Baca, the Baca House, was built by Manuel de Baca, son of José Francisco Baca y Terrus, for his family in 1835. The Baca house is roomier, with large windows that admit ample light, and the exterior defense walls and the *torreón*, once necessary to protect the inhabitants, are gone. The house is now comprised of three rooms, although there once had been more, and is protected from the elements and uninvited guests, human or animal, with *contraventanas* (shutters), and *rejas* (wooden bars) set into the windows. Construction utilized a labor-saving building technique similar to that of the *adobe* Casa Mayor with its more labor-intensive *adobes*, but employed the use of *terrones* (dried blocks of sod cut from marshes), some of which have been left exposed in the *cocino* wall to demonstrate the technique.

Descendants and friends of the Vega y Coca/Baca families held a family reunion at Las Golondrinas the summer of 2008. Attending were some 200 persons, descendents of the fourteen families that made the paraje home.

Some buildings at Las Golondrinas have been collected from northern New Mexican sites where they were in danger of demolition. Regrettably, many old structures were seen as a ready source of firewood and fell to the chainsaw, and *adobe* bricks were recycled. Salvaged utility buildings installed near the Baca house are the Fuerte (secured storage), the Dispensa, and the Soterrano (root cellar). Hispanic households often kept bull snakes in the *dispensas* to help control the rodent population.

Cocina in the Manuel de Baca House

Across the Placita from the Baca House next to the Tiendita (little country store) is the Hojalatería, the Delgado Tin Shop. Dedicated to tinsmith Francisco Delgado, who was largely responsible for a renaissance in Hispanic tin working the early 20th century, the Hojalatería (tin workshop) displays the workroom of a professional craftsman. Items made of the easily worked "poor man's silver," an alloy of tin and lead, became available when the U. S. Army arrived in the territory. The military imported foodstuffs and oil in tin cans, and thrifty Hispanics saw an opportunity to recycle the discarded containers into useful artistic and household objects.

Another attraction at the museum is the Almacen de Vino (winery). Here one will find El Viñedo Gallegos (the Gallegos Vineyard), originally planted with traditional Old World mission grapes, *vitus vinifera*. However, the grapes are not harvested. The cabernet sauvignon or pino noir grapes used during the Harvest Festival wine making demonstrations are obtained from the lower Rio

Grande region. Grapes are crushed in the traditional way employing barefooted children who line up to have their feet hosed down with water, and then climb into the cowhides vats to squash, press, and mash away. The juice is fermented for a few days, and a consortium of museum members makes wine throughout the winter. It is an annual challenge to increase the quality and quantity from the year before.

Before Prohibition, New Mexico produced more wine than all of California. In 1880, 3150 acres yielded 950,000 barrels of wine, most of them in the El Paso area. By 1920, drought and Prohibition diminished the total crop to eight acres.

5

Threats from the East

The Comanche—Juan Bautista de Anza—Trade Fairs and Cautivos

The Comanche

Spain paid little attention to the events in the vast wilderness of North America beyond the borders of New Mexico. In 1684, the daring French explorer and adventurer, Robert Cavelier de la Salle, proposed to colonize the mouth of the Mississippi. The hapless explorer missed his mark, and found himself well within Spanish territory four hundred miles to the west. Although his petty incursion was quickly driven off, it alarmed Spain. La Salle had previously led an expedition from the Great Lakes down the Mississippi River to its delta where he proclaimed the river and all adjacent lands possessions of the Sun King, Louis XIV. French Louisiana split the Spanish borderlands in two, separating their western flank south and west of Texas from their eastern lands in Florida, settled in 1565.

A growing rivalry between Spain and France for possession of the immense wilderness in the interior of North America found French fur traders establishing posts in Illinois and the eastern reaches of the Great Plains. Other pressures from the East forced mass migrations of native peoples. Plains Indians, the Pawnee, Osage, Wichita, and Kansas tribes moved toward the Southwest. By 1680, the Apache acquired Spanish horses through raids and barter. The horse allowed for a new means of swift and deadly warfare that made the Apache an ever-present menace. To complicate matters, other Plains tribes encroached on the hunting grounds of the Navajo and Apache. Hemmed in by Spanish and Pueblo towns in the west and the French and enemy tribes to the east, the Apache began to raid settled areas of the Río Grande with increasing regularity.

Spain needed a buffer to protect its valuable mining districts and densely populated areas of San Luis Potosí, Zacatecas, and Chihuahua against foreign invasion. In order to discourage French incursions, Spanish law barred all trade with foreigners, as did other colonial powers that jealously guarded their mercantile interests. But French traders soon learned that the ban could be circumvented. These enterprising folk avidly sought to trade with Santa Fé merchants who were eager to acquire wares from the east, and could pay for them with silver from the mines in northern Mexico. The colonists resented the Spanish commercial monopoly that excluded cheaper and sometimes better made foreign goods.

Plains Indian lodge

In the spring of 1720, Santa Fé received alarming reports that many Frenchmen were living among the Pawnee along the Platte River in Nebraska.

In response, the young and inexperienced Don Pedro de Villasur was sent with a small company to scout this territory. His company was massacred, but a few survivors returned to Santa Fé to report what happened. Spain responded by attempting to strengthen the eastern defenses.

A pictorial record of the 1720 ambush of New Mexican presidial soldiers, led by New Mexico Lieutenant Governor and Commander-in-chief Pedro de Villasur, is recorded on the bison hide painting known as Segesser II. It is now on display with Segesser I in the New Mexico State Historical Museum. Jesuit priest, Philipp von Segesser von Brunegg, sent the hide paintings of the Villasur battle to his brother in Switzerland. Two hundred years later, the paintings were purchased by the Palace of the Governors in Santa Fe.

In 1724, Miguel Vega y Coca testified concerning the ill-fated Pedro de Villasur expedition into Pawnee territory of the Great Plains.

When the French and Indian War ended in 1763, France ceded its vast Louisiana Territory to Spain to keep it from falling into British hands, only to have it returned to France in 1802. President Thomas Jefferson bought the entire of the Louisiana Purchase from Napoleon Bonaparte in 1803, and the fledgling United States claimed territory to the Río Grande River. The 1819 Adams-Onis Treaty renounced any claim of the United States to territory west of the Sabine-Red-Arkansas Rivers to the Río Grande. Anglo squatters and the Spanish found themselves face-to-face in Texas.

Meanwhile, the Spanish living on the Río Grande faced a mounting threat from Indian raiders. Pressures from Spanish colonials and incursions of Anglos from the east were creating turmoil amongst the native peoples. Apache bands arrived in historic times and dispersed throughout New Mexico. The Jicarilla, a name derived from the baskets they wove, moved to the Canadian River. The Mescalero Apache, who raided along the middle Río Grande, and the Chiricahua, their cousins to the west, suffered abuse by the Spanish and became formidable foes. The alignment of Indian forces grew more complicated when the Ute to the north and the Apache to the south acquired new neighbors, the fearsome Comanche (Numunu), who struck like bolts of lightning out of the northeastern plains. Together, the Ute and Comanche began raiding the Pueblos, the Spanish settlements, and the Jicarilla Apache.

The ever-growing Indian threat produced a deepening alliance between the Pueblo tribes and the Spanish settlers. Efforts by Spanish missionaries to extend an olive branch and coax the raiding tribes to come under Spanish tutelage failed dismally. Spain then resorted to *guerra a fuego y sangre* (war by fire and blood), but that too proved futile. In the long run, a policy of "peace by purchase," supplying the Indians with foods and other goods, proved more effective.

By the time of the American Revolution of Independence, The Kingdom of New Mexico was under intolerable stress from warring Plains tribes. The Comanche swept into Taos in 1760 carrying off fifty Spanish women and children. The colony was in danger of collapse from the raids, especially those of the Comanche who struck from West Texas, Oklahoma, and Southeastern Colorado with deadly force. The dreaded Comanche had a mounted strike force considered by many to have been the best light cavalry in the world.

In the summer of 1776, the hapless residents of La Ciénega, Cieneguilla, El Alamo, and Las Golondrinas suffered loss of life from the devastating Comanche raids. In 1778, one hundred twenty-seven persons were killed by the Comanche in New Mexico, and loss of life continued until 1881.

During his 1759–1760 visitation of New Mexico, the Bishop of Durango, Pedro Tamarón y Romeral, arrived at El Alamo, a large two story house with many corridors. Here an esteemed chief of one of the "peaceful" Apache tribes came to call on the Bishop, and warned of a pending Comanche attack. Tamarón took the opportunity to urge the chief to become a Christian. The Apache insisted he was too old to learn and recite the catechism.

Antonio José Mora, great grandfather of Carmen Mora-Lisano and Sarah Mora-Nigro, brought a bulto of San Antonio from Portugal and kept it in his home in La Cieneguilla. Neighbors would come, pray, and seek solace from the fearsome Comanche raids. The suffering became so great that the villagers made a promise to San Antonio that if the raids cease, his grateful petitioners would build a capilla to honor him. The attacks did stop, and the Mora-Lisano family constructed the Capilla de San Antonio shortly thereafter to fulfill its pledge.

Juan Bautista de Anza

By 1776, half of the villages and hamlets in the region were in ruins, and the remainder faced a precarious future. Relief came with the arrival of the gifted military leader, explorer, and diplomat of Basque heritage, Lieutenant Colonel Juan Bautista de Anza. Anza's career rivals that of any heralded frontiersman, but is mostly unknown outside of Hispanic America. Anza, accompanied in 1776 by the Franciscan Father Pedro Font, eighteen soldiers, muleteers and servants, made a reconnaissance through southern Arizona to San Francisco Bay where he designated the future site of the Mission San Francisco de Asís (also known as Mission Delores). With him also came some two hundred Mexican colonists with their cattle, pack-mules, and horses, to establish the *presidio* of San Francisco, and to plant the seeds for today's thriving City by the Bay. The Presidio was intended to stop anticipated Russian incursions from Alaska.

Today a commemorative monument stands in the Juan Bautista de Anza Memorial Plaza by the visitor's gate of El Rancho de las Golondrinas. A bronze plaque by Mexican sculptor Julián Martínez honors the memory of Anza's 1780 visit. It reads, "Don Juan Bautista de Anza, outstanding Spanish Governor of New Mexico (1778–1787), explored a new road from Santa Fe to Arispe, Sonora in 1780. This plaque is placed in commemoration of the two hundredth anniversary of the historic journey." Anza was searching for an alternative route between New Mexico and Sonora, hoping to enhance the economy and to provide for better defense.

Juan Bautista de Anza memorial plaque

> Governor Anza embarked on a mission of mercy to the Hopi nation in 1780 after receiving reports that its people were starving because of a three year drought. Hoping that he might improve relations with the Hopi people by offering food aid, his overtures were refused. The Hopi claimed they had nothing to give in return.
>
> The name of Las Golondrinas first appears in the journal entry of Juan Bautista de Anza dated November 9, 1780.

Not only were the Russians encroaching on the northern reaches of Spanish territory, Indian raiders were wreaking havoc along the two-thousand mile stretch between the Sea of Cortés to the Gulf of Mexico. The French were supplying arms to Plains tribes and the fearsome Comanche raiders, and the Spanish crown was under financial stress. Spain had thrown her diplomacy and financial support behind the American Colonies as they sought to break away from Great Britain, a fact little known or acknowledged by historians.

The colony along the Río Grande was on the verge of collapse from the pressures of the Indian nomads when, in 1778, Juan Bautista de Anza arrived in Santa Fé to assume his new role as governor. This *criollo*, born the son of a military officer on the Sonoran frontier and killed by the Apache, understood Indian warfare. A natural leader, Anza possessed determination and courage. By August 1779, he had assembled a punitive expeditionary force at Ohkay Owingeh Pueblo with the aim of eliminating the Comanche threat. The army numbered more than six hundred troops of trained and equipped regulars, Hispanic settler volunteers, and Pueblo Indians and a few Apache who were ill-equipped. Most of their horses were in such poor shape that Governor Anza declared them "almost useless."

Anza's command consisted of three divisions. He provided each volunteer with a sound horse, weapons, and other needed equipment. Two hundred Jicarilla Apache and Ute joined his force. Traveling by night and preceded by scouts, the army rode into present day Colorado in search of a Comanche war chief, Cuerno Verde (Green Horn), who came by his name because his headdress had one buffalo horn painted green. The Comanche leader, known as Tabivo Naritgante (Brave and Handsome), was a charismatic war chief of one of the more powerful Comanche bands, and had a burning hatred for the Spanish who had killed his father during a raid at Ojo Caliente.

Knowing that the pass east of Taos was watched by Comanche lookouts, Anza chose to travel up the western flanks of the Sangre de Cristo range (the southern tip of the Rocky Mountains), where his troops were hidden from view. He crossed the mountains above Pike's Peak, and then moved south along Fountain Creek to Wigwam. There Anza came upon the main Comanche camp, took a number of prisoners, and much booty for his Indian allies. There he learned that Cuerno Verde, accompanied by four military captains, had raided Taos and was expected to return to his camp below the Arkansas River. Moving to engage the war party, Anza and his forces surprised the unsuspecting Cuerno Verde. Before the battle ended, the proud Comanche perished along with his son, four sub-chiefs, and his primary medicine man. The mighty chief, a firebrand to the last, went down full of arrogance, pride, and feeling secure in his invincibility. Anza had crushed Cuerno Verde's military power in a stunning campaign against a war party of from 800 to 1,000 warriors. One must note that there was no single cohesive unit of the Comanche; rather there were many independent bands. Some would trade peacefully while others raided at will.

Victorious in war, Anza was also skilled in the arts of conciliation, for he understood Indian tribal structure and ways. Anza opened negotiations with Ecueracapa, the Comanche leader who had become head of a now unified Comanche nation, a move that resulted in the 1786 peace treaty. At Pecos Pueblo, a splendiferous Ecueracapa received the title of "General of the Comanche Nation" from Anza, serving as a representative of the crown, and was presented with Anza's personal sword and a banner. Ute leaders also attended the meeting, promising to keep the peace, and to join with the Comanche in a common war against their old enemy, the Apache. The peace treaty, little known today, was executed at Pecos Pueblo between the Comanche, the Pueblos, and the Hispanics. The pact lasted well into the American period.

There are striking differences in Spanish attitudes toward the Comanche. A prominent New Mexican, Pedro Baptista Pino, was chosen by lot to serve as the colony's deputy to the Spanish Cortes (Parliament) in Cádiz. On his arrival in Spain in 1811, he published an invaluable political and historical treatise, *The Exposition on the Province of New Mexico, 1812*. In this work, written after the 1786 Comanche peace treaty was executed, Pino contrasted the ferocious Apache, who were still at war, with the noble and chivalrous Comanche, who were now at peace. Pino glowingly described the "robust and graceful presence" of the Comanche, and his frank, martial air. Pino described the Comanche government as democratic and gave a respectful account of the Comanche religion, way of life, and funereal practices. Of the Comanche style of war he wrote: "None of the other [Indian] nations attempt to match their forces with those of the Comanche. The Comanche do not accept quarter, but grant it to those they conquer. They prefer death rather than subject themselves to humiliation. In their acts of war they never attack with use of trickery, but face to face and after giving warning by their whistles." By contrast, Pino described the "Apache nation is the most obnoxious and cruel of all . . . They are always naked, always treacherously killing and robbing. They torture their prisoners in the cruelest way. They are accustomed to scalping their victims while still alive and they cut up their bodies into small pieces. Finally, the Apache . . . has no check on his depredations other than his fear of the brave and honorable Comanche." Pino concluded by describing Anza's campaign against the Comanche. In contrast, before attitudes softened when the proud nation and its flamboyant chief were defeated by Anza, Governor Manrique had briefly and brusquely called Cuerno Verde "the scourge of this kingdom who has exterminated many towns, killing hundreds, and making as many prisoners whom he afterwards sacrificed in cold blood."

In 1803, Salvador Manuel Armijo, cousin of the last Mexican governor, Manuel Armijo, was ambushed and killed by Apache warriors at Las Golondrinas.

Remarkably, the treaty held. New Mexicans now carried on a vigorous trade with the Comanche, and plied them with trade goods and tobacco to secure the new relationship. The Comanche threat to La Ciénega and Las Golondrinas ended. Comanche warriors, sometimes accompanied by Spanish troops, rode against the Mescalero and Gila Apache, keeping them away from the mining areas of Northern Mexico. It is noteworthy that no Anglo-American could travel freely through the Texas-New Mexico borderland, but Pueblo Indians and Hispanic settlers moved about unmolested.

Trade Fairs and Cautivos

In a curious break with the tradition of chronic Indian warfare, the annual Great Taos Trade Fair and the Pecos Trade brought about a universal "blanket" truce among New Mexico's warring parties. Many Indians had been practicing the concept of a peaceful market, so they readily accepted a medieval concept of the Truce of God. Even the most unmanageable Indian tribe honored the universal respite until the fair ended. Then it was back to the business of fighting as usual.

The first New Mexican trade fair was held in 1650, but records of the fairs were lost during the Pueblo Revolt of 1680. By 1710, fairs were held at the old Pecos Pueblo, Taos, Laguna, Santa Clara and Jémez Pueblos. By 1790, single tribes were allowed to hold their own trade events in order to reduce opportunities for conflict. All tribes, be they enemies or friends, came to major autumn trade fairs laden with buffalo hides, buckskins, horses, jerky, and *cautivos* (captives) to exchange for Spanish hardware, textiles, bells, knives and hatchets, awls, needles and scissors, mirrors, other novelties, and Pueblo produce. Buckskins, the treated hide of antelope or deer, were so valuable that they often were used as the medium of exchange. On occasion, an illegal French trader slipped into Taos from the East. The tradition of trade fairs continued until the opening of the Santa Fe Trail in 1821.

Taller de Cuero leatherworking shop

> Before the Mexican American War, Plains Indian slaves in New Mexico were known as genízaros. After Spain lost control of the New World and Mexican rule took over, these persons came to be called cautivos, although the term genízaro remained in use. Many La Ciénega Valley residents held cautivos and participated in the widely accepted trade.

An elitist group of Spanish governors sought to maintain a monopoly of the valuable trade by barring ordinary citizens from attending the fairs. But after missionaries smuggled letters from outraged colonists to Mexico City, a royal order proclaimed the fair open to everyone. In order to prevent possible outbreaks of violence, the governor in Santa Fé, along with their own pack loads and soldier escorts, traveled to Taos for the duration of the event. Haggling and swapping went on twenty-four hours a day with gambling, horseracing, drinking bouts, and womanizing. Many a "grass baby" was born nine months later. The whole fair was such an unruly, scandalous scene that in 1761, an abashed priest could not bring himself to speak aloud of what he saw. He had to write out his account. No doubt the Great Taos Trade Fair was the largest, most colorful, noisy, and rough marketing system ever seen in the Southwest. Indians, Hispanics and a few French traders came in relative peace from far and wide to buy and sell, trade, gamble, party, visit, exchange news, and in general have a fine time.

> In 1726, the thirty-two-year-old Diego Manuel Baca, Miguel Vega y Coca's son-in-law and his "ambitious and greedy" companions, began to trade before the Pecos Pueblo Trade Fair was officially open for business. Diego was bartering for Indian *cautivos* when he and his companions stirred up quite a ruckus. His brother-in-law, Manuel Tenorio de Alba, Alcalde of Pecos, was there to preside over the fair and maintain order, and to purchase captives for friends, an act which was in direct competition with Diego. Tenorio de Alba withdrew from the fracas that ensued, and looked for witnesses to testify about Diego's outrageous behavior.

Alcalde Tenorio de Alba may have had a conflict of interest. Clients had arranged to have the alcade select a "good heathen child" for a Spanish resident of Santa Fé, and another young Indian for a Catholic priest. When the Indian traders came to do business, they brought but few captives. Tenorio delayed the start of the fair in order to select the choice from the scant supply. Diego Baca and others incited a riot, claiming that trading was not reserved for government officials. Subsequent investigation found illegal trade practices had been employed by the alcalde.

The *cautivo* trade concession was one of the largest at the fair. Native peoples and Hispanics alike traded for and took captives to market. No one abstained on moral grounds, least of all the colonists whose military campaigns against Navajo and Apache groups provided a convenient pretext for taking prisoners. The *cautivos* were then sold for use as labor for handsome profits. As early as 1618–1625, Governor Juan de Eulate issued *vales* (licenses) that permitted kidnapping of Indian "orphans" as rewards for military service. The license gave a soldier settler the right to take one Indian child where he found him or her, provided he treated the "orphan" well, and taught the youth Christian catechism. A strong eight-year-old girl could bring premium price, and as a rule she became an integral part of the new owner's family. Boys were less valuable because they were not easily pacified and tended to run away. Hispanics sometimes ransomed Indian slaves whom they Christianized and taught Hispanic ways, for use in their household domestics and field hands. When Indian children were brought into families as servants, they were given the family name, baptized, and became full citizens when they married. Most were freed at twenty-one years of age.

It was common practice for *ricos* (wealthy) to purchase a *cautivo* as a gift for a daughter on the occasion of her wedding; possessing a *criado/a* (Indian servant) was a mark of distinction. Even colonists of low status felt that they had not made their mark until they had one or more *cautivos* to train as servants in their homes, and to bear their names. Many Hispanics preferred the term "bonded servitude." A wealthy colonist's female slave often bore his children who then became available as wedding gifts for relatives and friends. The introduction of Indian blood expanded the limited Hispanic gene pool. To avoid the accusation of illegal chattel slavery, and to mollify their consciences, captives were often baptized and recorded by their owners as *piezas de indios* (individual Indians). Slaves could take their masters to court in order to obtain a change of master, but their children remained with their owner.

The 1740 will of Andres Montoya of La Cieneguilla records that he owed the following to the ". . . Son of Thomas Madrid, San Buenaventura: little Indian girl, 6 years old which I likewise order shall be paid from my estate." . . . "and to Miguel Gonzáles, resident of San Buenaventura, little Indian boy, 7 years old . . .. " He concluded, "If through forgetfulness, one should appear that it may be proved that I owe, and my goods fall short of paying for it, I ask my Creditors, for the love of God, to forgive me."

Juan Antonio Baca of La Cieneguilla, who engaged in cautivo trade, was brought before Governor Vélez Cachupín in 1762 accused of selling an Indian woman.

Nazario Gonzáles, María Rita Baca's husband, was born in 1818 into one of New Mexico's oldest families, became a prominent businessman, and held political offices. Nazario traded $60, a mule and a saddle for Guadalupe, a Navajo captive. She was subsequently discharged for quarreling with another captive.

María Antonia was three years old when she was purchased and taken in as a member of the Gonzáles family along with Guadalupe. María Antonia later married into the valley's Padilla family after she inherited part of the Gonzáles estate.

In all of New Mexico's history, slavery was technically illegal. But under the genius of Spanish legal theory and its "Just War" clause, taking and ransoming captives was allowable. As long as the parties were capturing or redeeming captives and raising them as their own, the practice was accepted. Although the Mexican Constitution of 1824 abolished the enslavement of Indians, it was condoned with the argument that the slaves received the gift of Christianity. The custom continued on after 1860, and even the Emancipation Proclamation issued by President Abraham Lincoln in 1865 made little difference.

Charles III, the Spanish King, provided a special mercy fund to redeem Spanish *cautivos* and to ransom *genízaros*. Plains Indian *cautivos* were regarded as the lowest of the low in Hispanic society. The king's well-intentioned ransom fund only exacerbated the problem, and the Comanche intensified their raids for *cautivos*. At the aforementioned trade fairs, the question on everyone's mind was the mood of the Comanche. Their surliness and inclination to fly off the handle were of great concern. In 1723 when the captive women the Comanche offered for sale found no buyers, the Indians flew into a rage and killed the lot on the spot. The Western New Mexican town of Cebolleta became the center of the trade in *cautivos*. It may have been illegal, but as late as the 1930s, Indian women who had been taken from their tribes as children still lived in Hispanic households. Some became so acculturated they refused to leave even when given the opportunity. Special Commissioner for Indian Affairs, William Griffin, tried to end slavery in the courts. In 1868, the agent brought 290 cases forward in Taos County alone, but all were ultimately dismissed.

6

Everyday Life in Colonial La Ciénega Valley

Transformation in Isolation—Land and Water—Agriculture and Husbandry

Transformation in Isolation

Change came slowly to the way of life of the families at Las Golondrinas and the rest of La Ciénega Valley. Children were born, elders died, saints were honored, crops harvested, sheep shorn, prayers said, seasons and visitors came and went, and life went on. Villagers lived in almost total isolation from Mexico and the rest of the world. Their only contact with the outside was with the travelers along El Camino Real de Tierra Adentro, and the merchants who did business from Mexico to Taos traveling to trade fairs. Their language, sprinkled with some native words, remained that of Cervantes, and their faith that of the medieval Catholic Church. Of necessity, villagers learned to be self-reliant for the crown could give them little support. The agricultural practices brought by the early colonists changed infinitesimally, but over time were modified by need and by example of their accomplished Pueblo neighbors.

Villagers were introduced to several varieties of corn, beans, squash, and medicinal herbs, along with nonfood crops of gourds and tobacco. Successful farm methods were demonstrated and shared. Colonists fed themselves primarily with wheat, corn, summer and hard-shelled varieties of squash, Anasazi, bolita, and pinto beans along with foodstuffs introduced from Mexico: mutton, lamb, milk, cheese, goat meat, wheat, and the indispensable chile. They raised a variety of melons, squash, cabbage, radishes, onions, lettuce, and the grains, sorghum, hard red spring wheat, and barley.

The corn varieties ranged from flint, which was ground into flower, to dent corn and sweet corn. Seasonal fruit produce from orchards and vineyards supplemented their diets. Wild fruits were plums, chokecherries, and *tuna*, the fruit of the prickly pear cactus. Sorghum molasses was the primary source of sweetening. Juice from the sorghum cane grown at Las Golondrinas can be observed being extracted in the old way during the annual Harvest Festival. Sugar was imported at great expense.

Stringing chile ristras

Melasera Vieja juices sorghum

Wild honey was sometimes obtainable; domestic honeybees were imported later. Apples, apricots, peaches, raisin grapes, and melons were sun-dried for use out of season and against lean times. Strips of venison, buffalo, and domestic meats were dehydrated into *cicinas* (jerky) to store, and as a mainstay of travelers. In times of scarcity, the villagers trapped or hunted wild game with bow, arrow, and spear to augment their diets. Trains of *burros* laden with kegs of Taos whiskey and *ardiente* (flavored liqueur) from El Paso and Bernalillo supplied requirements of the thirsty villager. Wealthy colonists could sometimes enjoy rice, saffron, olives, and olive oil shipped in ceramic containers at high prices from Spain and off-loaded at Vera Cruz, Mexico.

Chocolate, imported from Mexico, was perhaps the most esteemed food found in colonial kitchens. It was so valued that it was often kept in special lock boxes. A beverage of chocolate was often drunk cold, occasionally sweetened with honey or vanilla, and spiced with chile, but it was most enjoyed as a hot drink. Ground cocoa beans were heated with water, mixed with sweetener and cinnamon, and whipped into a frothy delight using a *molinillo* (wooden whisk).

> **The 1740 will of Andres Montoya, La Cieneguilla resident, records, "I declare I have an old chest for chocolate with its key."**

Corn and wheat tortillas were cooked on *comales* (flat sheets of iron or stone). Other foods were prepared in earthenware pots over open fires, and game was grilled on a spit. Most families ate from the common pot while seated on the floor using curled tortillas as edible spoons, and drank from gourds that had been split, emptied of their seeds and dried. Pueblo ceramic pots were used as storage vessels, cook pots, and to store water. Indian pots fired at low temperatures are porous and allow for slow evaporation; capillary action cools water. In wealthier families, food was served in pewter dinner ware or *majolica* (glazed pottery) brought from Mexico.

The cool days of autumn was the favored time to butcher animals, and Las Golondrinas *matanza de animales* (butchering area) was put to use. The *malacate* (hoist) suspended a slaughtered carcass so that it could be bled, skinned, eviscerated, and butchered. Slaughtering a pig in the fall, *la matanza del cerdo*, was a community event for family, friends, and neighbors when *chorizo* (sausage), *chicharrones* (cracklings), and *morcilla* (blood sausage) were shared. The Baca house plaza with its *matanza* buzzed with activity on such occasions.

Land and Water

Land suitable for irrigation in New Mexico was generally found on alluvial floodplains, while essential woodlands grew at higher elevations. With an average precipitation of less than fifteen inches in a year, agriculture in these high desert regions of New Mexico was dependent upon irrigation. More than one growing season came and went without enough moisture, and famine threatened. Efforts were made to ensure that each colonist received his or her share of irrigable bottomland, uplands, and forestlands. *Suertes* ("ribbon" or "long-lot" platting) that spanned the creeks were favored to provide water to as many farms as possible, and it was by this division that families willed their lands. Agricultural land was recorded in *varas* measured along the bank of the watercourse. The colonist owned the territory from the stream bed to the *acequia* (lateral irrigation ditch) laid out above. The land above the *acequia*, with its grass, firewood, and timber was for community use. The arrangement guaranteed that large numbers of settlers would be accommodated with access to limited water resources. La Ciénega long-lot farms extended over spring-fed Ciénega creek, and an 1895 Territorial plat map clearly delineates the long, slim parcels owned by Andres Gonzáles, Manuel Baca y Delgado, Miguel Bustamante, Pedro Pino, and others.

At the heart of all Hispanic farming communities was a water distribution system overseen by an elected *mayordomo* who determined the distribution and use of the water, and made the labor assignments for construction and upkeep. All decisions were based on the amount of water used and the amount of land irrigated by each farmer. The *mayordomo* assigned a section for the annual spring maintenance to each individual. *Acequia madres* and *contra acequias* (lateral ditches), had to be cleaned every spring. These annual activities allowed time for conversation and socializing between task assignments. By the time the first dwelling at Las Golondrinas had been erected, the *acequia* system was in place to irrigate the fertile bottom lands.

In La Ciénega Valley, as elsewhere, the need to share scarce water resources with villagers required a cooperative relationship. The Vega y Coca/Baca family and villager neighbors first drained the *ciénegas* (marshlands) of their *estancias* in preparation for the delineation and layout of fields. Next they surveyed and dug the *acequia madre* fed by water from Ciénega Creek. The source of the creek is six *ojos* (springs) in the upper valley; the water course flows from Arroyo Hondo through Ciénega Valley, El Rancho de las Golondrinas, and into the Santa Fé River below. Small rock, earthen, or wood dams up-stream in the *acequia* diverted water to lateral ditches, which in turn redirected water to fields surrounded by earthen banks. Water was then turned into small furrows that irrigated thirsty crops.

Men using plows, shovels, and hoes drained the *ciénegas* and cut away the brush and weeds, surveyed the terrain, and then laid out the fields. One simple survey level was designed with a piece of wood carved to resemble a boat and assembled with two matching sticks equidistant from front to back. The crude assembly was then placed in a shallow container filled with water and supported on a monopod. The surveyor sighted across the tops of the sticks to a range pole calibrated in tenths of a *vara*. With multiple sightings, an ideal grade of about one-foot drop in one hundred feet would be staked out. With a one percent drop, water ran fast enough to service the fields, but not so fast as to cause erosion of the ditch banks. Aqueducts were made of a series of *canoas* (wooden troughs) to span gullies and arroyos.

> A ready supply of water is indispensable, especially in semi-arid zones like New Mexico; passions over water allotments run high yet today. José Andres Gonzáles, living in the La Ciénega Valley, was seen illicitly diverting water to help his father, Nazario, to irrigate his crop at El Guicú. A neighbor, after threatening any who interfered with his water allotment, struck José with a shovel, killing him instantly.

Today's crops at Las Golondrinas are watered from the historic *acequia* using siphons and furrows. Any water left over from irrigation and the occasional powering of the *molinos* (grist mills), is emptied into a holding pond below there to be held for La Ciénega village needs. The ancient Las Golondrinas *acequia madre* is listed in the National Register of Historic Places in Washington DC.

A major use of *acequia* water was to power the grist mills. Juan de Oñate reported from his capitol of San Gabriel that "the wheat is growing well, and the *molino* is ready." The first planting in 1599 was of seven *fanegas* (about 62 acres). For those living in a community that did not have the services of a *molino*, or chose not to pay a fee for the milling of their own grain, the task fell to wives, daughters, and servants. Wheat does not lend itself readily to being ground on a *metate*, so one or more grist mills were established in every community.

Historic Golondrinas acequia

Three such *molinos* are on display at Las Golondrinas today, one collected in Truchas and reassembled on a branch of the *acequia*. The venerable log Molino Barela de Truchas (Truchas Mill), constructed in 1873 with its 32-inch *rodezno* (horizontal water wheel), and is powered by water diverted from the ancient *acequia* through *canoas* (log flumes). It is the only known tub *molino* constructed of logs in operation today. One operational tub *molino*, the Cordova Mill near Vadito in Taos County, has been primarily reconstructed using railroad ties.

Molino Barela de Truchas powered by a rodezno

Museum researcher Earl Porter has documented over 450 Hispanic *molinos* in New Mexico, and has studied many, all in ruins. As a result of his analytic and engineering skills, the venerable Truchas mill was moved from the mountain village, renovated, and made operational at Las Golondrinas. Porter reports that tub mills were housed in log structures because the vibration of milling caused *adobe* structures to weaken and fall. He demonstrates that the millstones can be adjusted to control the fineness of the flour; the upper stone is never allowed to rub against the base stone. Power to drive the Truchas mill is supplied when water strikes the *rodezno*, forcing the vertical axle to rotate counter-clockwise at a speed of 69 revolutions per minute, and is rated at about 1.0 horsepower.

The *molinero* (miller) monitors the amount of grain fed through the leather hopper and down a wooden chute with its *tarabilla* (dancing damsel) that keeps the grains from clumping together and restricting the flow. The axle drives the revolutions of the *mano* (grindstone) of vesicular basalt, a local porous lava rock, which turns upon the stationery basalt *metate* (lower stone).

The kernels are then sheared open between the two cylindrical self-sharpening basalt blocks. He controls the speed of the revolutions of the shaking bolter (sifter) by means of a crank arm and drive belt powered by the main shaft. Water is diverted from the *acequia* to power the mill and is never wasted, but returned to the *acequia*; to waste water was and is still illegal. A tub *molino* could process up to 400 pounds of flour daily. Families who owned tub *molinos* charged neighbors 10 percent of the yield for use of their services. In June, 2007 the Historic Preservation Division of the State of New Mexico placed the Barela Molino of Truchas on the State Register of Cultural Properties. It is estimated that one tub *molino* would serve from twenty-five to thirty families per year. The Barela *Molino* operates for all to view on El Rancho de las Golondrinas Festival weekends.

Rodezno powers the Molino Barela

The non-operational Molino Viejo de las Golondrinas was purchased from the Padilla family in Truchas, and installed on what is believed to be the foundation of the original Las Golondrinas *molino* that appeared in the 1815 inventory of the estate of Don Manuel Francisco Delgado. Both the Las Golondrinas Mill and El Molino Viejo de Talpa are static displays. Neither mill is operational as the working mechanisms have long since been scavenged. The Viejo de Talpa *molino* sits below the *acequia* that waters the historic fields where traditional crops are grown yet today, and was named for a small mountain town south of Taos.

Agriculture and Husbandry

Life in the colonial period was difficult at best. Because the first supply trains arrived every three to five years from Mexico primarily to supply the church and its missions, little was left to provide the village colonists with necessities, much less luxuries. Almost everything consumed or used had to be grown or made from the materials at hand. Resources were wood, dirt, stone, and the foodstuffs the villagers grew, bartered for, or gathered. From these local stocks, tools were made, transport provided, and shelters erected to protect against the harsh New Mexican winters and hostile Indian raids. Looms were built entirely of wood. Farm *carretas* rarely employed metal parts and were made by the same hands. Indispensable village *molinos* were constructed of timber on stone foundations.

Men, women, and children shared the labors of fieldwork, planting, weeding, and harvesting, but women did the *adobe* plastering, painting, and constructed the *hornos*. The men ditched, plowed, laid *adobe* bricks, worked with wood, and irrigated the fields. A primitive *arado* (plow) was fashioned from the sharpened end of a small cottonwood tree trunk with a large limb left in place to serve as a handle. If available, the tip of the plow was fitted with a precious piece of iron; metal was always in short supply. The assembly was fastened to a strong pine pole that served as the tongue which was then secured to a *yugo* (ox yoke), using rawhide lashings across the horns of a team of *bueyes*. The farmer used a *punta de buey* (ox goad) to drive the team. Some *arados* were pulled by *burros*. The wooden plow was inefficient at best, but it worked. The design of the *carreta* was just as inefficient as the plow. Two wheels were fashioned from thick cross-sections of cottonwood tree trunks. The bed of the *carreta* rested on an axle hewn from a pine log. Wooden pins inserted through the axel secured the hubbed wheels in place, and pine planks provided a four-foot square floor. Sometimes a cow hide was stretched across the floor of the bed, and a wickerwork basket of light poles enclosed the sides of the *carreta* where women and children, lambs, kids, chickens, produce, and any manner of things were transported. *Carretas* were used to collect and transport firewood, garden produce, and to carry wild hay from the fields. The man of the family seated himself on the tongue of the wagon or walked alongside, *punta de buey* in hand.

Cereal grains were often harvested by hand often with a *hoz* (sickle), a tool used since biblical times, and hauled to the *era de trillar* (threshing floor), situated high on a hillside to catch the breeze. The threshing floor had been leveled and plastered with *adobe*, beaten down, sprinkled, beaten and sprinkled again and sun-baked until the floor was hard as brick. Winnowing wheat and barley was done using a most primitive method. The grain was spread on hard-packed ground, and goats, sheep, *burros*, and horses were made to walk about and around until their hooves separated the grain from the straw.

Occasionally a *rodillo* (slatted roller) pulled by a draft animal served the same purpose. The grain and straw was raked up, pitched into the air, or flipped from a blanket or a shallow basket. The breeze blew the chaff away, leaving the kernels free to fall. "Blow, blow, San Lorenzo, San Lorenzo, beards of gold, *Viento, viento, San Lorenzo, San Lorenzo, barbas de oro*," was the *oración* (prayer) to St. Lawrence for wind. Sometimes a *criba* (sifter), made of perforated animal hide and attached to a wood frame, separated the kernels of grain from straw chaff and foreign matter. If a Harvest Festival guest is lucky, he/she will see the Las Golondrinas *churros* driven to winnow the wheat.

Visitor watches wheat threshing in Era de Trilla

Chief among the livestock on the *estancia* were the sheep. Imported from Spain, the hardy ancient Iberian *churro* breed was well adapted to the semi-desert conditions of New Mexico. *Churros* thrive in harsh climates with their long staple protective topcoat and soft underbelly. The coarse wool is an easily worked fiber suitable for *jerga,* and the *churros* produce quality meat. Las Golondrinas owns a flock of *churro* sheep, a breed nearly extinct because of breeding with merinos and rambouillets, and federal government intrusions.

Shearing a churro ewe

In an effort to ruin the economy of the unruly Navajo, the U. S. Army in 1863, under the command of Colonel Christopher "Kit" Carson, slaughtered great flocks of *churros* as the Navajo were exiled to the Bosque Redondo reservation on the lower Pecos River. A second slaughter was ordered by the Department of the Interior during the Great Dustbowl of the 1930s in order to reduce the size of flocks. Las Golondrinas *churros* were collected from a small population remaining on the Navajo reservation. Today, the *pastora* (shepherdess) can be seen during festival and theme weekends roaming the museum grounds with her *churro* flock, charming all visitors. *Churro* ewes, having a pair of horns, and the rams, sometimes growing as many as four horns, are favorites of Las Golondrinas guests.

Pastora and her flock

In addition to flocks of sheep, La Ciénega villagers kept *cabras* (goats) for milk, cheese, and leather. Goats supplied milk for the village families. One goat for every ten sheep in a flock was an easy way to keep track of numbers. Villagers simply counted the goats and multiplied by ten. What few head of cattle the villagers kept were primarily *bueyes*. A few *caballos, mulas* (mules), and the strong and hardy *burros* rounded out the inventory of livestock. *Aves de corral* (chickens) were an indispensable part of the husbandry although vulnerable to coyotes and other predators.

> In 1833, José Antonio Zubiría, Bishop of Durango, was the first prelate to visit the northern reaches of his bishopric in the only official visita by any bishop since colonization. In his journal, the Bishop noted the majada (sheepfold) of the Bacas at the first paraje before Santa Fé.

Orchards and vineyards in the valley provided peaches, apricots, cherries, apples, pears, plums, and grapes. Piñon nuts were gathered from the wild and roasted, and surplus fruit was dried and stored for the winter. Presses were used to extract juice from apples and other fruits as well as from wine grapes, and currant juice provided a fine cordial. A *vinatero* (vintner) oversaw the vineyard, and wine and grape brandies were made from crushing grapes in a *prensa de lagar* (grape press), the juice strained through a *colador* (strainer) and stored in *botas* (wineskins). The wine-making tradition is ancient. The varietal, *vitus vinifera*, was introduced to the lower Río Grande valley in the 1530s.

> A local legend tells of the town blacksmith, Facundo Romero, and his son, who died of exposure in brutal weather while foraging for piñon nuts. Facundo had made a manda, a religious vow that he would say a rosary to honor his saint upon completion of the construction of the home he was building. A light could be seen in the window of the uncompleted house every night as Facundo's ghost struggled to finish construction, the rosary said, and his manda fulfilled.

The Las Golondrinas Carretería Wheelwright Shop, moved from Truchas, was built to accommodate a *carretero* (wheelwright) whose task was to keep ranch equipment in good repair; cart wheels with spokes required special attention. Visitors to the museum during Festival weekends will find a skilled wheelwright at work in the *carretería*. The adjacent Carpintero (carpenter) Shop was moved from elsewhere on the ranch to demonstrate the carpentry skills necessary for remote colonial communities to thrive.

Trade caravans from Mexico made iron rods and *yunques* (anvils) available to the villagers of La Ciénega and Las Golondrinas. The *herrero* set up his *fragua* (forge) in a shelter of *adobe* or timber, and installed his *fuelle* or *bofes* (bellows) made of wood and leather. The indispensable *herrero*, an expert metalworker who also served as an armorer, was one of the most important persons on any of the *estancias*, served the needs of the farmers and home makers of Las Golondrinas.

Fruits of the harvest

From precious imported iron, he made hardware, farm tools, *frenos* (bits for bridles), *herraduras* (horseshoes), *chispas* (strike-a-light tools), adzes and ax heads, cooking pots and trivets, and all manner of useful things. When a piece of iron wore out or was broken, the *herrero* fashioned something new from it. Many a nail was made from a *herradura* or *cuchara* (spoon). The *herrero* (blacksmith) often worked as a *herrador* (farrier) who shod horses, mules, and oxen, and also served as the local veterinarian. After the fields were plowed, planted, weeded, harvested, and the produce stored, the animals in barns and corrals still required constant care. Weak or sick livestock needed his special attention. The Manuel Apodaca Blacksmith Shop at Las Golondrinas is operated by a skilled blacksmith on festival weekends.

Herrero (blacksmith) at work in Manuel Apodoca Blacksmith Shop

7

The Colonial Family in Transition

Honor and Marriage—The Changing Role of Women

Honor and Marriage

"La Constancia," the seventeenth century folktale, is told yet today in New Mexico. The lovely Constancia was married to José María. Admired for her great beauty, she drew the attentions of many men. A depraved vagrant became infatuated with her and tried to seduce her, but Constancia rebuffed him, so he determined to ruin her reputation. With the aid of a witch and Constancia's stolen necklace, the scoundrel persuaded naïve José that his wife had committed adultery with him. True to the morality of his times, José determined to avenge his honor by disposing of his faithless wife. He locked her in a box and threw her into the sea. Days later, the box floated onto a beach in Spain, and Constancia emerged in a nearby city to find a battle raging between Christians and Moors. An apparition of the Virgin Mary instructed Constancia to disguise herself as a man, don a suit of armor, and kill as many Moors as possible. Constancia did as she was told and single-handed forced the Moors from the city. The grateful Spanish monarch bestowed the crown of his kingdom on the unknown warrior. Having proved her innocence by her steadfast and valorous conduct, Constansia restored José María's honor by placing the crown on his head. She then removed her suit of mail and resumed her womanly role.

The moral of the tale is clear. Men can win and enhance their honor by vigorous heroic action, but the only option for a woman was to maintain or lose her virtue. Women must reside in seclusion while men can live in the great world, displaying their masculine qualities of domination and conquest that were essential to uphold family honor. Since maternity could not be denied but paternity could be questioned, females must be sequestered to prevent the bloodline from being "polluted." The unquestioned authority of the Spanish patriarch and his double standard of sexual behavior were based on these premises. To seduce a woman of inferior social rank was acceptable, for such women were considered fair game. To keep a mistress or concubine was tolerated, whereas adultery was not because it violated the couple's marriage vows. Some colonial clerics kept concubines. Numerous common law marriages were based on mutual consent. Church and state officials looked on interracial conjugal relations as concubinage. It was estimated that one out of every ten children born into New Mexican communities was a "child of the church," often left at the sanctuary door by the unknown mother. Slaves seldom wedded because sacramental marriage, being a symbol of honor and social status, was not readily available to them.

On the elite level, arranged marriages enhanced family honor, for they joined two *calidad* (social status) families of equal social status; the alliances also protected their assets. The "blind passions of youth" were not to be trusted in these matters. The Council of Trent (1545–1563) decreed that valid marriage must be based on free consent of the parties, witnessed by the priest and two others. In practice, the *patria potestad* (supreme authority) of the father over his family, enabled him to control the lives of all in the household, and he generally chose the marriage partners for all of its members. *Limpieza de sangre* (purity of blood) was most important early in the colonial period, but then it waned. The requirement supposedly ensured the bloodline would be free from any taint of Jewish or Moorish ancestry. Marriage in New Mexico was symbolic of social status, and was reflected in the splendor of gifts. The wedding feast showed the economic importance of the union. Unsuitable marriages threatened the privileges and status of the elite.

Under both canon and secular law, the purpose of marriage was procreation. Therefore males had to be at least thirteen years or older, and females at least eleven; most couples were older than these prescribed ages. Most women were married by age nineteen, while men tended to wait until their mid-twenties to take a wife. Lower class men frequently postponed weddings until they had saved enough to obtain appropriate gifts, and the couple may have lived in concubinage until that time.

A substantial dowry enabled an upper class woman to attract a husband of equal or higher status and helped the couple set up their household. It also provided economic security in case her husband died. In exchange for the dowry, the groom's family contributed moveable goods that automatically became the property of the bride, and all passed to her heirs upon her death. The groom often received an endowment of land or money from his parents to help the couple get started. Sons received their share of farmland, and were entitled to a certain number of *vigas* in the parental home, a way of dividing up interior space, or new quarters were built for them.

> Fabiola Cabeza de Baca told of a story that no doubt set tongues wagging in the tight-knit community. In 1814, twenty-two year old Manuel Salustiano asked his father, Don Manuel Delgado, to request the hand of the daughter of Don Juan Domingo Baca in marriage. The old gentleman went on the mission, but found Ana María Baca very much to his own liking and promptly married her. He requested her younger sister, María de la Luz, for his son. Don Manuel lived but one more year whereupon his young widow married another aging widower, Don Pedro Baptista Pino, who had served as Deputy from New Mexico to the Spanish Cortes in 1812.

During the Mexican period (1821–1846), the *casta* (caste) system disappeared with the exception of the classifications of *indio* and *genízaro*, and the old aristocratic values no longer dominated. Commoners could rise to higher status through economic endeavor and hard work. All persons of wealth, be they pure Spanish or *mestizos*, were given the honorific title of "don" or "doña." In New Mexico, even wealthy farmers worked in their fields and flocks with their laborers. Rich and poor worshipped and played together, and attended each other's baptisms, weddings, and wakes. They wore the same kinds of clothing, albeit the *ricos* dressed better, and spoke the same dialects. Freed from the control of the Spanish crown, New Mexico became an open, more inclusive society. Pedro Baptista Pino, in his report to the Spanish Cortes (Spanish parliament), observed that the hordes of beggars found in the large cities of Mexico and Europe were seldom seen in New Mexico.

The Changing Role of Women

Susan Shelby Magoffin, the eighteen-year-old American wife of a successful trader-husband, came to New Mexico in 1846. Her invaluable diary records, "Wednesday 7th. Camp No. 1. El rancho de Delgado [Las Golondrinas]. Lo, we are camping again! and after all it is quite as good as staying in Santa Fé. I was impatient to leave. Gabriel [Valdez] and William [Magoffin] are with us now. The wagons are all on ahead, and we'll not reach them yet for some days.

Left Santa Fé about 12 o'k came on fifteen miles to this place—a little farm, called a rancho—rather a poor place, only a little corn, beans, and an abundance of *chile verde* [green chile pepper], a few goats, sheep and jacks—the beast of all work—they pack wood on them, ride them, take all their little 'fixings' to market in baskets or bags swung on the long-eared animals back &c &c. We camped pretty near the house and of course the peepers were not a few."

Susan's astute observations of Spanish society, faithfully recorded in her memoir, provided a revealing picture of Spanish women's freedom in social relations and other rights unfamiliar to the Easterner. Another entry reads, "The women stand around with their faces awfully painted, some with red which shines like grease, and others are daubed over with flour-paste. The men stand back with crossed arms, and all look [at us] with as much wonder as if they were not people themselves." Women painted their faces to protect against sunburn. Young Susan could scarcely believe her eyes when she saw women dressed in petticoats and chemises, garments that American women wore only as undergarments. Over their heads and arms, women wore *rebozos* (large shawls) into which they tucked their infant children. Children ran naked, and women with bosoms covered by a loose white chemise and legs bare were "pulling their skirts up over their knees and paddling across creeks like ducks." Susan had to draw her veil over her face to hide her blush at the sight. She was appalled when she saw women smoking cigarettes, shopping, and paying visits to each other on Sundays. She noted that women even conducted their own businesses and sold whiskey, farm produce, and traded goods in stalls along village streets. Susan was distressed when a New Mexican woman suggested that her husband might be away with "his other *señorita* (unmarried woman)."

Susan's amazement is understandable, for back East women were denied the freedom women possessed in the relatively freewheeling society of New Mexico. A married woman lacked almost all legal rights; her property and her wages belonged to her husband. By contrast, New Mexican women retained their legal rights, wages, property and maiden names. Women could divorce their husbands, but only after all attempts at reconciliation failed. Both parties to an adulterous act received the same punishment. Differences in appearance also set New Mexican women apart from their Eastern sisters. Americans described New Mexican women as swarthy and copper colored. Women, as Susan noted, protected their faces from the sun with a paste of flour or bone meal and the juice of *alegría* (cockscomb blossom). Another observer, W.W. H. Davis,

United States Attorney in the new territories, wrote approvingly that New Mexican women were graceful, healthy, and athletic in their full short skirts and low cut blouses, costumes which allowed them to work free from encumbrance. He described their *adobe* houses as easy to clean, cool in the summer and cozy in the winter, with little corner fireplaces for heating and cooking. Homes were almost devoid of furniture. Families slept on thin mattresses that were rolled up in the daytime and placed against the walls to serve as seating. Only the rich had bedrooms with beds, carpets, draperies, kitchens with silver table service, and servants to maintain them. But Davis condemned the sexual freedom of New Mexican women. "The standard of female chastity," he wrote, "is deplorably low." In reality, promiscuity was less common than Americans thought.

Some Americans judged New Mexican women harshly because, in their view, the women refused to regard idleness, frivolity, or dancing as sinful. One American sourly claimed that, "the *fandango* and *siesta* (afternoon rest) form the diversion of time." Critics ignored the fact that Mexican women were often times more pious than their men, attending church more regularly, and participated in pious religious societies. It was their role to teach their children manners and moral principles. However, other anglo accounts described New Mexican women as cheerful and hardworking. One observer wrote, " . . . maidens with merry faces sported baskets of purple grape clusters on their heads, and chatted merrily as they filled their water jugs at the springs." Another recalled seeing mothers spinning yarn outdoors as they nursed their babies. Women waded into the river to launder clothes. Women were ranked in terms of their professions: seamstresses, stocking-knitters, midwives, shepherds, bakers, weavers, servants, or prostitutes.

The simplicity of a New Mexican woman's home and costume allowed her to take part in the many social affairs. She probably used some of her time to replenish the energy needed for the frequent *fandangos* where she appeared radiant in her tinkling jewelry. Everyone from the priest to the ragged peon was welcome to join the party, and everybody took part in the dancing. *Fiestas* featured races, cock-fights, puppet shows, miracle plays, tumblers, horse races, pyrotechnics, and, of course, consumption of wine. Puppet shows were political and bawdy, not entertainment for children. Jacinto Ybarry was accused of staging an "indecent" puppet show and was summarily arrested. Women gambled at *chuza* (game similar to roulette) side-by-side with the men. George W. Kendall, editor of the *New Orleans Picayune,* saw the women as "joyous, sociable, kind-hearted creatures, easy and graceful in their manners." The attitude toward work in the fields was egalitarian; women and their children cheerfully labored alongside their men, giving "life and gaiety to the surrounding scenery." Lieutenant William Emory recalled the "high glee of men, women, and children as they see-sawed on the lever of a molasses press."

George W. Kendall had accompanied the Santa Fé Expedition in 1841, and reported entering "the largest home in the place . . . It had but two rooms, the earthen floor and scant furniture of which gave them a prison-like and desolate appearance. Not a chair or table, knife of fork, did the occupants possess, and we were given to understand that we were in the house of the 'first family' of Anton Chico."

The relative independence that New Mexican women enjoyed ended when, in 1846, the United States army invaded New Mexico. The Americans strongly disapproved of New Mexican natives in general and in their lifestyles in particular. Within fifteen years after the American conquest, New Mexican women had to surrender to the will of their husbands, and abandon their pretty costumes to the tyranny of whalebone corsets, hoop skirts, numerous petticoats, and bonnets. Legal rights that the *alcalde* courts had upheld were nullified, and American ethnic discrimination scorned their festivals and folk art. Their children were forbidden to use their Spanish language in American schools, secular Sabbath activities were banned, some cultural traits were lost, and their way of life changed forever.

8

Faith of Their Fathers

Children of the Medieval Church—The Penitentes—Our Lady of Guadalupe—The Art of the Santero

Children of the Medieval Church

The Catholic religion of the Spanish colonists was reflected in every aspect of their existence; it went far beyond mere religious ceremony.

Faith in their Lord and their saints was the consuming, driving force in the life of New Mexican colonists. As children of the medieval church and the Counter-Reformation, the Spanish viewed the observance of their religion, not as a perfunctory service, but the very condition of their being. The changing political climate and increasing spiritual isolation caused the faithful to cope in their own unique ways. Their faith fashioned thoughts, behavior, and their very souls, enabling them to endure the hardships in their thirsty and ragged edge of the world. Without God's love, nothing would flourish; with it, all was possible.

The practice of their faith was the lasting foundation of the colonists' world. Many greeted the dawn with a hymn, and kneeled at the end of the day to offer a prayer of thanksgiving. The following *alba* (song of praise to the dawn) was collected and translated by folklorist Enrique R. Lamadrid, and may be found in *La Música de los Viejitos: Hispanic Folk Music of the Río Grande del Norte* by Jack Loeffler.

Cantemos al alba, ya viene el día. Let us sing to the dawn, the day is coming.
Daremos gracias, Ave María. Let us give thanks, Hail Mary.

Cantemos al alba, ya viene el día. Let us sing to the dawn, the day is coming.
Daremos gracias, Ave María. Let us give thanks, Hail Mary.

Quien al alba canta muy de mañana. Whoever sings to the dawn early in the morning,
Indulgencias al cielo gana. Will win indulgences from heaven.

En la calle arriba está la custodia. On the path above is the monstrance.
Los ángeles cantan arriba en la Gloria. The angels sing above in heaven.

Cantemos al alba, ya viene el día. Let us sing to the dawn, the day is coming.
Daremos gracias, Ave María. Let us give thanks, Hail Mary.

Benedita sea la luz del día. Blessed be the light of day.
Beneditos sean San José y María. Blessed be Saint Joseph and Mary.

A la madrugada nació el Niño Dios. In the early morning the Infant Lord was born.
Al amanecer, dió su luz el sol. At daybreak, the sun gave its light.

La mula se espanta con el resplandor. The mule is surprised at the brilliance.
El buey con el vaho calentó al Señor. The ox with his breath kept the Child warm.

Los tres Reyes Magos del Cielo han venido, Three Kings from heaven have come,
A darle las gracias al Recién Nacido. To give thanks to the One just born.

El Rey Baltazar que el era mayor, King Baltazar was the oldest,
Presentó el incienso al Niñito Dios. And gave incense to the God Child.

Bendita sea la luz del día. Blessed be the light of day.
Bendito sea Quien nos la envía. Blessed be He that sends it to us.

Bendita sea la claridad. Blessed be the clarity.
Bendito se Quien nos la da. Blessed be He that gives it to us.

Angel de mi guarda, noble compañía, My guardian angel, noble company,
Vélame de noche, guíame en el día. Watch over me at night, guide me during the day.

Cantemos al alba, ya viene el día. Let us sing to the dawn, the day is coming.
Daremos gracias, Ave María. Let us give thanks, Hail Mary.

Estas sí son flores, estas sí que son. These are truly flowers, these truly are.
Gracias a María, gloria al Señor. Thanks be to Mary. Glory to the Father.

Los gallos cantaron, las aves salieron. The roosters crowed, the birds came out.
Toditos los campos ya se florecieron. All of the fields are blooming.

Cantemos al alba, ya viene el día. Let us sing to the dawn, day is coming.
Daremos gracias Ave María. Let us give thanks, Hail Mary.

María divina ya no pudo ver Divine Mary could no longer see
La cuya fiera de Lucifer. The beast Lucifer.

Cantemos al alba, ya viene del día. Let us sing to the dawn, the day is coming.
Daremos gracias, Ave María. Let us give thanks, Hail Mary.

Devout farmers planted their seeds using three digits, the thumb and two fingers, in recognition of the Holy Trinity, and housewives used the same symbol cut into the crust of their loaves in hopes that their bread would rise and turn out well. All relied on San Ysidro Labrador, the patron saint of agriculture, to watch over their fields, and San Ignacio de Loyola for protection against witchcraft. Colonists venerated one or more manifestations of the Virgin Mary, most especially the Mexican Our Lady of Guadalupe, and held The Holy Child of Atocha near and dear.

San Ysidro, Patron Saint of Las Golondrinas

Possibly the most notable visitor to La Ciénega Valley was not of a person, but a sacred image now known as La Conquistadora. She came to New Mexico in 1625 with Fray Alonso de Benavides. When the colonists fled during the Pueblo Revolt in 1680, she was bundled up and taken to El Paso del Norte where she remained until Don Diego de Vargas returned with her in 1692. Later, the practice began for La Conquistadora to visit parishes, and the much revered bulto is believed to have stayed in La Ciénega Valley homes overnight.

Central to every home was a devotional shrine, a place for private family worship. Here images beloved by the family were displayed and tended with loving care, and the saints became members of the family. The colonists knew their saint could intercede with the Virgin Mary and her Son to grant favors. If the saint did not manage the intercession, the offending one might find itself out of favor. To this day, chastisement takes the form of turning the *bulto* or *retablo* (two-dimensional line painting of sacred figure, usually on wood) to the wall, or exiling it to a cupboard until all was forgiven. When reconciliation was achieved, the saint again basked in the good graces of the family.

Family shrine in the salon

For a truly imposing favor, the fortunate supplicant might provide an all-night *velorio* (vigil) for the saint of *alabados* (songs of praise) and prayers. Children often bore the name of the saint on whose special day they were born. Villages adopted a saint that they venerate on the chosen saint's special day. There were, and still are, plenty of saints to go around.

San Ysidro, Labrador (Feast Day—May 15) was born into a poor family near Madrid, Spain in the year 1070. As a youth, Ysidro worked for Don Iván de Vargas, a wealthy landowner, knight, and ancestor of Don Diego de Vargas. The most popular tradition tells that Iván de Vargas grew angry with Ysidro. The *patrón* believed his fields were being neglected because the farmer spent so much time at his devotions. When Ysidro assured Vargas that all was in order and asked his *patrón* to check his claim, Vargas and Ysidro's skeptical fellow *peones* (laborers) found an angel working Ysidro's oxen as they plowed the field. A second version of the tradition tells the story that María, Ysidro's wife, insisted he work on a Sunday rather than attend Mass. When Ysidro acquiesced, the Lord threatened him with torrential rain, then a plague of locusts, and finally, worst of all, a bad neighbor. Only then did Ysidro leave his plow and attend Mass. When he returned to his fields, Ysidro found that God had sent an angel to work with his team. San Ysidro was canonized in the year 1662. María was also canonized and appears with Ysidro in Las Golondrinas museum's *capilla reredo* (altar screen).

San Antonio de Padua (Feast Day—November 30) is routinely asked to locate lost items, and to help find suitable husbands for unmarried daughters. He may also be solicited to assist with pregnancy, suggesting how intimate and personal is the reliance on saints in Hispanic lives. Few New Mexican kitchens are without a *bulto* or *retablo* of San Pascual Bailón (Feast Day—May 17), the patron saint of cooks. It is believed that San Pascual was relieved of his duties in the kitchen so he could pray before the Blessed Sacrament. San Pascual is also the patron saint of shepherds.

A story tells of Agueda C'de Baca of La Ciénega and her younger brother traveling to an Indian pueblo to attend a fiesta. The pair journeyed by train to Los Cerrillos (the railroad town) where their cousin was to fetch them by wagon and carry them to the pueblo and back again. The return trip found the party in a downpour that muddied the road, delaying their return trip to the train station. Foolishly they elected to take a shortcut crossing an arroyo. Before long they were in danger of being swept away by a flash flood when Agueda appealed to San Antonio for a milagro (miracle), "¡San Antonio Bendito! ¡San Antonio Bendito! ¡San Antonio sálvamos! Save us, San Antonio!" With one tug, the wagon pulled free of the mire, and they made it to the station in time to catch their train. They never told their mother what happened.

Santiago (Saint James, Feast Day—July 25), patron saint of Spain and warriors, is portrayed on the white horse he rode when he allegedly helped defeat the Moors in Spain. Gaspar Pérez de Villagrá's 1610 chronicle of the colonization of New Mexico tells how the warrior saint appeared to help the conquistadors as they stormed the Pueblo of Ácoma. Santiago is a symbol of courage in battle, and was called upon to aid New Mexicans who fought in World Wars I and II. A famous *bulto* of Santiago is displayed in a glass case to the right of the crucifix of Our Lord of Esquípulas on the altar in the Santuario de Chimayó in the village of Chimayó.

Nuestra Señora del Rosario (Our Lady of the Rosary, Feast Day – October 7) is invoked to bring peace, protect against peril, and ensure a peaceful acceptance of death. The bulto of La Conquistadora, now in the Cathedral Basilica of St. Francis of Assisi in Santa Fe, is another expression of Our Lady of the Rosary. She is celebrated for helping Vargas re-conquer Santa Fé in 1693 after the Pueblo Revolt. La Conquistadora is so much revered and well known that, when youthful thieves spirited her out of the cathedral in 1973, they were thwarted in their attempts to extort a $150,000 ransom and immunity from prosecution. The story of her recovery would read well in modern detective fiction. An all-points-bulletin was issued throughout the United States to alert antique dealers far and wide, and the telephone company traced calls to a juvenile suspect's home. The teenage kidnappers broke down and confessed where they had hidden the purloined image in an abandoned mineshaft in the Manzano Mountains south of Albuquerque. One might have thought the naïve culprits had stolen the revered *tilma* (cloak of maguey fibers) that bears the image of the Virgin of Guadalupe from the Basilica de Guadalupe in Mexico City, so great was the consternation her disappearance caused.

The legend of El Santo Niño de Atocha tells of a time when Spain's Moorish overlords held many Spanish Christians in prison. The Moors forbade anyone to enter the prison save little children. Knowing the prisoners lacked enough food, water, and spiritual consolation, their wives and mothers prayed for Divine aid. One day a small child, dressed like a pilgrim, arrived at the prison with a basket of bread in one hand, and a staff with a gourd full of water suspended from its tip in the other. To universal surprise, the bread basket and the water gourd never ran empty even after all had been fed, and each prisoner was given his blessing. According to the legend, the Christ Child had come to serve in answer to the women's prayers.

El Santo Niño de Atocha (The Christ Child, Feast Day – December 25) is much-loved and holds a special place in the hearts of New Mexicans. Many charming stories are told about Santo Niño de Atocha, the patron saint of prisoners and travelers. He is believed to travel through the countryside under cover of darkness doing good deeds. It is said that once the Holy Child was so moved by the sad sight of drought-stricken fields that he caused a great rainstorm that flooded the thirsty crops. The next day an image of Our Lady was carried to the same fields to show her the havoc. "Look what your bad little boy did!" was the villagers' cry.

Santo Niño de Atocha

No matter how poor or small, every New Mexican Hispanic settlement had a religious center. A visitor to a colonial village needed only to look around to see that the *iglesia* (church) was the most important edifice, whether it be a Franciscan mission church or a humble chapel built by neighbors. Churches were constructed of local materials, timber, mud and stone, materials that dictated a similarity in planning and execution. Builders lacked professional training or instruction of any kind, and had to design and construct the edifice using instinct and common sense. The mission church was often a "fortress church," although not necessarily designed with that in mind. Many communities took refuge within its walls when threatened by marauding Indians. Made of *adobe* or undressed stone, and roofed by log *vigas* and *latias*, the high altar was often illuminated by transverse clerestory windows. Chapels or transepts were absent, and the apse was narrower than the nave in order to focus attention on the high altar. Side windows were few and small, or non-existent. A mission church generally consisted of two parts, the *santuario* (sanctuary), and the *convento* (living quarters for the missionary).

One of the traditional *iglesias* that has survived to this day is the jewel, San José de Garcia, in the village of Las Trampas. At the time it was built, the villagers gave one-sixth of each family's proceeds from their meager crops to cover the costs. The bishop gave his blessing for a church to be built in honor of St. Joseph, and the construction began in 1760. Services have been held in the sanctuary for more than two centuries.

The much revered *capilla*, El Santuario de Chimayó, is another example of a traditional house of worship. In 1814, the charismatic leader of the Brothers of Our Father Jesús the Nazarene, Bernardo Abeyta, received permission from the See of Durango, Mexico to build the massive *adobe* structure. The chapel is venerated by Hispanic Catholics as the most sacred edifice in the Southwest. Built on the site of an ancient Tewa Indian shrine with reputed curative powers, it was dedicated to "Our Lord and Redeemer, in his Advocation of Esquípulas," who was crucified on the tree of life. A bulto of Santo Niño de Atocha resides in the annex of the chapel and has become associated with El Posito (the sacred source of the healing earth).

El Santo Niño de Atocha figures prominently in the story of New Mexican survivors of the Philippine Bataan Death March at the start of World War II. All had been members of the 200th Coast Artillery regiment of the New Mexico National Guard in the Philippines, when it was over-run by the invading Japanese

Army. Only half of the original contingent of eighteen hundred came home; the rest succumbed to disease, maltreatment, and starvation in Japanese captivity. In 1949, those survivors made a pilgrimage to the Santuario de Chimayó to thank El Santo Niño for deliverance from their ordeal.

The *capilla* at today's El Rancho de las Golondrinas museum is a portrayal of a traditional colonial place of worship. The *capilla* was installed in the 1970s, and the addition of religious art helps to create an atmosphere conducive to devotion and reverence, but is not a consecrated sanctuary. Many happy couples have exchanged marriage vows there. During colonial times, families at Las Golondrinas no doubt worshiped in the church of San José de Guicú in La Ciénega. This church was blessed by the Archdiocese in 1817 and licensed in 1821, and was served by a circuit priest.

Community life revolved around the church of San José de Guicú in La Ciénega. The most popular annual event is the March 19 anniversary of the patron saint. Legends speak of the revered bulto of San José and an unauthorized journey. One version tells of a time long past when a priest attempted to remove the sacred image from the capilla vieja (old chapel). It would seem that the statue was reluctant to leave its home in Ciénega because the farther away the ox drawn wagon traveled, the heavier the load became until it was hopelessly mired in the mud. Alarmed villagers hurried to rescue the saint, and the closer the party came upon its return to La Ciénega, the lighter the burden became. An alternate version of the story credits thwarted thieves, believing the image was stuffed with gold, as responsible for the unauthorized removal. A newer sanctuary is now the home of the wandering bulto with the sad eyes.

A grant from the Oliver S. and Jennie R. Donaldson Charitable Trust financed the *reredo* and the Stations of the Cross at Las Golondrinas. The inscription reads, *"Se pintó este Reredo colateral el Mes de Abril, Año de 1994."* Instead of the traditional crucifix in the *nicho* in the center of the *reredo*, the magnificent *bulto* of San Ysidro stands, a creation by *santero* Alcario Otero. San Ysidro is the patron saint of El Rancho de las Golondrinas, of agriculture, and of Madrid, Spain. At the far end of the *capilla* is the *Sala de Fundadores*, the Founders' Room, where the first meeting of the Colonial New Mexico Historical Foundation was held. The hall is now used for special exhibits.

Reredo in the Capilla

Franciscans, one of several regular orders of the Catholic Church, shaped the Catholicism that came to New Mexico with Juan de Oñate. Although the Franciscans were responsible for the spiritual welfare of the colonists, their primary concern was to convert the Indians and guard against their lapse into paganism. The Franciscans sought to indoctrinate the natives in religious matters. Spanish military, civil, and economic practices were the responsibility of the government. The overall intent was to turn the Indians into Spanish subjects in religion, language, technology, and all things cultural. Eight priests and two lay brothers composed Oñate's Franciscan contingent who made Kewa Pueblo their ecclesiastical capital. From this center, the Franciscans ministered to the Santa Fé parish from 1610 until 1821 when, with Mexican independence, some returned to Spain as they chose not to take the required oath of allegiance to the new nation of Mexico. Were it not for the rights to evangelize held by the Franciscans, Juan de Oñate's colony may well have failed. The dedication to and the financial support of the missionary efforts by the crown provided the transportation and communications necessary for the colony to survive.

The ambitious and indefatigable Portuguese Fray Alonso de Benavides came to New Mexico in 1625 to 1629 as *custos* for the New Mexican missions, and as agent of the Inquisition of the Franciscan Custody of St. Paul. Benavides needed the crown's commitment to finance El Camino Real de Tierra Adentro supply trains necessary to support his missionizing endeavors. In support of his request for monies to finance the trail, he traveled to Ágreda, Spain. There he interviewed Sor María de Jesús de Ágreda, the Conceptionist Franciscan nun. The blue cloaked holy woman was reported to have been miraculously transported on the wings of angels to Gran Quivira Jumano Indian bands where she was believed to have preached, ministered to their needs, and cured illnesses. The blue nun, as she came to be known, encouraged the Jumanos to go to Santo Domingo to request missionaries to baptize and teach them. Fray Benavides used this account to appeal to the crown for the financing needed to promote mission interests. The crown committed to sending thirty more priests plus monetary support for the supply trains. By 1631 there were 66 Franciscans in New Mexico to minister to thousands of mission Indians. After the Pueblo Revolt in 1680, there were none.

Franciscans returned after the Vargas re-conquest somewhat chastened. They were less demanding in their efforts to missionize the Pueblos, and concentrated on the colonial population instead. By 1740, there were forty religious in New Mexico. As circumstances deteriorated, Fray Francisco Atanasio Domínguez, a church inspector posted at Zuni Pueblo and accompanied by missionary Fray Sylvestre Velez de Escalante, were charged in 1775 by their ecclesiastical superiors to survey all churches, and to report on what they found. The party discovered twenty-two priests serving in pitiful facilities with little activity.

Later, Pedro Baptista Pino's *Exposicion sucinta y sencilla de la provincia del Nuevo México of 1812* reported that twenty six Indian pueblos and one hundred and two Spanish settlements were served with but twenty-two missionaries and two secular priests. By 1820 and Mexican independence, the financially strapped Mexican government paid no missionary subsidies, and abolished all but "absolutely indispensable" expenditures.

> Manuel Francisco Delgado is credited along with Pedro Baptista Pino as having responded to the Viceroy's request for a donative *voluntario* (voluntary gift) soliciting 5000 pesos from prominent merchants and sheep men to help suppress the Morelos revolution in Mexico. They were reminded that

the crown was maintaining New Mexico with about 50,000 pesos annually.

A letter from Fray Francisco Atanásio Domínguez, who was inspecting New Spain Missions, reported Comanche raiders struck the flocks in La Ciénega Valley on June 21, 1776. Sheepherders and laborers in the fields were at great risk as they usually tended their flocks armed with little more than a slingshot.

Domingo Ortega was living at the Baca ranch when he was killed in 1776 without receiving the sacraments, leaving three children. José António Sandoval, also living at Las Golondrinas, was killed by the Comanche while resisting capture. Manuel de la Coca, son of María Vega y Coca and Diego Manuel Baca, was taken prisoner while he and a servant were guarding the estancia's livestock. His two children were taken captive in the same attack. Surviving Manuel was Olaya Segura, coyote (Indo-Hispanic), pregnant by the then deceased Manuel. Six other hapless victims died during the Comanche rampage through La Ciénega and La Cieneguilla. A scouting expedition from the Royal Presidio in Santa Fé was dispatched to search for those abducted, and reconnoitered for ten days without success.

Spain's distresses at home and abroad had a catastrophic impact on the church in New Mexico. The mother country was involved in a series of costly and exhausting wars and, in 1810, *criollo* leaders throughout Latin America took advantage of Spain's difficulties and began a struggle for independence. In 1821, Mexico won her autonomy, and New Mexicans became citizens of the Republic of Mexico. But Mexico, splintered by factional struggles between liberals and conservatives, had not the time, energy, or resources to be concerned with the problems of her distant northern province. Spain had supported the military and the civil governments of New Mexico as well as the missions, but little funding from Mexico remained. The shortage of clergy was but one of the results; only eight Franciscan priests remained to serve all the missions.

After 1821 and Mexican Independence, Spain ceased to finance the Franciscan missionaries, and when in 1834 the missions were secularized, the Society for the Propagation of the Faith assumed the task of funding and providing personnel. The Diocese of Durango took over administration and assigned secular priests to New Mexico, but these clerics did not stay long, preferring more appealing assignments in places where living was less arduous. By the end of the Mexican period in 1846, one Franciscan and seventeen secular priests of the

Diocese of Durango remained to serve the immense territory of Texas and New Mexico.

Villagers lost most of their clergy on whom they depended for leadership and spiritual guidance. No bishop had visited since 1760. Many colonists saw a priest only once every few weeks or months, and priestly services were expensive. Burial costs were so prohibitive that it was said that it was more costly to die than to live. Generations of raids by nomads caused great suffering along with problems of inadequate spiritual leadership and little to no effective military. The vacuum bordered on intolerable.

The Penitentes

An often misunderstood religious *cofradía* (confraternity), Los Hermanos Penitentes (The Penitent Brothers), came into being in northern New Mexico and southern Colorado. Isolation and hardship, coupled with the need for a pious society to observe rituals and to provide assistance to underserved communities, contributed to the proliferation of the folk religion. The history of the lay society is obscure. *Santero* and anthropologist Charles Carrillo found documentation of the existence of *moradas* (Penitente chapter houses) in New Mexico as early as 1791 to 1793. By the time of Mexican Independence in 1821, the Penitente movement had developed as a lay-led folk faith. It roughly corresponded to official Catholicism, and offered "cradle-to-grave" care according to the Reverend Monsignor Jerome Martínez y Alire, rector of the Cathedral Basilica of St. Francis of Assisi in Santa Fe. The religious lay society called itself Los Hermanos de Nuestro Padre Jesús Nazareno, or Los Hermanos Penitentes. Edward Romero, former ambassador to Spain and 13th generation of the family in New Mexico, holds that the Penitentes came to New Mexico with the Franciscan priests as part of the Oñate expedition in 1598. Los Hermanos regard the year 1833, when the Bishop of Durango, José Antonio Laureano de Zubiría y Escalante, made a *visita* (visit) to New Mexico and found the organization active as the date marking the official existence of the society in New Mexico.

The Brotherhood, also known as La Hermandad, was organized for religious and social purposes, and had two basic divisions, membership being fluid with members moving from one branch to the other. Los Hermanos de Sangre (The Brothers of Blood) were devout souls who performed self-mortification by scourging themselves with *disciplinas* (yucca whips) or other means of inflicting pain, carrying heavy crosses, or who performed various corporal acts of *penitencia* (penance). The Penitente sought to purge himself of sins by enduring corporal penance. The more he suffered, the more Christ-like he became as he sought to expiate his sins. Permission to flagellate himself had to be obtained from the *morada's hermano mayor* and from the would-be penitent's wife or mother in order to guard against excessive zeal. Los Hermanos de Luz (The Brothers of Light), those who had came through their novitiate and penances, and made up the general population, acted as officials of the *morada*.

Penance, in Catholic thought, is a sacrament involving the confession of sin and a voluntary act of reparation for wrongdoing. One cannot "look on the face of God" unless one dies in a state of grace obtained by the expiation of sins. Purgatory in Catholic belief is a condition in which those who have died in the grace of God redress their sins by doing penance. Penance during one's lifetime is practiced in order to shorten the time the soul must reside in purgatory. Penance did not necessarily entail physical punishment; it often took other forms. The *hermano mayor* (elected head) could assign communal activities that would serve as penance. An individual penitent might provide a load of firewood for a widow, or perform other activities that required sacrifice in materials and labor. An entire *morada* would sometimes build a family a home, or bury its dead. Such activities had to be performed with no thought of reward or credit. While most penance was self-imposed, the offense of revealing secrets of the organization and dissidence was dealt with severely by the organization. The worst offenses usually led to ostracism or expulsion. Less serious infractions were on occasion punished by floggings by the *celador* (Penitente warden), or by other imposed penances.

The Penitentes developed and flourished above all in *genízaro* settlements that experienced a shortage of priestly services. The *genízaros* were Hispanicized Plains Indian captives. Many were used by the colonists as military personnel. To reward their service, they were given land to create communities, and to act as a barrier to guard their own and other colonial districts. Truchas, Trampas, Carnue in Tijeras Canyon, Tomé, and one plaza in Belen protected Santa Fé and Albuquerque from the Comanche, and Abiquiú buffered other Hispanic settlements from the threats of the Ute and Navajo. In the Mexican period, some *genízaros* of Comanche ancestry were found farther east in San Miguel de Vado. Thoroughly Hispanicized, many were members of the pious Confraternity of Los Hermanos de Nuestro Padre Jesús Nazareno with its important contribution to New Mexico's unique Catholicism.

Loading firewood on a burro

Generally, only men were members of the penitent confraternity although women served as auxiliary *Carmelitas* (Carmelites). However, *santero* Charles Carrillo speaks of two of his wife's female relatives, who belonged to the confraternity, practicing their penance in their own venues. It was the women who ultimately decided whether their husbands and sons had the lifetime commitment to join the order.

Although the church was at the heart of each village, the *morada* with its Penitentes and their patron, Nuestro Padre Jesús Nazareno, was important to the community. When communities found themselves without the services of learned clerics, the leaders of the pious Hermandad, relying on collective memory, assumed some of their responsibilities; exempted tasks were saying Mass and administering the sacraments. Any one of the faithful could baptize infants, for with the high infant mortality rate in the territory, who could wait until a priest arrived? The Brotherhood held wakes and buried their dead in a prescribed manner. An activity of the Penitente community was to call on members to visit the sick and take care of their needs when families could not or would not assume the role.

Only sincere candidates, age fourteen or more, were accepted as Hermano *novatos* (novitiates) when the community deemed the candidate was mature enough to accept lifetime responsibility. After an examination of the novitiate's knowledge of the elaborate rituals and regulations, the applicant, accompanied by his sponsor, presented himself for the actual rite of initiation. He then served some three to five years of active penance during Holy Week and Lent before being entitled to hold office.

At the center of the Hermandad belief system was the concept of *caridad* (charity). Every member in the community knew where to go for spiritual comfort, prayer, and assistance. Succor was provided through prayer and spiritual ceremonies in the *moradas*. Widows and orphans relied on extended family first, and from then on their Penitente neighbors for help in difficult times. The most significant trait of the Penitente remains the practice of penance, and charity is regarded as an act of penance.

The Hermandad was dedicated to the spirit of penance and the Passion of Jesus Christ, especially during *Semana Santa* (Holy Week) when activities reached a climax. In all the villages, conical *adobe hornos* baked bread and *panocha* (gruel made from sprouted wheat); the ovens were blessed so the bread would not turn soggy and heavy. During the week, special *charolitas* (small bowls) containing *torrejas con chile* (egg fritters in chile sauce), *panocha* and *rueditas* (fried dried squash), were exchanged throughout the village. Eating meat was forbidden by the church during the four Holy Days, Tuesday through Friday. Ancient crosses were retrieved and placed outside the door of the *morada*. On Good Friday, as the Penitentes exited the *morada* after prayers and *alabados*, took up their crosses and followed by the Hermanos de Disciplina (flagellants), dragged their heavy burdens up the rocky trail to *El Calvario* (Calvary Mount) in imitation of Christ's ordeal at Golgotha.

Calvario de Morada de la Conquistadora

As darkness descended on the eve of Holy Thursday and Good Friday, the public ritual of Las Tinieblas (darkness, lower world, death) was held in the *morada*. Sixteen lighted candles were placed on a *tienebre* (triangular wooden candelabra), a yellow candle for each of the Apostles, and one candle each for the three Marys who accompanied Christ to the cross: Mary, mother of Christ, Mary Magdalene, and Mary, the wife of Cleofas. A white candle at the top of the *tienebre* represented the risen Jesus. To the accompaniment of chanted *alabados*, the candles were extinguished one by one; the snuffing-out of the upper-most candle symbolized the death and burial of Jesus. At the Biblical sixth hour, "there was darkness over all the land unto the ninth hour. . . . And behold the veil of the temple was rent in twain from the top to the bottom; and the earth did quake, and the rocks rent; and the graves were opened and many bodies of the saints which slept arose." (St. Matthew 27:45-46, 51-52) There followed a cacophony in the darkened *morada*, achieved by using *matracas* (wooden clackers) and all manner of noisemakers, chains, flutes, drums, and clapping and stamping, in order to simulate the Biblical storm and earthquake. Lulls in the deafening storm allowed for prayers to be offered for the dead. When a lit candle again glowed and others were lighted from it, Jesus was symbolically resurrected.

An *alabado,* sung during a Good Friday simulated rite of crucifixion, was collected by Lorin W. Brown of the Federal Writer's Project, and published in his *Hispano Folklife of New Mexico.*

> *Oh Jesús, por mis delitos,* Oh Jesus, for my faults,
> *Padeciste tal dolor;* You suffered so much pain;
> *A tus pies arrependito* At your feet you see me
> *Me ves, dulce Redentor.* Repentant, Sweet Redeemer.
>
> *Agonizante en el huerto.* We meditate upon Your agony.
> *Contemplemos al Señor,* In that garden of old, Our Lord,
> *Postrado en tierra su rostro* With His face bowed to the earth
> *Con un sangriento sudor.* Covered with bloody sweat.
>
> *En el pretorio le vemos* In the Pretorium we see Him
> *Azotado con furor;* Suffering furious scourges;
> *Es de cadenas cubierto* Chains are loaded on Him
> *Por los hombres el Señor.* Our Lord is treated thus by man.
>
> *Con afrentas y Dolores* With affronts and cruel blows
> *Ciñe la tropa feroz* These fierce troopers bind
> *Una punzante corona* A cruel crown of thorns
> *En la frente de su Dios.* Upon God's holy brow.
>
> *Al cordero manso cargan* They make the Gentle Lamb
> *Con el leño del dolor;* Carry a cross, emblem of pain;
> *Su pesada cruz a cuestas* With His cross upon bent shoulders
> *Marcha el dulce Salvador.* Our Savior marches to Mount Calvary.
>
> *A Jesús en cruz clavado* Look, oh sinner, on the Christ
> *Contémplale, oh pecador;* Jesus nailed to the cross;
> *Ve al hijo del Eterno* Look on the Son of the Eternal
> *Expirando por tu amor* Expiring for love of you.

Los Hermanos helped families at the time of a death. Since only a priest could administer the Last Sacraments, communities without clergy often substituted a *rezador* (reader) to recite prayers at the end of life. At death, he called out the name of Jesus three times and *alabados* were sung. The *velorio de difuntos* (wake for the dead) followed. The bathed and fully clad corpse was laid out in the main room of his or her home surrounded by lighted candles, and there it remained until burial. Neighbors would greet *los dolientes* (the mourners) with messages of condolence, and prayed over the body of the deceased. Throughout the night they sang *alabados* and offered more prayers. *Luminarias* (small bonfires) were lit and the men gathered outside to visit while the women prepared *la cena* (supper) served after the midnight rosary service. If the deceased was a member of a Penitente family, the body was often laid out in the *morada*. Such activities lent an opportunity for communal support and provided an outlet for personal grief.

Many Hispanics in New Mexico were philosophical about death, and there was a strong communion between the living and the dead. Masses, prayers, and *novenas* were often said for those who have passed on, thus lessening the time of their stay in purgatory. *Novenas* were prayers over nine days asking for special favors. While not inviting death, none were fearful of it. "¡Sea por Dios! (God's will be done!)" an expression used upon the loss of a loved one, illustrates the Hispanic's acceptance of the inevitable.

After the all-night *velorio*, the deceased was taken in procession to the burial place. If a priest was not in attendance, the cleric would bless the burial site and say Mass upon his next visit. Bodies were placed in a coffin or wrapped in a *mortaja* (shroud) and placed on a platform, a door, or a *palajuela* (ladder) for transport, and then interred. Funeral processions, whether originating in a church or *morada*, would halt for rest on the way to the *camposanto* (cemetery) for burial. At each *descanso* (resting place), *sudarios* (prayer for the departed) were said and *alabados* sung. The funeral party then marked the *descanso* with a small wooden cross. Descanso symbols have come into modern use as small roadside shrines where someone has met an unexpected and often lonely death.

Descansos mark resting places of the deceased

The practices of Los Hermanos and their need for privacy have been misunderstood and widely criticized by scandalized Anglo Protestants and some Catholic clergy. Not unlike the Indians, who sequester their sacred rituals from the outside world, the Hermanos choose to keep non-members from viewing their rites and ceremonies with the exception of public occasions. From the Penitente point-of-view, to describe the organization as secret is not appropriate, for the confraternity is openly recognized.

The Hermandad's practice of seclusion began during the first *visita* of the Bishop of Durango, José Antonio Laureano de Zubiría y Escalante, to New Mexico in 1833. Meeting with Padre Antonio José Martínez, the Bishop expressed amazement at the singular folk Catholicism of the Hermandad because they were operating outside of the authority of the church. He issued a decree forbidding the Hermandad practices. On his second visit in 1845, he found the organization still very much alive, and ordered the Hermandad to surrender its real property to the diocese. As a result, the Hermandad did not comply, grew cautious, and drew into itself.

Prying curiosity and condemnation by Anglo outsiders forced Los Hermanos to shield themselves away from inquisitive and disapproving eyes. Early in the twentieth century, there emerged uninvited parties known as "Penitente Hunters" who considered the Hermanos exotic or superstitious, and made it their business to hunt down and exploit the practices of the Hermandad. From his undercover observations of the processions and sacred crucifixion rites of the penitents, Charles Lummis gathered much of his inflammatory material for his widely read *The Land of Poco Tiempo,* and his various journalistic pieces. Carol Taylor, a correspondent for major news outlets including *Newsweek,* the *New York Times,* and the *San Francisco Chronicle,* relied on Lummis' reports that further promoted the sensational and negative image of the Hermandad. Relentless adverse publicity created so much antagonism that in 1931, Judge M. A. Otero of the First Judicial District Court in Santa Fe, found it necessary to move by court order to protect the Penitentes from molestation.

Docents accompanying visitors through the Morada de la Conquistadora at Las Golondrinas exercise discretion in their presentation of the Penitente story, for it is necessary to interpret the whole of the narrative. The Hermandad not only practiced sacred rituals, but looked after the welfare of their communities, cared for the ill and infirm, and administered law. An offending party was brought before an informal court hearing conducted by the *hermano mayor,* the *alcalde* in charge of the justice system. The Hermandad passed the folk religion with its rituals and devotions to Jesus' passion from one generation to the next. "Not easily explained in modern psychological terms, this strange religion has a terrible beauty that must be judged in its own context," said a reviewer of *Los Hermanos Penitentes* by Lorayne Horka-Follick.

The *morada* at Las Golondrinas, as it sits on a high hill overlooking the whole museum complex, is often mistaken for a church. The handsome structure, constructed in 1972–1974, is a faithful two-thirds scale replica of the south *morada* in the *genízaro* village of Abiquiú. The Hermanos from Abiquiú served as advisors for the construction, and archaeological plans, collected by the Smithsonian Institution, were consulted. It took three years to obtain permission from Los Hermanos to construct the Las Golondrinas *morada*. The replica is so faithful to the concept that fourteen brothers from Arroyo Seco were present to bless the edifice at the dedication ceremony. The *morada* is not sanctified, but Father Questa, the former pastor of Cristo Rey Church in Santa Fe, blessed the edifice.

Los Hermanos have prayerfully dedicated the *morada* to La Conquistadora. Although never a chapter house, some devotees have worshipped there. The Brothers ask that no photographs be taken of the interior as it is considered a sacred space.

Traditional fields below the Morada de La Conquistadora

As is traditional, the first room is the chapel with a traditional altar, a crucifix, *santos*, candelabras, and Stations of the Cross. The magnificent figure of Cristo, Nuestro Padre Nazareno, stands to the right of the altar, and is clad in a crimson tunic. The icon depicts His passion during Holy Week exemplified by the tortured countenance and the oversized hands bound by a cord. Were the life-size image, with its articulated arms and flowing robes, taken in procession, it would appear lifelike. The same figure can portray Christ in torment, crucified on the cross, or portrayed as He lay in the tomb. The viewer feels an overwhelming compassion for the image. The creator of the piece is Alcario Otero.

To the left of the altar sits the Angel of Death, Doña Sebastiana. She is not a saint but an allegorical depiction of death. She appears as a skeletal woman clad in black, holding a bow and arrow and other instruments of death. Doña Sebastiana serves to caution the viewer to avoid a "bad death," and to prepare for a "good death" which will assure admittance into heaven. Doña Sebastiana warns one not become too attached to things of this world, but prayerfully make ready for the next. Also evident in the room are a pair of *tenebre* (branched candelabrum) along with *matracas* and other noise makers that represent the ritual of Las Tinieblas on Thursday, the last hours of Jesus Christ in the Garden of Gethsemane when his apostles abandoned him, and from whence he was taken and crucified on the cross.

The second room in the *morada* replicates the sacristy with its *fogón* where meals were served and penitents rested. A third is a *depósito* (repository) in the rear where crosses used in past processions are kept; it is also the room where the penitents would have bathed their wounds with *romero* (rosemary) medicated water in a tub. A large cross stands on the hillside to the south of the *morada*, *El Calvario* (Calvary). Next to the *morada* is a replica of a *camposanto* with its weathered crosses. Wooden fences were typically constructed around burials to keep animals from digging up the remains in the shallow graves. Many of the Las Golondrinas *morada* crosses and fences were collected elsewhere. No *camposanto* has been found on the grounds of the museum.

> A frequently asked question is, "Where was the cemetery?" No trace has been found. Nor is there evidence of a pre-existing chapel. However, Nazario Gonzáles and María Rita Baca de Gonzáles gave 100 varas of land for a new chapel in 1858, and according to an article in The Santa Fe New Mexican, José Baca y Delgado was buried at the chapel at Las Golondrinas that he erected at his own expense.

The church's former hostility to the Penitentes has given way to friendly acceptance and understanding of the society as it officially abandoned corporeal mortification. The Archdiocese of Santa Fe annually issues a certificate of acknowledgment to the Hermandad. In 1947, Archbishop Edwin Byrne and the Penitente Hermano Superior, Miguel Archibeque wrote a new constitution for the Hermandad, and the Cristo Rey Confraternity of New Mexico and Southern Colorado was formally accepted back into the Catholic Church. The confraternity is now a benevolent fraternal order with its own constitution, and is incorporated with the State of New Mexico guaranteeing it certain legal rights. Each *morada* chapter writes its own bylaws. Every time a new Archbishop assumes his term of office, or a new Hermano Superior is installed, the Brotherhood's constitution is again ratified. The Most Reverend Michael J. Sheehan, Archbishop of Santa Fe, recently observed that, "We have about eight hundred active *hermanos* presently in the Archdiocese, and approximately 125 *moradas*, of which some ninety have an active membership in the Cristo Rey Confraternity of New Mexico." A minority of *moradas* do not choose to be part of the confraternity and remain separate under their own jurisdiction.

After World War II, the membership in the Hermandad surged, but many new members could not speak Spanish. Admission to membership requires the applicant be Hispanic and Catholic, and able to speak Spanish, for only Spanish is spoken inside the *morada*. A bi-lingual book of *alabados* has been published and distributed to new members to assist them to achieve the essential mastery of the Spanish language required for membership.

Our Lady of Guadalupe

Prominent among the religious icons seen at Las Golondrinas and elsewhere in New Mexico is the Mexican Virgin, Nuestra Señora de Guadalupe, Our Lady of Guadalupe. She is the subject of one of the *retablos* in the *reredo* of the *capilla*. Our Lady's story begins with an event alleged to have taken placed in December 12, 1531 on Tepeyac Hill at the eastern edge of Mexico City. The legend relates that Juan Diego, an Aztec peasant and neophyte, was making his way to Mass, when the image of a beautiful lady, surrounded by a body halo, spoke to him. She was his "Compassionate Mother," she told Juan Diego, and wished to love and protect "all folk of every kind." She requested that a temple in her honor be built where she stood. A temple to Tonantzin, an Aztec goddess worshiped as "our mother," is believed by some of the devout to have stood on the site. The Virgin sent Juan Diego to tell the bishop-elect of Mexico, Fray Juan de Zumárraga, of this miraculous event. The skeptical Zumárraga dismissed the humble peasant and his story. The next day, the apparition again appeared to Juan Diego, and this time the bishop demanded proof of Diego's claim. On the third day, Diego sought to elude the apparition, for he was seeking a priest to administer last rites to his dying uncle. The Virgin again appeared to him, informed Diego his uncle had recovered, and asked him once again to urge the bishop to build her temple. As proof of the truth of his story, the Virgin then plucked "Castilian garden flowers' from the mid-winter barren hilltop, and placed them in Diego's tilma. When he appeared once more before Zumárraga, and proceeded to open his tilma, the flowers fell at the prelate's feet. A portrait of the Sacred Image of the Ever Virgin Holy Mary, Mother of God miraculously appeared on the cloak. Finally the bishop accepted Juan Diego's claims. Today this garment hangs in the Basilica of Guadalupe in Mexico City. The Nahuatl name for Juan Diego was Cuautitlán, or Eagle That Speaks, a name reserved for Aztec nobility although the neophyte was considered a commoner.

No reference to the incident appears in Zumárraga's writings, but in 1754, Pope Benedict XIV declared La Virgen de Guadalupe patroness of New Spain. During the reign of Pope John Paul II in 1990, the Aztec neophyte, Juan Diego, was beatified. Almost five hundred years after Our Lady of Guadalupe is believed to have appeared to Juan Diego, the Pope visited Mexico in July, 2002 to complete the canonization of Juan Diego. In the same year, a former Mexican bishop, Guillermo Shulemburg, reigniting a centuries-old debate, asked the Pope to rescind his decision, claiming that there is little or no proof that Diego ever lived, and that the canonization would propagate a lie. The late Fray Angélico Chavez, well-known New Mexican Catholic priest, scholar, and author, is quoted as saying, ". . . there is no factual proof surrounding the legend of Guadalupe, and it has never been proven." He does concede that the legend had united the Mexican nation. The Vatican, however, certified that Juan Diego performed a miracle, a requisite for sainthood. It is alleged that Juan Diego interceded when a mother prayed for her son's life after the nineteen-year-old youth plunged from a second-story window in Mexico City, fracturing his skull. By a miracle, the youth survived his fall.

Our Lady's core image is an elongated three-quarters profile of an olive skinned figure clad in a rose-colored dress and blue-green mantle. She holds her hands in a supplicating position, and stands on a half-moon held aloft by an angel. On the Virgin's head is a crown, and a burst of sunrays surrounds her figure. Clergy, who thought the icon needed enhancing, added details to the image on the tilma. For Catholics, Our Lady of Guadalupe, a dark skinned madonna, is the most venerated and reproduced holy image in all of Meso-America.

The devotion to Our Lady of Guadalupe came at a time of growing self-consciousness on the part of the *criollo* elite that foreshadowed their coming struggle for independence from Spain. Miraculously transformed into an Indian woman, the Virgin became mother to New World people, and an enduring and essential emblem of faith in Mexico and New Mexico. The tradition of Our Lady of Guadalupe did not appear in New Mexico until after the *entrada* of Diego de Vargas in 1692. "Our Lady of Guadalupe made her own quiet *entrada* into the devotional practices in New Mexico," wrote scholar Jacqueline Orsini Dunnington. Our Lady is the premier Marian symbol in New Mexico.

The Art of the Santero

Newcomers to New Mexico are often surprised at the rustic simplicity of the sacred art. American Third Calvary officer and ornithologist, Lieutenant John G. Bourke, wrote in 1881, "To the traveler, the greatest charm of New Mexico will be lost when relics of a by-gone day shall be superseded by brighter and better pictures framed in the cheap gilding of our own time . . . because its [New Mexico's] religious observances are so crusted over with the picturesque medievalism, or savagery, if you will, . . . the traveler endures uncomplainingly bedbugs, fleas, *coroquis* [sic], sand, grease and chili colorado. Today, collectors highly prize the folk art relics for this very reason, and the devout cherish them as a bond to the past."

When French born Jean Baptiste Lamy, the first American bishop, came to Santa Fe in 1851, he was appalled by the unorthodox, rough plainness of the Catholic images that were revered by his New Mexican flock. He imported baroque plaster figures from St. Louis to replace the detested works. Happily, his effort to coax his devotees into abandoning the rustic old images did not succeed. So who were the makers of this truly indigenous form of art? As a rule, the *santero* was a rural person without formal training in image making who supported his family as an itinerant carpenter. He used local materials for his *bultos* and *retablos*. Cottonwood root and pine logs were his basic supplies. Cottonwood root carved easily, was light in weight, and did not splinter. For colors he made tempura of egg yolk thinned with water and mixed with mineral pigments. Vegetal colors did not hold fast, so colorful minerals were employed. To make a base coat for the pigments, *yeso* was composed of baked gypsum, pulverized and dissolved in water, and mixed with animal glue. Varnish, made from piñon pine resin and homemade grain alcohol, protected the finished piece. The *santero* used brushes of yucca fiber, chewed willow sticks, or fine feathers, and applied color to large areas with swabs of wool or cloth.

The *santero* drew outlines in cartoon fashion in black or brown and applied color in simple terms, contrasting dark with light. Composition was dictated by the *santero's* limited knowledge of the iconography of holy figures. He had few printed images to study and so took his clues from older pieces, or he adapted the suggestions of the local priest. His *retablo* began as a slab of seasoned pine or cottonwood cut into a rectangular shape, and often thinned at the top so that it would hang flat when suspended by a thong or cord. Sometimes a semicircular half clam shell lunette, typical of Franciscan art, topped the panel. The wood, sanded with pumice stone, was painted with successive thin coats of quick drying gesso to form an absorbent surface. The finished coat was smoothed with fine sand. The *santero's* color palate was limited; he used iron oxide or ochre to achieve the red spectrum, select clays for creams, yellows, and oranges, and charcoal for black. Ground azurite provided the blue he needed. He depicted his images as his imagination dictated. He preferred to picture his saints alone in attentive poses, as if listening to a spectator or expressing their thoughts to God. The artist did use some conventional treatments, an oval face, and a single stroke for a nose, or an eyebrow over an almond-shaped eye. It was his prerogative to portray costumes, human features, and objects from everyday life in his creation.

Some older images, often skillfully executed, were drawings on tanned hides of elk, buffalo or deer. Plains Indians had been using this medium in their decorated masks, shields, and teepees long before white men arrived. The priests found a distinct advantage in hide paintings for they were tough and easy to roll up and transport. No doubt, too, the durability of tanned skins preserved the images for longer periods than wooden *retablos*. Unfortunately, in the early 1800s, the Archbishop of Durango declared hides to be a sacrilegious material unfit for religious purposes, and ordered them destroyed. Few pieces survived.

Bultos, figures of saints or other holy persons portrayed in the round, were created during the secular period by largely untaught native craftsmen. The *santero* carved the torso from a piece of cottonwood root. Larger *bultos* were hollowed-out to make them lighter. He then created the head, limbs and other members from sticks of pine, and secured the separate pieces with wooden pegs and animal glue. At times he made plaster of Paris from gypsum, applied it to the figure, and then traced details with a knife. A thin coat of *yeso* sealed the entire figure. The *santero* used the same pigmented medium to color his *bultos* that he employed in his *retablos*. A *bulto* was often secured to a solid base with wooden pegs and glue. Some *santeros* carved the figure, but when anatomical features were not important, it often consisted of a wicker frame over which leather or *yeso*-soaked cloth was draped. Departure from traditional anatomy allowed the artist to depict emotions and call attention to attributes he wanted to accentuate.

In the New Mexico *santero* tradition, an image was judged holy if its rendition reflected powerful traditional icons. "This is one of those art forms you cannot separate from the people. We write our own history by what we say and the art we do," said *santero* Charlie Carrillo. One intuitively senses that the religious art of the Hispanic Southwest is an integral part of the matrix that makes New Mexico unique.

Noted scholar and student of the ethos of New Mexico, Thomas J. Steele, S.J., writes that, "*Santos* are a kind of 'liberation theology' written in the language of wood, plaster, and paint, an understanding of Christianity empowers the poor to free themselves from unjust socioeconomic and cultural structures in the larger world and within themselves."

9

The Emergence of New Mexico Society and Culture

Mexican Independence—Law and Order—Fashion—Schools
and Literacy—Curanderas

Mexican Independence

The news of the declaration of Mexican independence of August 1821 arrived in New Mexico weeks after the fact, and was greeted with anticipation and jubilation. Gone were the crown policies that restrained commerce. Gone was the monopoly of Mexico's only trade partners, Spain and her colonies. Indeed, trade with Spain stopped. Gone, too, were the overt controls of the church, although New Mexicans remained very Catholic in thought and practice. Most Franciscan missionaries and many *peninsulares*, who would not swear allegiance to new republic, chose to return to Spain. No longer subject to Spanish social and trade controls and the political turmoil that accompanied the process of independence, today's New Mexican culture evolved.

The years after the achievement of Mexican nationhood were far from tranquil. The new state was a mixture of peoples of widely differing cultures with little or no concept of what nationhood signified. Its first leader, Agustín de Iturbide, ruled precariously over an empire that in 1824 became the Estados Unidos Mexicanos, the Mexican United States. The new nation acquired a constitution that provided for a federal republic of nineteen states, four territories and a federal district. Civil strife between conservative centralists and liberal federalists kept Mexico in turmoil for another ten years. The competing parties had little time or energy to worry about the country's northernmost region, New Mexico.

The constitution of 1824 made some sweeping changes in the formal political and social conditions of all Mexicans. Freedom of speech and press were proclaimed, all male inhabitants, including Indians, were enfranchised, and slavery and the caste system were officially abolished. Catholicism remained the state religion, but in New Mexico the mission system collapsed, and the newly secularized churches had to support themselves. When available, friars were replaced with diocesan priests. By 1830, there were only nine priests in the entire of New Mexico. Later in 1898, Archbishop John B. Salpointe reported that of the 239 Franciscan priests who had served during the colonial period, thirty had been martyred.

New Mexico's isolation bred an independence of spirit and disdain for authority that Spain or Mexico would never have tolerated had not the northern colony been so remote. Its population was widely dispersed; New Mexicans continued to rely on their own skills and resources to survive. Needs were simple and supplied by one's own labor, by the community's collective effort, and by trade with the Indians. After Mexican independence, life remained as hard as before. Farmers were still subject to attacks by marauding Indians, to epidemic illnesses such as smallpox, and to the threats posed by rattlesnakes, grizzly bears, lightning, drought, and floods. Religious art reflected fatalism in the face of these many dangers and the uncertainties of life.

Society was composed of self-sufficient communities peopled by *paisanos* (compatriots) who relied on ranching and sheep husbandry for much of their economy; many were subsistence farmers. New Mexico had been sheep country ever since the *entrada* by Juan de Oñate. Sheep were trailed to Chihuahua, and later large flocks were sent to California to supply miners in the gold fields. A *patrón,* using the *partido* system (system of shares), would allot two thousand sheep to a *pastor* to tend for one or more years. In return, the herder was entitled to a share of the lamb crop, often 10 percent. By this means the shepherd hoped to start or increase his own flock. The herder used dogs trained to guard against predators. At night, the *pastor* posted his canine guards, using *saleas* (sheepskins) as sleeping pads by which the dogs recognized their beds by their unique smells.

The *patrón* took care of the family of the *pastor* during his absence, kept track of expenses to be deducted from his share, but held the shepherd responsible for all losses of stock to predators, theft, disease, or accident. It was easy for the *pastor* to become mired in debt. No one living at Las Golondrinas owned enough sheep to be considered a *patrón*.

In 1829, José Francisco Baca y Terrus, a wealthy La Ciénega landowner, inventoried 1,000 sheep along with 140 head of livestock on the *estancia*.

Some notable *patrones* in the Río Abajo were the Otero, Luna, Perea, Chávez, Ortiz, and Armijo families. In 1899, five million sheep roamed New Mexico's pastures and plains, more than twenty-five sheep for every person in the territory.

The general poverty of the land, the low level of economic activity, and the scarcity of specie (gold and silver coin) coupled with low wages, forced many New Mexicans to become debtors. Some fortunate village families had been granted title to land as soldier-citizens, but other farmers relied on sharing communal lands, and reciprocal labor that often resulted in economic bondage. Severe economic stagnation continued until the introduction of gold pesos by 1750, and the general circulation of specie in the 1770s. Even then coin was scarce.

New Mexicans welcomed the new freedom allowed by Mexico to trade with whomever they pleased with few restrictions. Increasing foreign commerce along the Santa Fe Trail and El Camino Real de Tierra Adentro made more and better goods available at cheaper prices. The cost of imported merchandise dropped by two-thirds after the Santa Fe Trail opened. With increased business traffic came more ways of conducting one's own business affairs. The opening of the Santa Fe Trail may be regarded as a forerunner of NAFTA, the 1992 North American Free Trade Agreement. The pact provides for the eventual elimination of tariff barriers.

Law and Order

The Spanish legal system, Las Leyes de las Indias, generally remained in place from 1621 until the Mexican-American War. The Juzgado General de Indios (General Indian Court), designed specifically for Indian litigation, exemplifies the crown's obligation to defend Indian rights. The Protector de Indios (Protector of the Indians), who did not have legal powers, would often appear in court and argue for the natives. John S. Calhoun, first civil governor of the New Mexican Territory, was amazed at the regularity with which Pueblo Indians pursued resolution of their grievances through his office. The many years of experience with Hispanic jurisprudence gave them the insight to use the system.

There were no *abogados* (lawyers) or *jueces* (judges) in colonial New Mexico, so parties involved in the dispute hoped for the presiding *alcalde* known to have good judgment and common sense. There were three different *fueros* (jurisdictions) of law. Clergy could not be arraigned before a tribunal, but were to be tried by ecclesiastical superiors. Military cases were tried in military courts, and civil charges against laymen were heard before an *alcalde*. Trial by jury was unheard of. On occasion, a convicted felon would be sent to the Chihuahuan prison and sweatshop, such as La Hacienda de Encinillas. The longest sentence served there was ten years. Prisoners were paid a pittance, but the amount could be assigned for restitution to the victim. Sentencing often included compensation to the victim of the crime through fines or servitude; other punishments were whipping or exile of the culprit. A debtor often became the creditor's servant until he satisfied his obligation by working for very low wages. Deduction of his maintenance could keep him in perpetual servitude. Capital punishment was rare in colonial New Mexico throughout the Mexican period, and imposed only for premeditated murder, treason, or rebellion. Appeals of a death sentence on humanitarian grounds were common. Robert Tórrez, former New Mexico State Historian, notes that there are only two documented death sentences in the 250 years of colonial rule. A Cochiti mother and daughter pleaded guilty to murdering the daughter's husband in 1773, and were summarily hanged. Then in 1809, two Santa Cruz de La Cañada men were executed for the murder of a French merchant. In general, it can be said that punishment was humane, creative, and practical.

Alcaldes combined civic duties with the administration of justice. As a rule they had little knowledge of formal law, and did not administer it to the letter. The *juez* (judge), often nearly illiterate, attempted to make decisions based on tradition, common sense and compassion. The parties involved in disputes were brought together in a *careo* (confrontation), a face-to-face encounter intended to ferret out the truth. Testimonies were read, charges were dropped, or the suspect confessed and was found guilty. A formal reading of the sentence was acknowledged by the culprit. In case of appeal, it was forwarded to the *alcalde mayor* in Santa Fé. A charge of blasphemy, insulting the church, could result in a large fine in pesos and exile. It fell to the *alcaldes* to be defenders of public morality and, in many instances, to serve as the court of first resort in marital difficulties. *Alcalde* courts had jurisdiction over children whose rights or property was threatened. Guardians were appointed, especially when a piece of property was to be held in trust for the child.

A symbol of authority used by the *alcalde* was the *VARA*, a symbolic staff of justice. The Rod of Justice accompanied the *alcalde* anytime and anywhere that the official was acting in authority. Curiously, the height of the Rod of Justice and the length of a *vara* used to measure distance are the same. After American occupation, Indian Agents, as representatives of the Federal Government, gave Pueblos, Comanche, and other tribal authorities similar canes— symbols of tribal autonomy.

The businessman Josiah Gregg, author of *Commerce on the Prairies*, was a gifted although critical observer of the New Mexican social scene. He made a condemning observation that New Mexican mores were "a convenient cloak of irregularities." The lawyer W. H. H. Davis, another chronicler and social critic of New Mexico, wrote that three out of four of the married population of New Mexico had lovers, probably an excessively high figure, but that society accepted this state of affairs. He also claimed that concubinage, a Spanish tradition, was more common than marriage, possibly because marriage was costly, and some priests had concubines and families. The public at large accepted concubinage but not adultery; the church condemned both. Because marriage fees were so high, and there was no equivalent to civil marriage, some couples chose cohabitation. Natural children were common across the classes, birth records recording the mother's name and the father recorded as "unknown." But promiscuity was less tolerated than American newcomers assumed. *Alcaldes* served as protectors of the public morals against habitual adulterers, fornicators, and prostitutes. "Spurious" children, those born to a priest or to an adulterous or prostituted relationship, bore the most dishonor.

As mentioned before, New Mexican women enjoyed legal rights unknown to their American counterparts. It was not uncommon for women to bring complaints to the *alcalde* court against their husbands. Servants of both sexes could seek redress of grievances before the *juez*. Widows were not liable for their husband's debts as was the case in the United States. They maintained ownership of assets brought into a marriage, and could inherit, sell, loan or pawn property. If the *alcalde* could not solve a conflict between the parties, each named a *hombre bueno*, an arbitrator recognized by the community as an honorable person, who would examine the evidence and advise the *juez* who then rendered a judgment. If neither plaintiff nor defendant could agree, the case was dropped or appealed to the governor for a verdict. The one thing the *alcalde* courts could not do was grant a divorce. Divorce was obtainable only from an ecclesiastical court, and then only after all attempts at reconciliation and appeals failed.

In this male dominated and family oriented society, a woman living alone did not enjoy the same legal protection as her married sisters. She found herself fair game for men, and was suspected of being a temptress. If she was no longer young and attractive, she could be rumored to be a *bruja* (witch), a powerless and unintended way that sometimes protected her. The only respectable options for a woman alone were to become a domestic servant in the house of a wealthy family, live with relatives, or voluntarily enter a convent, an alternative that required traveling to one of the population centers in Mexico. Those unfortunate enough to have none of these options and resorted to prostitution were subject to harsh punishment, the loss of all legal rights, and possible banishment to a convent.

Bruja repellant hangs above the Baca cocina door

Gambling was carried on everywhere, much to the dismay of the Yankee, Josiah Gregg. *Chuza* was a favorite of the ladies who played for large stakes. *Monte* was the favorite card game. Bull-baiting and cock fighting were popular amusements accompanied by heavy betting. *La corrida del gallo* (rooster pull) was often performed on St. John's Day.

Inevitably, the favored amusement was a *baile* (dance) attended by everyone including the priest who danced the *fandango* with even the humblest peasant.

The sexes mingled with scant supervision and little fear of public condemnation given for the stolen kiss or moment of familiarity. But, fear of lustful behavior prompted some clergy to exhort women to refrain from the *baile* because the provocative movements of their uncorseted bodies might tempt men to indulge in naughty behavior. Favored musical instruments were the fiddle and *guitarra* (guitar), sometimes accompanied with a little Indian *tombé* (drum). The night air was filled with youthful male harmonizing and punctuating some of the phrases with a high falsetto. The high cost of alcohol limited drunkenness, but local wine was always available. All smoked corn husk wrapped *cigarrillos* (cigarettes). According to Josiah Gregg, the vice of smoking by the ladies was most intolerable. Social pleasures were many. Saints' days, following each other in rapid succession, marked the changes of seasons. Villagers honored the occasions by carrying a flower-decked figure of a patron saint on an *andita* (litter), often the farmer's friend, San Ysidro, about the villages and fields in procession; other favorites, notably the Virgin Mary, were also taken in processions. *Fiestecitas* (parties) invariably followed.

Baile class

Fashions

New Mexicans quickly adapted European fashions after textiles from the East became available after the opening of the Santa Fe Trail. Only the occasional *caballero* of the *rico* class still retained his traditional picturesque image. Typical of his dress was the wide brimmed and low crowned *sombrero,* the *chaqueta* (jacket) flamboyantly embroidered with barrel-buttons and braid, the *calzones,* leather over-pants open down the outer side of the leg and trimmed with filigree buttons, and topped by a splendid sash drawn smartly about the body. A *sarape* (blanket) completed the dashing figure. The *caballero's* mount was decked out in a similar manner. The embossed saddle trappings sometimes weighed one hundred pounds or more. The bridle was often the most costly part of the equipment, often made of silver alloy and ornamented with buckles, slides and stars. Iron or silver spurs sported shanks up to five inches long and with rowels up to six inches in diameter. For the working man in the saddle, the *armas de pelo* (shaggy goatskin chaps) were laid across the pommel of the saddle for use in case of rain, or worn over trousers for protection against brush and brambles, much as chaps are worn by today's ranch hands.

A countryman or craftsman of the *pobre* (poor individual) class wore a hat, wide brimmed and with a low crown. His shirt had a high collar and long, full sleeves, cuffed and tied in the front of the wrist. His knee breeches had a drop front and leg openings wide enough through which to slip the foot. His above-the-knee knit stockings were held in place with a garter, and his feet sported leather shoes with a low heel, a high tongue and a buckle.

Traders imported hoopskirts to be worn by wealthier women, and silk from the Orient and velvet from Chihuahua. Ladies copied styles from New York and Paris, but never gave up their favored *rebozos* (shawls). *Fiestas,* parties, and church-going were the favored occasions to display finery. Blouses of colorful cotton prints trimmed with lace and ribbons in bands of flashing colors, were worn with a skirt embroidered with a bold China Poblana floral motif, graced the figures of upper class women.

Persons of lesser means aspired to similar finery but of coarser material. Common velveteens, corduroys and thick cotton cloth were used along with the woolen products of the country. Ladies never wore hats, preferring *rebozos* of silk, linen, or cotton drawn over the head. The *enaguas* (petticoats) of coarse blue or scarlet flannel was secured around the waist with a contrasting girdle that held a loose white chemise in place, creating the "graceful sort of undress" mentioned by Josiah Gregg. Women were fond of jewelry, and bedecked their necks, arms, and hands with pieces of decorative ornaments; they would rather go barefoot than give up their necklaces, bracelets, and earrings. Their costumes scandalized puritanical easterners, both men and women. The newcomers also found offensive the habit of besmearing female faces with crimson alegria (cockscomb blossom), or a combination of clay and starch, a mudpack used to protect the skin from the sun. With a scrub and a rinse before a *fiesta* or a *baile*, their complexions appeared fresh and ruddy.

Except for ornamental jewelry and items such as ribbons and sashes, the poor rarely had a change of dress. Laundering was typically an annual warm-weather affair. At this time women, clothed only in their chemises, washed the bedding and family wardrobe in a hot spring or in the river. Although seldom laundered, the purifying New Mexican sun and wind made garments useable. After large metal kettles became available, wash water was drawn from a well or a stream, and heated over an open fire.

Poor children of both sexes, including the babe in arms, rarely appeared fully dressed. Some wore only a shift, others were in a complete state of undress. When they reached the age of about eight, the children began to wear adult clothing, but boys remained hatless and shoeless until their early teens. Wealthier families took pride in dressing their progeny as elegantly as their means permitted.

Schools and Literacy

Not surprisingly, a society that changed little in three hundred years, with a primitive economy, poor roads and transportation, limited education, and scarce access to doctors or medicine, cared little for formal instruction. Why teach youngsters to read and write when the land offered a living, and they could learn all they needed to know by watching and working with adults? Tilling and harvesting crops, building shelters, creating religious art, weaving *jerga*, tanning hides, dipping candles, learning to honor the saints, and a myriad of other tasks did not require being able to read. If a letter had to be written or records prepared, scribes were available.

Taking a turn at the plow

Some colonists saw a need for a literate society. Juan de Páez Bustillos was one of the colonists from Mexico City who received a Santa Cruz land grant from Governor Vargas. Poor health forced him to sell his grant, and he relocated to Santa Fé where he became the earliest known schoolmaster in New Mexico. It is unknown how many *estudiantes* he taught. Many colonists, including Miguel Vega y Coca who came at the time of the re-conquest, were able to read and write.

In 1717, the Viceroy of New Spain sent a royal *cédula* (decree) to Fray Antonio Camargo, the Franciscan Custodian in Kewa Pueblo. In it he ordered steps be taken to establish schools in all of the missions where there were children of Indians and Hispanic settlers. Expenses were to be paid by Indians with donations of corn, and by settlers who were to cultivate a *milpa* designated for that purpose. But nothing came of the edict, as education was generally left to the family in the home. The children of the wealthier class could be taught in the homes of Franciscan friars, and in the early 1800s in the *presidio* school of Santa Fé. Fray Antonio de Acevedo of Santa Fé is recorded in 1727 as having taught school for both boys and girls. However, the religious in their missions selected only boys to be raised and educated as *doctinarios*. By reading texts and interpreting the content to other *estudiantes*, these children served as culture brokers and teachers, and played a vital role in the Hispanic catechizing of the Pueblos.

Although it was uncommon for Indian children to receive a formal education, a Comanche student in Santa Fé was the son of Ecueracapa, the Comanche chieftain who helped to implement the successful treaty executed with Juan Bautista de Anza after the defeat of Cuerno Verde. His father wished his son be educated in the Spanish language and culture. A later report by Pedro Baptista Pino referenced a son of Comanche chief Maya who also attended school in Santa Fé in the 1790s.

By 1806 there were efforts made by the Spanish to bring education to Santa Fé. The Royal Cantábrico Seminary was established. The "eminent faculty" professed to teach religion, the study of classic authors, political education and physical education. In 1808, 140 children were enrolled in the presidio school of Santa Fé where twenty were judged able to write, 108 to read, and twelve could recite their prayers. The same year, a Santa Fé military company survey observed some fifty-nine children attending two schools, and it forecast that the citizenry would become more motivated to seek an education. But in 1812 Pedro Baptista Pino reported to King Fernando VII that only those who can afford to hire a schoolmaster were able to educate their children. It is believed that Pino presented a gloomy picture of the state of education in New Mexico in order to persuade the crown to provide more support.

A New Mexican, who saw the value of a well rounded education and owned the second largest private library in the territory, was the enlightened Manuel Francisco Delgado who owned Las Golondrinas. The illustrious Manuel Delgado entered the history of La Ciénega Valley and Las Golondrinas about 1804. Born of noble blood in Real de Pachuca north-east of Mexico City, he joined the military in 1761, achieved a brilliant career, and eventually moved to Santa Fé. His name appeared in the presidio census of 1790 immediately after that of Governor Fernando de la Concha. He mustered out of the army as *capitán retirado* (retired captain) whereupon he became an importer of wine and brandy for thirsty citizens of the capital city, and a recognized leader in business circles. Don Manuel married María Josefa García de Noriega in 1778. Las Golondrinas, "known throughout the province for its fertile fields and unfailing springs . . ." was but one of his farm and ranch properties.

The inventory of the sizeable estate of Manuel Francisco Delgado, who died in 1815 after having served in the military, and as a businessman in Santa Fé with ties to merchants in Chihuahua, revealed a man of considerable wealth

and apparent intellect. In addition to 9,000 Mexican pesos, the declaration included a flock of 2,240 breeding ewes and the now well-known El Rancho de las Golondrinas. Delgado's personal library contained the works of Charles V, the biographies of Charles XII and Estevancillo (Estebanico), books on natural history, the Hebrew monarchy, military ordinances, Holy Week, the Conquest of Mexico, daily exercise, faith, criminal practice, several novels and a nine volume set on how to entertain one's self.

Documents disclose that Manuel Francisco Delgado had a dispute with a neighbor, Juan José Silva, sometime between 1798 and 1799. Silva claimed Delgado had despoiled his farmlands and his rights to pasture land. The lands were eventually awarded to Delgado.

Recognizing the extent and uniqueness of the holdings listed in Manuel Delgado's will, The Museum of Spanish Colonial Art in Santa Fe proudly dedicated a room, La Casa Delgado (The Delgado Home), that exhibits a "realistic glimpse of life in a colonial New Mexican home through a variety of objects whose historical equivalents are represented in the collections at the Museum of Spanish Colonial Art."

Few books, even works of devotion, were brought into the province. As late as 1803, the Church ordered seizure of "seditious" or "heretical" works such as the *Social Contract* by Rousseau. One Franciscan stated, "May God forbid that free trade should lead to the introduction of free thought!" Efforts at controlling the import of condemned materials failed as Josiah Gregg imported 1,141 volumes of many persuasions to New Mexico, and smugglers brought in many more. No printing press, much less an adequate supply of paper, existed in the territory until shortly before the American occupation. Priests, officials, and clerks provided the little instruction in reading and writing that was available. Franciscans organized mission schools for *doctrinarios* (educated mission Indians) and taught crafts, music, reading and writing. Priests used puppets to teach Biblical stories to their Pueblo charges, and taught a few Hispanic children on the side. Mexican independence saw the exodus of many Spanish, thus eliminating numerous persons qualified to teach. Only the sons of *ricos* received formal education, some attending the seminary in Durango, Mexico or, after the Santa Fe Trail opened up, Union College in St. Louis where they learned to speak English and French. New Mexican merchants found it useful to have sons well educated so they could function reliably as traders.

In 1827 the Mexican government posted regulations for a prescribed curriculum. They included religious instruction, often continuing through the weekend. The *maestro* (primary school teacher) was provided housing, but could not leave the village for any reason. *Maestros* were forbidden to use corporal chastisement because, "such harsh punishment embitters the children and robs them of their dignity." *Maestros* were expected to treat children with paternal love. Despite rules to the contrary, they engaged in physical punishments of many kinds, some severe. Mexican schools required strict surveillance by instructors. *Estudiantes* were to learn to respect and honor civil, religious, and military authorities. Quarreling, discourtesy, and obscene language were forbidden. The entire school would assemble after Mass on Sunday for the visitation by the *ayuntamiento* (local assembly). Days began at six o'clock in the morning and finished at five-thirty in the evening with breaks for students to go home to eat breakfast, and then again for lunch.

In 1829, D. Marcelino Abreu opened a Lancastrian School in Santa Fé, but complained that the ninety-four pesos due him went unpaid, and that school attendance was not required. The Lancastrian System substituted especially bright pupils for teachers. *Estudiantes* were taught in groups and made to read from copy on large placards, thus eliminating expensive textbooks. In 1833, the Mexican Congress secularized public education and created the Dirección de Instrucción Pública (Administration of Public Instruction), decreeing the development of a system of *escuelas primarías* (primary schools).

Average citizens had to find capable instructors from their own number, sometimes resident presidial soldiers or secular priests. The few mentors traveled widely to private homes that provided supplies in order to teach rudimentary reading, writing and Christian doctrine. Promised salaries often went unpaid, and the patience of teachers was sorely tested. Parents lost faith when teachers and local authorities quarreled. Many were already convinced that schools had no role in the frontier. Some officials, upset by the parental practice of using their children for farm and domestic labor, accused them of imprisoning their sons and daughters in their own homes. Relations between the *ayuntamiento* and the teacher were often strained. Instructors could be autocratic, and the *ayuntamiento* had absolute control, not only of students and the school, but of the teacher as well. The *ayuntamiento* felt it was responsible for the moral conduct of citizens and for the expulsion of subversive ideas from schools.

> Don Manuel Echevarría, school master in Santa Fé in 1837, had charges brought against him by Pedro Baptista Pino, Manuel Francisco Delgado, and two other residents of Las Golondrinas, for what was considered extreme punishment of a boy. Another Santa Fé school master, Don Serafín Ramírez, was fined for severely punishing a student.

Among the dedicated individuals providing instruction to children was Antonio José Martínez, the famous Taos curate and a luminary of the period. A brilliant man, he had all but finished a six-year scholastic theology course at the Tridentine Seminary of Durango, Mexico when he received a petition to prepare several young men for entrance to the seminary. The accommodating Martínez taught them morals and Latin grammar, and later expanded his class load to include those who wanted instruction in rhetoric, reading, writing, and arithmetic.

Critic Josiah Gregg noted the shortage of educational opportunities, and estimated that three-quarters of the population in 1844 could neither read nor write. He reported in his journal, *Commerce of the Prairies*, "... although a system of public schools was afterwards adopted by the republic, which, if persevered in, would no doubt have contributed to the dissemination of useful knowledge, yet its operation had been suspended about ten years ago for want of the necessary funds to carry out the original project.... The only schools now in existence are of the lowest primary class, supported entirely by individual patronage... [with the result] that at least three-fourths of the present population can neither read nor write.... Female education has, if possible, been more universally neglected than that of the other sex, while those who have received any instruction at all have generally been taught in private families."

Drawing on primary sources from the Archives of the Santa Fe Archdiocese and Spanish Archives of New Mexico, in his *Literacy, Education, and Society in New Mexico 1693–1821*, historian Bernard P. Gallegos has disputed the notion of massive native illiteracy in colonial New Mexico. The researcher studied signatures on documents and counted those who could sign their names as literate. He argues that in order to write a name, one had first to be able to read and then learn to write, a universal symbol of literacy. He maintains the large number or reliable documents, wills, military enlistments, baptismal records, Inquisition accounts, and other reports contradict the myth that most New Mexicans were illiterate. From the examination of the signatures, Gallegos concludes that the male literacy rate for the entire period was about 32 percent.

According to historian Marc Simmons, Cleofas Jaramillo of Santa Fe, who died in 1956, reminisced about her early education in a one-room *adobe* house in a remote northern village. Children had to bring their own chairs, and the teacher provided the only desk. The single textbook belonged to the teacher who wrote copies on pieces of cardboard that were then passed among the *estudiantes*, a practice adopted from the Lancastrian system of the Mexican period.

Curanderas

Faith and fatalism, "Que se haga la voluntad de Dios" (God's will be done) was an element of folk medicine dispensed along with what nature provided. An occasional reference has been made to the presence of *médicos* (doctors) and other health-care workers. An officer of the Juan de Oñate expedition of 1598, Juan de Caso Barahona, must have practiced medicine on the side. In his manifest were medicaments, surgical instruments, a syringe, and instruments to perform a phlebotomy, the bleeding of patients. A shoemaker who came to live in the Santa Cruz Valley in 1793, Francisco Xavier Romero, was credited with being a physician. Barbers were often proficient in bloodletting, a supposed remedy for nutritional deficiencies and the parasites that plagued colonial settlers. The practice of medicine was not profitable. According to Josiah Gregg, all a physician could expect as payment for his services was "¡Dios se lo pague!" (May God pay you!) Formal study of medicine was unavailable.

The poor continued to view death and disease with medieval fatalism, seeking relief from suffering with empirical remedies and witchcraft. They built up an extensive folklore of miraculous cures, and adopted many practices of their Indian neighbors. Even now, older *curanderas* (healers) practice a healing trade based on psychological and various medicinal aids. The *curandera* was midwife, nurse, pharmacist, and doctor. Her tools were the herbs and roots that God provided, prayers, chants, faith, self-reliance, witchcraft, and a store of ancient knowledge passed on to her by her culture. If payment in coin was scarce, the *curandera* would accept produce as payment. Corn, beans, chile, and onions were always welcome.

Processing produce for winter storage

It is little wonder that the services of a dedicated *curandera* were so valued given the few cures that were available for the control of disease and discomfort. A passage taken from *Healing Herbs of the Upper Río Grande* by Leonora S. M. Curtin, reads, "Often when I visit one of the *médicas* (curanderas) in her modest *adobe* house, her clothes perhaps frayed and worn, I am amazed at her ability and her memory, at her self-reliance, and at the good that she has accomplished among her people. She has brought comfort and relief to suffering, armed only with her simple remedies derived from nature. I look about me and there is no equipment. Her cures are in her mind, in her garden, far out in the mountains, or out on the plains. Her tools are her wonderful hands, so small, so magnetic and eloquent of healing. She is the Temple of Hope for those in need, as she is the source and essence of this book." Legitimate *curandera/os* shunned black magic and refused to treat cases of bewitchment, fearing that in case of success they might be suspected of possessing dark supernatural powers.

Poor families slept on the floor in poorly ventilated rooms on sheepskins and *jerga* that were seldom laundered. The habitual infestation of flies, fleas, bedbugs, mites and lice were a constant harassment and incubator of disease.

Respiratory infections were the most devastating illnesses after diarrhea. In summer months, when residents took their bedding outside to sleep, the sun and fresh air brought some relief. This practice had its own risks for the marshlands bred malaria-carrying mosquitoes. Only the few *gente fina* (high class people) had large residences that would accommodate bedsteads and mattresses. Lice that laid their eggs on the fibers of rich and poor alike, could be removed by laundering, often in an *acequia*, but a more efficient way was to spread the bedding on an anthill; ants would quickly devour the lot. Body and head lice were an ever-present scourge. Bathing, now considered a requisite for good health, was seldom practiced. Outdoor baths taken in warm weather were more for refreshment than sanitation. Rural New Mexicans generally relieved themselves outdoors. In cold weather, body wastes were captured in a *bacín* (chamber pot) and then disposed of on farmland or tossed into ditches or streets. Europeans of the same time period were no more fastidious in their personal habits.

Hispanic colonists made their own soap from buffalo and sheep tallow, rendered over open fires in large kettles, and mixed with caustic potash lye leached from wood fire or corncob ashes. The soft brown soap, *jabón de lejía*, was poured into wooden molds to cool and then cut into bars. The addition of soda produced a finer hard soap. Many soap makers were also candle makers, crafts that evolved into cottage industries. Even though the means to better hygiene was available, it varied from one household to the next. Poor families rarely changed clothes, perhaps because there were no changes to be had. Children wore their lone garments until they literally fell from their bodies. Women and girls carried bundles of clothing, rugs and bedding on their heads to the banks of *acequias* for the occasional laundry. There water was boiled in kettles, poured into log *canoas* along with lye soap or amole, the dirty laundry scrubbed in the suds, and then rinsed in the stream. Garments were tossed over tree limbs and brush or spread over the grasses to dry.

Healing herbs and roots, not readily located in the wild, were grown in herb gardens as demonstrated by the small plot at the Mora House in the Sierra Village at Las Golondrinas. The *curandera's* medicine and spice cabinet was a series of poles suspended from the ceiling from which she hung herbs upside down to dry. From one or more choices she made a decoction, a medicinal tea, or prepared the herbs in some other form. Some of the herbs also provided colorant to dye wool, and many served as spices for food.

Some favorite herbs are:

Ajo (garlic), an Old World crop, is an herb widely favored today. It was used to prevent diphtheria, and strung on a string worn around the neck to protect those exposed to other diseases. A crushed bulb, pressed against the gum, relieved toothache. A fresh poultice applied three times daily was one of the treatments for snakebite, hornet, and scorpion stings. Garlic, roasted and boiled in sugar water then strained, was consumed to cure stomach and intestinal disorders. As a vermifuge, it expelled intestinal parasites from both animals and humans. Earaches were soothed with a mix of garlic and salt placed on a swab of lamb's wool and placed in the ear. In addition to all of the above, garlic made a fine food seasoning.

Alegría (cockscomb) produced a mild astringent for use on irritated mucus membranes and as a douche to relieve vaginal itching. Combined with red wine, cockscomb helped treat mild heart disorders, and alleviated intestinal infections and diarrhea. Its crimson juice was smeared on the faces of women to provide a sunscreen.

Amole (yucca root) is truly a plant without parallel according to Leonora S. M. Curtin. The *yucca* grows in hostile soils and bears towering shafts with clusters of white-flowered splendor, and is known as "Our Lord's Candles." Pulverized roots swished in water yield an excellent lather valued by Hispanics and Pueblo Indians alike. When the Spanish were driven out in 1680, Popé, the San Juan Medicine man and leader of the rebellion, instructed the Indians to go to the rivers to cleanse themselves with *amole* to remove any taint of baptism. Indians made a practice to shampoo their hair with *amole* suds before ceremonies, for it gave their black tresses a glossy sheen. The colonists used the suds for their laundry and to wash the fleeces of the *churro* sheep, as well as a hair shampoo. The Penitentes not only used the yucca fibers for their scourges, but the plant yielded a stimulating red, wine-like liquid drunk by the Hermanos before their atonement. It made them "*muy bravo y valiente.*"

Chamiso blanco (rabbit bush) provided not only a rich yellow dye, but served as a laxative tea, and as a cold and stomach remedy. Roots and tops boiled into a tea controlled bloody diarrhea, and crushed leaves placed in tooth cavities eased the ache. Hot tea promoted sweating to break fevers, and added to bath water helped reduce swelling and the pain of arthritis. In other words, *chamiso blanco* was an all around aid to better health.

Yucca provides amole soap suds

Chicória (dandelion) was most likely imported inadvertently from the Old World in sacks of grain and on animal pelts. Dandelion foliage was not only used as a salad green and potherb, it was made into wine. Its tea was used as a spring tonic, blood thinner, a reliable laxative, and was employed for nonspecific heart distress, heartburn and digestive problems. The fleshy root in tonic was used to purify blood, for yellow jaundice, liver, and kidney complaints, and as a diuretic. A paste of ground leaves was applied to wounds, fractures and bruises. Root water made a coffee-like and caffeine free beverage used to relieve pestilential fevers, and to bathe sores. Uses were endless. Indians viewed the dandelion as "strong medicine."

Cota (aster family) was used as a beverage before coffee and tea were imported. It was boiled with sugar after the sweetener became available with the opening of the Santa Fe Trail, and drunk to reduce fever. A weak solution soothed a baby's chafed skin. It was valuable as a diuretic and served as a laxative and to "clean out" the stomach. Cota helped with blood circulation and the control of blood pressure. Red-brown and yellow dyes were obtained from the flowers.

Malva (mallow) came from the Old World, and was quickly adopted as a favorite in New Mexico. Its emollient, when used as a poultice, eased pain and reduced inflammation of tissues. Decocted tea was good for sore throats and tonsillitis, and soothed bladder and urethra irritability. Expectant mothers drank its tea to help facilitate labor in childbirth. Mixed with raisins, it was taken to help expel afterbirth. Its tea relieved infant thrush and diaper rash.

Mariola (aster family), its fall blossoms soaked in water, provided a wash that eased the pain of rheumatism, and tea from dried stems was a blood tonic. Tea from the dwarf yellow species proved useful for the control of gonorrhea.

Oshá (parsley family) was the local wonder drug. It controlled stomach gas and flatulence, and when the powdered root was taken with hot water and sugar, it reduced fever, especially if supplemented with whiskey. An ointment was effective in the treatment of sores, cuts, and bruises. The Penitentes used the salve after their Holy Week rites. A paste was used to draw poison from snakebites, and shepherds spread powdered roots around a bedroll in an attempt to protect against snakes. The root was carried as a talisman to ward off the spell of witches. *Oshá* provided a cough syrup, and its tea was useful to control nausea and vomiting. Its applications were endless. An ancient recipe for piñonero salve lists piñon tree resin, bees wax, *oshá*, and olive oil.

Plumajillo (yarrow) was regarded as a potent love charm, especially if collected by a maiden pining for passion. New Mexicans mixed ground dry leaves with boiling water for a drink to reduce fever, act as a purge, or break up a cough. A poultice of the plant was applied to broken bones and sprains. Fresh leaves applied to an abrasion promoted the clotting of blood and soothed hemorrhoids. Cool tea helped relieve chills and ague, and hot tea induced sweating to break fevers.

Poleo (penny royal), when brewed into a tea, treated dizziness, biliousness, and spots before the eyes as well as nausea, poor digestion, and general stomach ailments. When mixed with *oshá* and *manzanilla* (chamomile), it was used for stomach disorders and fever. Tea brewed from the dry herb controlled abnormal menstrual bleeding and acted as a laxative. It served as a remedy for mouth blisters and is still used today in soap and perfume.

Pragué (field marigold), when brewed into a tea, helped clear the baby's colic. Used as a tea or chewed raw, it relieved stomach disorders.

Punche has a nicotine content of nine percent, and is highly addictive. The dried plant, crushed into a powder and spread about gardens, acted as an insecticide.

Punchón (wooly mullein) was a natural tobacco substitute, and its smoke helped relieve asthma. A tea made from its leaves provided a mild sedative for the lungs.

Romero (mint family) was used to treat arthritis, baldness, headaches, stomach upset, pains, strains, cuts, scrapes, and bruises.

Yerba de tusa (coneflower), the "herb of the prairie dog," provided relief for a patient suffering from large red pustules. If the body was bathed in a boiled coneflower bath and wrapped in a sheet, angry spots disappeared overnight. The bath relieved rheumatic conditions, and finely powdered root applied to an aching tooth reduced throbbing.

As noted above, El Rancho de las Golondrinas has an herb garden in the Sierra Village in front of the Mora House. A wide assortment of herbs, only a few discussed above, are planted in a modest garden setting using a limited water supply of water. In earlier times, the plants would have been gathered in the wild.

10

Doing Business on the Santa Fe Trail

El Camino Real de Tierra Adentro—The Santa Fe Trail—Trappers and Ciboleros

El Camino Real de Tierra Adentro

The venerable Camino Real, the only means of commerce, immigration, and communication between colonial New Mexico and the larger Hispanic world, has seen its heyday come and go. From the first it was known as El Camino Real, the Royal Road, a name applied to all primary roads in Spain and its possessions in the New World. In New Mexico, it was commonly referred to as El Camino Real de Tierra Adentro, the road to the interior. For more than two and a half centuries, this road or corridor was the only link between Santa Fé and the distant viceregal capital of Mexico City. Conquistadors, colonists, Franciscan friars, governors, military, Indian retainers, and caravans with wagons, mule and donkey trains, livestock, mission supplies, and trade goods had endured the hazards of the long, arduous journey of over 456 *leguas,* the equivalent of twelve hundred miles. Add the distance from Veracruz on the Carribean coast, the port from which European goods were brought to Mexico City, and the length of the Royal Road increased to 608 *leguas*, or sixteen hundred miles. Over time, new ideas and concepts hitchhiked along the trail.

A system of old Indian trails predated the Spanish Camino Real. Over these ancient pathways, the Pueblos traded with other tribes in the Mesoamerican world. Casas Grandes in western Chihuahua was a prosperous trade center in the 13th and 14th centuries, and became the primary hub for trade goods moving throughout the Southwest. This vast network of trade routes brought an abundance of goods: marine shell, coral, copper bells, parrot and macaw feathers, and exchange of cultural traits. The Pueblo Indians exported turquoise, pottery, salt, flint, cotton, pottery, and processed bison products traded by Plains Indians.

Mission trains, initially intended to supply the Franciscans and their missionizing efforts, were to make the journey every three years, but in fact it sometimes took as long as five to seven years before supplies arrived. Early caravans, largely made up of pack animals rather than carts or wagons and managed by crown authorities, were the sole source of goods and communication with the outside world. After 1631 and the transfer of control to Fray Alonozo de Benavides, *custos* for New Mexican missions, the caravan schedule became more regular. The Franciscans had taken over the sponsorship of the mission supply caravans previously managed by agents of the crown. Annual caravans of some thirty-two wagons, each pulled by teams of eight mules, were accompanied by a contingent of twelve to fourteen soldiers. Up to one thousand head of cattle moved along with the wagons. *La Conducta*, "miniature traveling societies," with its government officials, settlers, friars, cattle, wagons, and two hundred mules with their burden of four hundred pounds each, and Indian *cautivos* destined to work in mines in northern Mexico, would travel twelve to fifteen miles per day.

The conquistadors used these trails in their colonizing efforts, and the Pueblo Indian routes along the Río Grande became part of El Camino Real de Tierra Adentro. Don Juan de Oñate earned the title of "father of El Camino Real" when he brought the first successful European colonists north from Zacatecas. By 1530, the Spanish were already using these native trails for slave raiding, mainly in the region of what is now Arizona. The terrified Spanish fled during the Pueblo Revolt in 1680 to El Paso del Norte over the New Mexican stretch of the *camino* (road). Over that same *camino*, Don Diego de Vargas and his colonists journeyed to Santa Fé in 1692–1693 to restore Spain's primacy over New Mexico. El Camino Real de Tierra Adentro "was probably the most significant of all of the early trails on the North American continent. It was the first road in North America, and for nearly a century the longest," writes Douglas Preston, author of *The Royal Road: El Camino Real from Mexico City to Santa Fe.*

The region over which the road passed posed some formidable natural barriers. The great sand dunes of Los Médanos de Samalayuca south of El Paso del Norte forced heavily loaded carts to detour for two days to San Elizario, often traveling at night because of the heat. The *Jornada del Muerto* (Journey of the Dead Man), east of the present-day town of Truth or Consequences, New Mexico was a challenging ninety-mile stretch that provided little fuel, shelter, or water. Travelers were forced up and away from the Río Grande because of insurmountable natural barriers, and *La Bajada* (The Descent), the volcanic escarpment just south and west of El Rancho de las Golondrinas. For those choosing to climb or descend the 900 ft. black basalt cliff, teams had to be doubled. Of La Bajada, journalist J. H. Beadle wrote in 1871, "Down the face of this frightful hill, the road winds in a series of zigzags, bounded in the worst places by rocky walls." The eastern most branch of the camino passed through the Galisteo Basin and accommodated most of the wagon traffic.

The western most branch of El Camino Real de Tierra Adentro, that primarily accommodated pack trains, approached through the Río Grande river basin, following the Santa Fé River upstream, proceeded through the village of Agua Fria, forded the Santa Fé River west of El Santuario de Guadalupe, and entered the Santa Fé plaza via La Calle Real, now San Francisco Street. Another route found the venerable road coming up La Ciénega Valley past the *parajes* of Las Golondrinas, El Alamo, and Cieneguilla, and on to Agua Fria. Trade to the Taos Pueblo and the colonial village of Taos was conducted primarily by pack train, thus making Taos the final terminus of El Camino Real de Tierra Adentro.

Since many people made for more safety, large numbers of families and their retainers came together. One priest called these large groups "miniature traveling societies." The travelers relieved the boredom and stress that inevitably accompanied these long journeys by holding *fandangos* in the evening. Some entertainment was provided by troubadours who celebrated the events of the day, noting births and deaths, budding romances, recitation of threats of attack by nomadic Indians and the like. Itinerant puppeteers provided lively entertainment performing plays with religious and political themes. The latter sometimes contained bawdy subject matter. Of necessity, wagon trains were self-contained and self-sufficient enterprises. As a rule, *parajes* like Las Golondrinas did not offer board or lodgings, but provided protection, water, firewood, and pasturage for livestock. Regrettably, we have no diaries or journals that recorded the experiences of the groups that traveled on El Camino Real de Tierra Adentro in its early days.

After 1700, private contractors took over. On return trips, traders transported *efectos del país* (local products) to the markets in Chihuahua. Because of the ever-present threat of Apache attacks, governors issued proclamations announcing the dates when the caravans should leave. This sound policy required all parties to travel in convoys. Rendezvous sites were designated so that travelers would know where to join the train. The columns left in late October or early November after the harvest season, for a successful operation required the services of persons of many skills who were free to travel. Livestock was driven ahead of the convoy so it could be more easily watched. Wagons were circled at night to provide a natural fort and a corral for the horses, oxen and other domestic animals.

The French participated from the late 1720s in an illegal textile and small manufactures trade with New Mexicans. They knew there was an eager market, and on occasion, Mexican authorities turned a blind eye. Trade fairs circumvented the ban with the French because Comanche traders served as middlemen. They had access to Louisiana merchandise and French guns, and colonists were fearful that these weapons would fall into unfriendly hands. Most often the middlemen at the trade fairs were *comancheros,* usually New Mexicans of mixed blood who traded with Plains tribes. Pecos Pueblo served as the gateway between the Rio Grande colony and the vast indigenous and French trade network to the east. Pecos hosted trade fairs throughout the 18th century.

Crown policy gave Chihuahuan merchants a monopoly on commerce that resulted in a negative balance of trade for New Mexico. In 1810, Pedro Baptista Pino reported to the Spanish Cortes that annual exports from New Mexico had a value of 60,000 pesos, but imports were valued at 112,000 pesos. In general, inter-colonial trade was forbidden so that Spanish imports would have no competition, but contraband trade flourished. By controlling the trade, twelve to fifteen Chihuahua merchant families, whose policy of buying cheap and selling dear, impoverished the province. The imbalance was compounded by heavy taxes on goods and numerous permit requirements. This state of affairs kept New Mexicans in perpetual debt.

Almost all business was transacted by barter with prices based on hypothetical sums of money. Some specie was used, primarily the *peso de plata,* silver coins minted in Chihuahua and other New World mints. In exchange for New Mexican hides, salt for mining, piñon nuts, buckskin and buffalo tongues preserved in barrels of salt brine, and Pueblo and colonial textiles including footless woolen stockings, Chihuahua merchants provided arms and munitions, medicines, textiles, Chinese shawls, hardware, spices, and religious articles. The annual Manila Galleon supplied jewels, silk, porcelain, furniture, and tin from the Orient. The trading ship was unloaded at Acapulco on the Pacific coast, and the goods, sealed with royal insignia, were transported to Vera Cruz on the Gulf coast and shipped to Spain. Some items were returned to Mexico for sale to the wealthier colonists.

The Santa Fe Trail

In 1806, young Lieutenant Zebulon Montgomery Pike, sent by the United States to search for the headwaters of the Arkansas and Red Rivers, breached the security of Spain's imperial borders. Thinking he was still on American soil, or so he claimed, Pike constructed a stockade on a tributary of the Río Grande River. A company of Spanish cavalry soon called his error to his attention. Although treated with courtesy, he and his men were sent to Santa Fé and then to Chihuahua where they were subjected to intensive questioning. They were subsequently expelled to American territory in Louisiana, but all records of the expedition, including maps, had been confiscated. Pike, not to be denied and without his seized records, published a popular account of the affair in 1810. He reported that there was a vast market in New Mexico just waiting to be tapped and included information on the high prices charged by Chihuahua merchants.

Mexico achieved her independence from Spain in 1821, but civil and political strife kept the Mexican government too busy tending to its own chaotic affairs to be concerned with developments on the far-off Río Grande. The centuries-long prohibition of foreigners was suddenly, without warning, no longer there. American traders, eager to establish trade, were at a disadvantage because the Mexican government periodically imposed taxes and numerous restrictions, collected heavy export duties, and prohibited the import of items that would compete with the products of Mexican industry. Josiah Gregg estimated that Mexican officials embezzled half of the revenue they received in customs fees. Only *churro* wool, regarded as inferior for use by American manufacturers, was exempt from fees and taxes. To evade them, merchants developed a lively contraband trade of textiles, carpentry, hunting and farming tools and housekeeping gear. Income from these taxes and various and sundry charges financed the provincial government in Santa Fé.

William Becknell, the "father of the Santa Fe trail," perceived a money-making opportunity. Following the proclamation of Mexican Independence in 1821 and the loosening of the border, he and four other traders brought a number of pack mules carrying cotton goods that sold at $3.00 a yard. The following year, Becknell's trip, using mule drawn wagons loaded with trade goods, netted a tidy $10,000, a 2,000 percent profit. Trade ballooned, Santa Fé traders were freed from the domination of the Chihuahuan merchants, and New Mexico's trade imbalance disappeared. From the outset, the Santa Fe Trail was used for commerce, not for the movement of immigrants and supplies to support the missions and the New Mexican colony as had El Camino Real de Tierra Adentro.

Becknell began his first trip from Arrow Rock, Missouri although St. Louis was his primary source of goods and supplies. Independence, Missouri later developed a bustling industry outfitting Santa Fe Trail traffic. The Santa Fe Trail spanned nine hundred miles of Great Plains from Missouri to northern New Mexico, and included five hundred miles over the vast prairie "seas of grass" with its ample forage for animals. Some 150 traders, driving about eighty wagons, passed over the Santa Fe Trail annually until the railroads arrived in the 1880s. The trail divided near Great Bend, Kansas into northern and southern branches, the northern branch passing through the future site of Dodge City and Cimarron, Kansas. There it branched again, and the mountain route paralleled the north side of the Arkansas River. At Bent's Fort the mountain trail crossed the river, continued on through Trinidad, Colorado, Las Vegas, New Mexico, and passing by the historic San Miguel Chapel, terminated at the plaza in Santa Fe. The Cimarron Cutoff, also known as La Jornada, was the original, shortest, and southern most route, but offered little water or fodder for an arid sixty miles, and some trail ruts can still be seen today, recalling the much feared Jornada del Muerto of El Camino Real de Tierra Adentro.

American goods flowed into Santa Fé over the Santa Fe Trail and on into Mexico via the Chihuahua Trail, the new name of El Camino Real de Tierra Adentro, for it was no longer a "royal road." Ramifications of this new and vigorous international commerce were felt as far away as Shanghai, China, the Philippines, and London, England. Combining the trails resulted in true international trade traffic.

The story of one of the much loved American Girl dolls, Josefina Montoya®, begins as Josefina waits for her abuelito (grandfather) to return home from a trading trip to Mexico over the Chihuahua Trail. Little did Manuel de Baca suspect that his *adobe* house would one day become the model for Josefina's fictional home. Here pre-teen guests to Las Golondrinas visit the very kitchen illustrated in Vol. 1 of the set of six books, *1824 Josefina, an American Girl.*

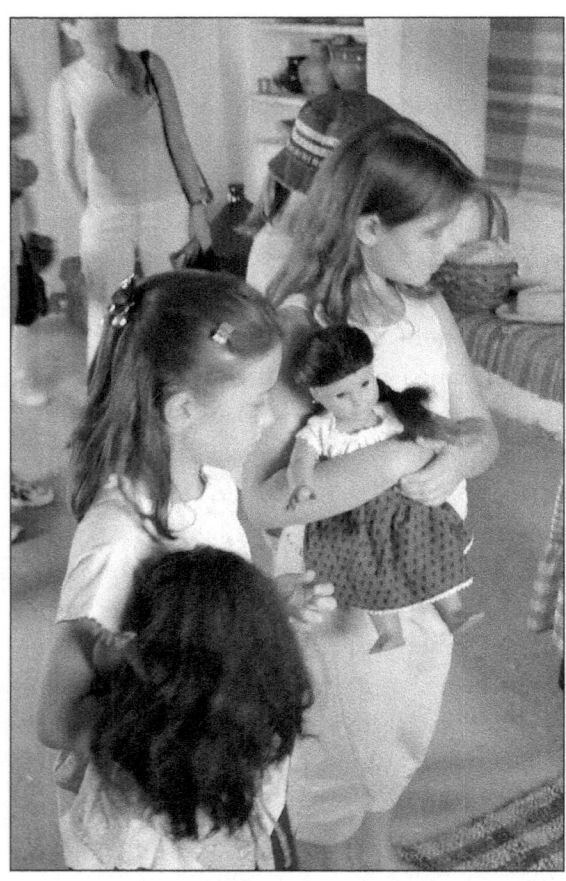

Visiting the home of the fictional Josefina Montoya

New Mexico's busy capital became a cultural crossroads. New Mexicans in *sombreros* and *rebozos*, Indians wrapped in native blankets or fur robes, and Americans in buckskin or frock coats, formed a new social mix. Santa Fé had a population of only 4,200 people, but New Mexico as a whole represented a potential market of forty-three thousand customers. The city of Chihuahua had ten thousand people and a thriving mining industry, but the Mexican economy was in shambles, largely because it had no industry. New Mexico traders traveled to Independence, Missouri to sell serapes, *jerga* and the like, and returned with U.S. manufactures and European imports that were freighted as far south as Chihuahua. Most trade was still conducted by barter.

During the glory days of the Chihuahua Trail, New Mexicans dominated the trade. Mexicans quickly adopted the light American Conestoga wagons, far superior to their own unwieldy *coches de paseo* (wooden carriages), Josiah

Gregg's "wheeled tarantulas." The American wagons had greater capacity and were easier to defend against marauders. After completing their Santa Fe Trail trip, Anglos sold most of their rolling stock to New Mexicans and Mexicans along with their trade goods. The conveyances were a boon to northern Mexico.

The Santa Fe Trail trade brought about a marked improvement in the New Mexican standard of living, and did a brisk business until the coming of railroads in the early 1880s. Imagine what a wonder it was to obtain quality manufactures in a matter of weeks instead of months, and at less than half of the previous cost. The market was flooded with textiles of every kind, percale, velvet, denim, pongee, flannel, linen and muslin, to name but a few, and iron and steel tools for farming, construction supplies, hardware, time pieces, gun works, toiletries, medicines, and kitchen wares. Most New Mexicans gradually adopted European fashions, although some dashing *caballeros* remained faithful to their picturesque traditional dress. The demand for bottled spirits kept profits high; empty bottles were returned to Missouri for reuse. Common drugs like Epsom salts, bicarbonate of soda, Seidlitz powder, balsam, sulfur, and assorted pills for ailments appeared in the stores and trade stalls along with cologne. Trade passed by Las Golondrinas *paraje* with the coming of the Santa Fe Trail and its plethora of goods.

Gloria Mendoza recalls her La Ciénega Valley family speaking of a store in a private mid-19th Century home where all trade was conducted by barter. Its location was near La Loma, the future summer home of the Curtin women, on the hill above the developed part of Las Golondrinas museum. It has long since disappeared along with the now-silent village.

Constructed of logs, La Tiendita, the period general store exhibit at Las Golondrinas, was collected in Trampas, New Mexico, and moved to the museum. It is stocked with typical wares of the Mexican and early Territorial periods. Here the visitor finds Tarahumara burden baskets from the Sierra Madre Mountains in Mexico, and calico cottons from the textile mills of New England.

Mexican silver was the single most important trade item transported to the East. Western states and territories suffered from a perennial shortage of ready cash, and often resorted to easily counterfeited paper money and unstable bank notes. The influx of silver from Santa Fé and the Chihuahua trade helped stabilized the monetary system.

The Missouri mule became an economic necessity. Josiah Gregg compared the relationship of the mule to a New Mexican with that of the camel to an Arab. Most merchants made handsome profits, and hired young men in their late teens to do the heavy work, paying them a miserly six to eight dollars for a month's work. Daily, the *mulatero* (muleteer) had to feed, water, hitch, and unhitch draft animals, pack the animals that carried a three to four hundred pound load each, and look after the animals on the hoof, a skill much admired by the Americans. The workday was eighteen hours long, and the only meal served was dried goat meat, or mutton, tortillas, and beans. A tortilla with a slice of onion served as a snack twice a day. The lone set of clothing issued to the drover rarely left his body, and a pair of *tewas* (moccasins) shod his feet. Outbreaks of cholera and other diseases were frequent afflictions on the trail.

New Mexicans, justly celebrated for their horsemanship, did not attempt to improve their mounts by selective breeding. Fear of losing horses to predatory nomads may account for some of the disinterest in careful breeding. Mustang stock, easily available, descended from the Spanish barb, was small, quick, spirited, stouthearted and long-lived. The best were chosen for *caballos de silla* (saddle horses), and were well trained. More care went into the breeding and care of mules. Josiah Gregg admired the dexterity and skill of the *mulateros* as they harnessed and loaded the beasts with their packs. Hoisting incredibly heavy loads onto the backs of the mules, it took two men only five minutes to make-ready each animal for the trail. The *carga* (cargo) was secured by an *aparejo* (packsaddle), a leather pouch stuffed with hay, and secured with a wide binding of rawhide or grass, laced securely so the burden would not shift and chafe its bearer. Mules can travel with unwieldy loads of up to four hundred pounds each.

The cultural influence of the new commerce is more difficult to estimate than its economic consequences. One way an Anglo trader could beat the protectionist system was to join a New Mexican firm; another was to convert to Catholicism and marry into a New Mexican trading family. In either case, Americans were required to swear allegiance to Mexico. George and Charles Bent, Céran St. Vrain, and other American traders learned Spanish and took New Mexican wives or mistresses. Some New Mexican traders and merchants, wishing their children to become bilingual, sent them to study English in eastern schools. In the process of acquiring a new language, their children came to understand the alien culture.

Under Mexican rule, life in the province was not all peace and tranquility. Following the seizure of power in Mexico by General Antonio López de Santa Anna in 1834, the liberal constitution of 1824 was replaced in 1836 by one that reduced semi-autonomous states to departments dominated by the central government. Santa Anna sent an army officer, Colonel Albino Pérez, to assume the role of New Mexico's governor. An "outsider" and aloof in manner, Pérez alienated many members of the upper class on whose support governors usually relied for the smooth running of their administrations. He also estranged the Hispanic villagers by reducing their rights of self-government, promoting Santa Anna's centralizing policies, and by imposing onerous new taxes to finance expensive education reforms. New Mexicans were convinced that monies collected from their subsistence economy would go directly to the bankrupt coffers of Mexico City. Since New Mexicans had provided for their own defense and managed their own affairs, they saw no reason to pay more taxes for services they themselves supplied. Although he had a wife in Mexico City, the new governor added to his disrepute by having with him his mistress and housekeeper by whom he had a child.

Popular discontent with Pérez, a lover of an extravagant lifestyle in the face of the hardships and starvation of his militiamen, soon flared up into a revolt commonly known as the Chimayó Rebellion of 1837, also remembered as the Río Arriba Revolt. Under the command of Juan José Esquivel, *alcalde* of Santa Cruz, a rebel force from between one hundred and fifty to two hundred men, small farmers from the Río Arriba district and some pueblo Indian allies, began a march on Santa Fé. From the rebel encampment at Santa Cruz de Cañada on August 3, 1837 they issued a public declaration. In this manifesto, prefaced with the cry, "For God and the Nation, and the Faith of Jesus Christ," they pledged to shed the last drop of their blood if necessary to defend their liberties, and to reject the new departmental system and its taxes. They insisted they only sought redress for their grievances, and pledged loyalty to the Mexican Republic.

Governor Pérez tried to raise an army with little success, and some who joined defected to the rebels. On the 8th of August, his force suffered a crushing defeat at the hands of the insurgents. Pérez and his cabinet attempted to flee the capital, but were captured by the rebels; Pérez was assassinated on Agua Fria Street in Santa Fé. Josiah Gregg reports that the governor was decapitated, and his head . . . "carried as trophy to the camp of the insurgents, who made a football of it among themselves." A small memorial plaque, once at the site of the decapitation, is now on display on the grounds of the Palace of the Governors.

The approach of the rebel army created panic among the capital's American and Mexican elite. "Native residents and American merchants alike," wrote historian Marc Simmons, "quaked behind their barred shutters, expecting that a mob of soldiers would be turned loose to plunder the town." But there was no reign of terror and no pillaging. The insurgents chose as provisional governor the *genízaro* José Gonzáles from Ranchos de Taos, and subsequently disbanded to return home in time for the fall harvest.

Their disbandment proved to be a serious mistake, reflecting the naiveté of these peasant revolutionaries. The revolt, in reality a class struggle with its implications of radical social and political change, alarmed both sections of the province's upper class, the Anglo merchants, and the *ricos* of southern New Mexico. Some American merchants had advanced money and goods to Pérez and other slain officials, and were bound to suffer financial loss by their fall; others feared the harmful impact of the revolt on trade. Before long, the formation of a counter-revolutionary force, with Governor Manuel Armijo as its commander, was under way. Missouri merchants contributed more than four hundred pesos to Armijo's war fund. Other financial aid came from the wealthy ranchers around Albuquerque. Armijo's band of six hundred men, reinforced by the timely arrival of Mexican regulars, met and defeated an insurgent force at the Pass of Pojoaque on January 27, 1838. The rebel governor, Gonzáles, already in jail, was barely given time for confession before he faced a firing squad. Other rebel leaders met with the same fate. Counter-revolution had triumphed, but this was not the last time that Río Arriba villagers rose in revolt against what they regarded as oppressive authority.

Meanwhile in the United States, an expansionist movement proclaimed ever more vociferously that it was the "manifest destiny" of the country to reach from ocean to ocean, the phrase coined by journalist John L. Sullivan for the *New York Morning News*, ". . . our manifest destiny to overspread the continent allotted by Providence for the free development of our yearly multiplying millions." The expansionists proposed to acquire California, the key to the markets of the Southwest, Oregon, China and perhaps Mexico. American immigrant wagon trains began entering the New Mexican territory as early as the 1830s, often following inter-fort trail routes. The use of wagon trains slowed after 1880 when the railroads began providing immigrant cars on freight trains to transport entire households, including livestock, to the Western Frontier.

There was a rising American interest in sources of information about the territory west of the settled frontier in letters, journals, and diaries like those of Josiah Gregg and Susan Magoffin. In time, this interest, tinged with romanticism and acquisitiveness, would spawn a new genre of American literature, the "western." Soon, "penny dreadful" and "dime novels" were regaling Americans with lurid stories of hapless señoritas, half-breed villains, fair-haired heroes, Indian raids, scalpings, stampedes, buffalo hunts, prairie fires, and all manner of hair-raising episodes.

Deeply rooted in this new expansionism and the literature that dealt with the West was an Anglo-American prejudice against Spanish culture, and especially its Catholicism, a bigotry that had long existed. Typical was a comment by American Stephen Austin who had sworn . . . "to fulfill rigidly all the duties and obligations of a Mexican citizen," but then became leader of the 1836 Texas revolt against Mexico. He proclaimed the Mexicans to be degenerate and unworthy to rule over Anglo Americans. "To be candid, the majority of the people of the whole nation as far as I have seen them want nothing but tails to be more brutes than apes." Josiah Gregg was exasperated by what he considered New Mexican indifference to the capitalist virtue of hard work. He condemned what he saw as a pernicious system of the *siesta* (afternoon rest) because everything closed down and no one could do any business. The *siesta* was a practice brought from Spain where the harsh heat of the early afternoon forced all to retreat and rest. These antagonisms and misconceptions contributed to the disasters between 1846 and 1848 that cost Mexico half of its territory. They helped create a mindset that favored the Texas revolt, and supported the Mexican-American war forced by the United States on a Mexico that was militarily weak and generally unprepared for hostilities.

In the troubled interval between the Texan revolt of 1836, and its annexation by the United States in 1845, the short-lived republic of Texas sought to resolve an acute financial crisis by demanding the right to participate in the lucrative Santa Fe commerce. The Congress of the Texas Republic claimed all the land up to the Río Grande River as its territory. In 1841, Texas sent a military expedition to New Mexico to enforce its claim, but the party was captured by General Manuel Armijo and packed off to jail in Mexico. After a failed military venture, the Texans resorted to less savory methods to achieve their ends, allowing individuals commonly described as "land pirates" to operate in the disputed territory. They sometimes murdered Mexican traders and confiscated merchandise and property from pack trains passing through what they regarded as Texan land. The annexation of Texas by the United States in 1845 put an end to these troubles, and the Compromise of 1850 resolved the issue of the boundary when one-third of the land claimed by Texas was ceded to the United States in exchange for $10 million dollars.

In May, 1846 the United States declared war on Mexico. By a certain irony, the Santa Fe Trail facilitated the invasion of New Mexico by providing American troops easy access to the territory. In a swift campaign that met little resistance, Colonel Stephen Kearny and his Army of the West conquered New Mexico, and the ancient land became a territory of the United States. The fulfillment of America's "Manifest Destiny" had begun.

Trappers and Ciboleros

Fickle fashion played a role in the commerce of New Mexico. On the East Coast and in Europe, elegant gentlemen demanded the latest in headgear, the tall beaver "stovepipe" hat. To satisfy their demand, the mountain man, clad in buckskin and shod with moccasins of deer or buffalo leather, set out in the fall to trap beaver for its thick winter pelt. New Mexicans did not trap professionally according to Josiah Gregg, *Commerce of the Prairies*. Licenses were issued to foreigners, provided the trapper took along a Mexican to teach to trap. Most likely the mountain man contracted to work for one of the following companies: Hudson Bay, American Fur, Rocky Mountain Fur, or Mission Fur Company. The trapper departed from Taos after he outfitted himself, traveled alone or with a companion, and carted his equipment on two horses while he rode a third. He packed along several dozen flints, twenty-five pounds of powder, a good supply of lead and, of course, some Taos Lightning. The much romanticized mountain man was as tough a customer as one could find, and a teller of many a tall tale.

Fiercely competitive, he was wary of other trappers, dangerous animals, and unfriendly Indians. Often a trapper carried two flintlock pistols tucked into a leather belt, along with a skinning knife and a hatchet. He also carried a rifle with a thirty-six inch barrel, a bullet pouch, a powder horn, and the fringe on his buckskin shirt supplied thongs for diverse uses.

A trapper might take as many as four hundred pounds of beaver pelt in a good season. A plew (prime pelt) would bring as much as six dollars, a very attractive sum. He skinned the beaver on the spot, and stretched the skin on a willow twig frame. He roasted the carcass for his meal with the broad, flat tail, as a pièce de résistance. Not all hides were prepared for trade because many, specifically buffalo, were needed for use at home. In addition to beaver skins, the trapper's payload included hides of deer and elk, buffalo, antelope, bear, and lynx that the trapper brought to his broker in Taos, or floated on a raft down the Río Grande River to El Paso del Norte. The latter course was a favorite means of bypassing tax officials. By 1840, the stovepipe hat of beaver felt fell out of fashion, and dandies required hats of silk from China. With the market for beaver gone, and the numbers of beaver now diminished, mountain men bid farewell to the beaver trade.

New Mexican buffalo hunters were lucky to reach old age because it was a hard and dangerous business. Taught their skills by their fathers or uncles and Comanche friends, hunters charged into the stampeding herd, and swiftly downed their prey. Known as *ciboleros* (Hispanic buffalo hunters) to the rest of the Spanish-speaking world, they provided their communities with much needed protein, and were regarded as local heroes. During colonial times, there were endless herds of bison on the plains, and every mountain village had its own *cibolero* or *lancero* (lancer). After harvest along about October, the *ciboleros*, equipped with bow, arrows and lances, would mount their horses and join the *corrida* (hunt).

Guns were rarely used because they were often old and not in repair, and ammunition was scarce and expensive. It took less time to arm a bow with an arrow than to load and fire a rifle. They used lances with razor-sharp points to drive into the animals' hearts, quickly dismounted to retrieve their weapons, and then mounted their horses to continue on, each rider bringing down many buffalo in a single chase. The riders would also dispatch arrows with great accuracy.

Flint knapping is but one activity

The *cibolero* trained his special mount, a horse that he allowed no one else its use. The rider guided his horse with his knees and legs, leaving arms and hands free to bring down the game. The *cibolero* had to kill the buffalo quickly, because running the animal made it over-heat, especially in the still warm days of October, and the meat spoiled rapidly. Often with the help of wives and other family members, the hunters skinned and butchered the buffalos, sliced the meet into thin strips, and dried it for *cecinas* (jerky). The smoke from the fire of the buffalo chips helped preserve and flavor the meat. Smoked bison tongue was considered a special delicacy and brought a premium price when sent to Mexico. Nothing was wasted; the hide provided rawhide for rope, storage boxes, utensils and clothing, and the wool was woven into fabric or stuffed into mattresses. The hollow horns were used as utensils and to dispense gunpowder, hence the term "powder horn."

The hunting party of *ciboleros* rode into Comanche and Kiowa territory, or as far north and east as necessary to find the herds. They took with them trade goods of hard oven bread, dried *calabazas* (squash), chile, piñon nuts, beads, steel arrow heads, red cloth, and vermillion, the bright red mercuric sulfide pigment that the tribes preferred for ceremonial body paint. A *mayordomo* (overseer) estimated how many bison the hunters needed to take home to supply their villages, and then negotiated with the tribes for permission to hunt in their territory. Nomadic tribes were even more dependent on the buffalo herds for their existence than the Hispanics, and were therefore fiercely territorial. The Comanche warned the *ciboleros* not to trespass beyond the treaty lands or interfere with the nations to the north. The son of Captain Damasio Salazar was foolish enough to cross into Cheyenne territory to hunt without permission; he lost his life in the war that his folly provoked.

Reflecting the days of the *cibolero*, the *adobe* hide-tanning exhibit near the molasses mill at Las Golondrinas, built by volunteers, is a recent acquisition. Here visitors can try their hands at scraping skins, and help with the preparation of deer, elk, buffalo and cow hides for leather and robes. Museum docents who portray mountain men sometimes prepare the hides for use in creating their period costumes.

Preparing animal hides for tanning

11

Folkways of New Mexico

Oral Traditions—Dichos and Proverbs—Witchcraft—Fiestas, Folk Dramas, and Morality Plays

Oral Traditions

A living culture expresses its own unique character, its vision of itself and its worldview, through its traditions, stories, music, dance, art, and religious and secular celebrations. Here we examine New Mexican folklore, *cuentos* (stories), *dichos* (proverbs), witchcraft, *fiestas*, folk dramas, and morality plays.

Harvest Festival musicians

For reasons rooted in New Mexico's history, a vast body of its Hispanic and Indian folklore remains in oral form. A New Mexican literature, accurately speaking, did not exist before the twentieth century. Governors and friars owned the sparse collections of books. The few volumes owned by settlers were primarily devotional and medical in character. Most Hispanics had to rely on their rich, expressive language and oral modes of expression to preserve their cultural heritage.

Linguist Dr. Garland Bills observed, ". . . the Spanish of New Mexico is a treasure secluded in this remote, unchanging part of the world, both the language and the worldview of its inhabitants . . . frozen in time." Only after penetration of New Mexico by American influence in the Territorial Period and statehood did language and culture change perceptibly. Scholars have traveled to the remote villages of northern New Mexico and southern Colorado in order to study the Castilian spoken in Spain's Golden Age of literature, the times of Miguel de Cervantes, Lope de Vega, and Tirso de Molina.

Oral and written literary practice in New Mexico has ancient roots, and is why folklore echoes medieval romances, epic poems like the *Cantar del mio Cid,* Grimm's collection of fairy tales, and accounts of medieval witchcraft trials. There is also an element of Pueblo oral tradition, not surprising considering the numbers of Indians in Hispanic colonial households and the proximity of the Pueblos. Folk audiences do not expect historical accuracy; a folk story only needs to conform to folk values, hold the listener's interest and be somewhat believable. New Mexican folktales are rich in fantasy.

The pioneering linguist J. Manuel Espinosa collected hundreds of folktales, riddles, ballads, and dichos early in the twentieth century. Other compilers of such precious material include Marta Weigle, Loren Brown, José Griego y Maestas, Rudolfo A. Anaya, and Nasario García. A sampling of these tales in summary form shows recurring themes—clever wives save dull husbands from disaster; animals are assigned human voices and qualities; greed, jealousy, and other human frailties receive their just reward. Frequently there are poignant references to the unfair gulf between rich and poor.

"Cuentame un cuento (tell me a story)" beseeched children by New Mexican hearths after the day's work was done and the supper meal put away. The tale of "La Llorona"(The Crying Woman) was perhaps the story most often told. It may have originated in Spain, taken to Aztec Mexico, and subsequently transformed as New World generations passed. As with all oral transmissions, there are many variants to the story; historian Marc Simmons found no less than forty-two versions. The goddess Tonantzin and Malinche, the Indian mistress of the conquistador Cortés, appear in some. One more modern version relates that in La Villa Real de la Santa Fé there lived a pretty girl named María. She came from a hard-working family and her parents provided her with many lovely things, but she was never content. When she grew up she told her *abuelita* (grandmother) she would marry the strongest, most nimble and handsome man in New Mexico. The *abuelita* cautioned that she should look for a man with a good heart, not just a pretty face. But María would not listen—old people just don't understand!

One day a handsome *vaquero* (cowboy) came to town. He could handle any horse, play the guitar and sing beautifully. The foolish girl would not listen to her parents' warning that Gregorio wouldn't make a good husband because he lived a wild life. Against all admonition, María was determined to have her own way. She pretended to pay no attention when Gregorio came to serenade at her window, then feigned giving in and soon married him. The couple had two children before her irresponsible husband went back to his old ways. He courted other women and paid attention to the babies, but not to the envious María. Consumed by jealousy, she threw her children in the river where they were pulled under by the current. Driven by guilt, she ran along the river trying to reach the drowning children, but stumbled and struck her forehead on a rock. She was found dead and her babies gone. The priest would not allow her to be interred in the *camposanto,* and gave instructions that she be buried where she died. Some claim that they know where she was buried—she lies by the Santa Fé River. From her first night in the grave, she was up, clothed like a corpse dressed for burial, and crying like the wind, "¿Donde están mis hijos? (where are my children?) ¡Aaaaaiiii . . .!" To this day children are told that they must be home before dark or the crazy La Llorona, looking for her lost children, will carry them away, never to be seen again. Some form of this tale is heard throughout the Latin American World.

A visitor to the *morada* at Las Golondrinas will see the skeletal figure of Doña Sebastiana, an allegorical figure, in the *Carreta de Muerte* (Death Cart). She is there to remind all of us to prepare for the fateful day when she arrives to take us to be judged. Story tellers José Griego y Maestas and Rudolfo A. Anaya collected the following *cuento*, "La Comadre Sebastiana." One day a poor woodcutter stole one of his wife's setting hens, and took it into the mountains to roast and eat it. There he was approached by a stranger of noble stature who introduced himself as the Lord, and asked if He might eat with him. The woodcutter refused, saying that he thought the Lord favored the rich and neglected the poor. So the Lord went away. Shortly came a woman who said she was the Virgin Mary, and asked to share his meal. Again, he refused because he thought her Son neglected the poor like him; she should intercede with Him, said the woodcutter, to make everyone equal.

The next visitor was Doña Sebastiana, Death herself. The woodcutter invited her to share his food because she did not play favorites, treating the young, old or ugly, alike. After the meal, Doña Sebastiana offered to grant the poor man any favor he wished. He replied that she should decide on the favor. Accordingly Doña Sebastiana made him a *curandero*, but told him to cure the sick only when she appeared at the foot of the sickbed. She cautioned him never to cure anyone if he saw her seated at the head of the bed, no matter what the individual promised. To do so would go against God's will. But when the *curandero* was called to a rich man's deathbed who offered a fortune for a cure, he broke the commandment. The woodcutter saw Doña Sebastiana at the head of the bed, overpowered her, wrestled her to the foot, and cured the rich man. On his way home, she intercepted him, led him to a dark room, and showed him two candles, one burning low and flickering, the other burning tall and brightly. She told him that once he had been like the tall candle, and the sick man like the short one. Now, he was the dying candle, and the man he cured the tall one. At the moment the short candle's flame died, the *curandero's* soul was added to Doña Sebastiana's death cart as it made its way into eternity.

Griego y Maestas and Anaya also collected and translated the story, "The New Bishop." A long time ago when Archbishop Zubiría traveled to Santa Fé to administer the sacrament of Confirmation to Children, a *fiesta* was planned, and the local priest prepared his parishioners to prepare to receive the important dignitary. The people had never seen a bishop, and were excited to meet such an august person. The day of the bishop's arrival, he met with the people in the sacristy. In their enthusiasm, the people forgot how to address the bishop properly. The first bowed and whispered, "¿Cómo le va, San Joaquín?" The second, a woman was so nervous and excited that she said, "¿Cómo le va, María Santisima?" The third, more sophisticated than his fellows, said, "¿Cómo le va, su *Señoric?*" When greeted as befitted a man of his station, the bishop whispered to the welcomer, "Isn't it a disgrace that these people are so ignorant and shy that they do not know how to address a bishop?" The man answered, "Yes, we *paisanos* (compatriots) are humble folk. Who else would mistake Your Excellency as the Virgin Mary or a saint when it is obvious that you are neither?"

The two authors also collected the story, "The Boy and His Grandfather." In the old days, many generations lived under the same roof in harmony. An aging grandfather was not getting along with his daughter-in-law. She claimed he was always in the way, and she prevailed upon her husband to send him to a small room away from the house. Out-of-sight, he was often ignored and many times went hungry. One bitterly cold day, the grandson visited his grandfather who asked the boy to find a blanket to warm him. The youngster ran to the barn and did not find a blanket, but a rug instead. He asked his father to cut the rug into two pieces, but the father told him to take the entire rug. "No," the boy responded, "I can't take it all because I want to save the other half for you so that when you grow old, you will not be cold." The boy's reply caused the father to realize how badly he had treated his own father. He brought the old gentleman back into his home and placed him in a warm room. From that day on, the boy and his father saw that the grandfather was fed and had company every day.

Dichos and Proverbs

Everyone has a favorite *dicho* that conveys a serious message in a few words. From the many dichos and proverbs of New Mexico, the following are a few of the nuggets from *Dichos* by Charles Aranda courtesy of Sunstone Press:

En boca cerrada no entran moscas. Flies will not enter a closed mouth. (Silence is golden.)

De tal palo salta la estilla. The splinter takes after the log whence it comes. (A chip off the old block.)

El que quiera saber sus defectos, que se case y el que quiera saber sus cualidades, que se muera. If you wish to know your defects, then marry; if you want to know your character, then die.

No es desgracia ser pobre pero es muy inconveniente. To be poor is no disgrace but it's very inconvenient.

Para saber hablar, hay que saber escuchar. If you would know how to speak, you must know how to listen.

Uno es el arquitecto de su propio destino. One is the architect of his own destiny.

Mujer hermosa es muy peligrosa. A beautiful woman is very dangerous. (You cannot keep a beautiful woman for very long.)

Mientras en mi casa estoy, rey soy. As long as I am in my house, I am king. (A man's home is his castle.)

Las canas no quitan ganas. Gray hair does not weaken your desires. (You are as old as you feel.)

El que perdona a su enemigo, a Dios tiene por amigo. He who forgives his enemy has God for his friend.

El traje no hace al hombre pero le da figura. Clothes do not make the man, but they do give him quality.

Witchcraft

Fears of witchcraft and other superstitions troubled Spanish missionaries as well as simple laymen. The Franciscans brought with them the European medieval belief in the forces of evil, and then blended these beliefs with similar Indian mystical beliefs. The Pueblos, themselves, were steeped in witchcraft. Scholars, even specialists in Southwest studies, seldom concern themselves with the occult even though witchcraft in all its aspects, casting of spells, enchantments, sorcery, divination and the like had many practitioners and was widely accepted as a reality in old New Mexico. Some folklorists have shed light on the occult lore of the Río Grande, and following are some examples:

What should an aggrieved wife or lover do if her *amante* (lover) proves unfaithful? The answer may be found in the records of the Inquisition. Fifty sworn statements tell of a lamentable state of affairs in Santa Fé in 1630. Soldiers had been unfaithful to their wives, and the inquisitors found ample evidence that women trafficked in love-potions and the use of occult practices designed to return wayward lovers to home and hearth. Recipes, often obtained from Mexican Indian servants attached to households, were decocted and slipped into breakfast cups; included were such ingredients as cornmeal, herbs, fried or mashed worms and urine, either that of the disloyal one or his mistress.

How can a young lady rid herself of an undesirable suitor? The remedy—choose a junction of two roads and "make a cross" on the ground using two crossed pins and a bulb of garlic. Of course she must coax the would-be lover into walking over the charm. If successful, she will be free of his attentions forever.

In 1708, Doña Leonor asked the governor to investigate the causes of her bewitchment. "Being extremely ill with various troubles and maladies which seem to be caused by witchcraft . . .," she wrote and continued, "Being, as I am, a Catholic Christian by the goodness of God, I know that there have been many examples . . . of persons of my sex who have been hexed by devilish art . . . ." She then proceeded to name several women, including her sister-in-law, as suspects. The governor found her near death, and immediately ordered a judicial inquiry. The investigation found one of the accused had years before been her husband's concubine, suggesting the victim was jealous and sought revenge. Vindictiveness prompted more than one charge of witchcraft.

When Father Félix Ordoñez y Machado died mysteriously in 1766, troops were dispatched to Abiquiú to destroy a stone with "diabolical" inscriptions and other evidence of witchcraft. An Indian girl accused a man and his wife of using supernatural forces who, along with other villagers, were arrested, tried, and found guilty of bringing about a priest's demise. All parties were condemned to a period of servitude in Christian households. When a Sandía Indian was found guilty in 1796 of being a sorcerer who used black magic to assist a party of Apache to run off some of the town's livestock, he was suspended from the roof of a kiva and lashed until he died.

Almost every town on the Río Grande had its stories and traditions of supernatural events, were-animals and witches. All were careful to avoid Satan's lackeys, cats with glowing eyes, hooting owls and night-flying objects. Juan Perea, a male *bruja* from San Mateo, deposited his eyes in a saucer and borrowed those of a cat. A dog upset the table, ate the eyes, and left Juan forever with the cat's green eyes.

At night, grandparents spun tales of horror around the family fireside. Every naïve child and adult knew that *brujas* possessed the power to fly high over the Río Grande, and at great speed. Their means of transport included meteors and comets as well as the common household broom. *Brujas* launched their flight with the cry, *"sin Dios y sin Santa María* (without God and without the Virgin Mary)."

One story tells that Luís de Rivera signed on as a *mulatero* with a caravan in 1628 bound for New Mexico. An insecure young man who was convinced he was possessed by demons, he hoped to change his run of bad luck. Unfortunately, a stampede of cattle and mules caused serious losses during the journey.

Fellow drovers and stock handlers were convinced that an associate of the *diablo* (devil) was responsible for the disastrous stampede. The simple fellow, his self-confidence shattered, confessed to a friar that he was indeed responsible. The priest immediately denounced him to the representative of the Inquisition at Kewa Pueblo where Luís threw himself on the mercy of the court. The tribunal concluded that his act was the result of youthful ignorance, and imposed only a mild penance. Luís was lucky; the Inquisition had no qualms about sentencing practitioners of evil to harsh punishments.

Brujas were believed to have practiced their dark arts as a means of revenge against enemies. They had served apprenticeships with older witches skilled in the ways of sorcery. Advanced practitioners held formal classes. Graduates were known as *arbolarias* (herb healers), and were skilled in the techniques of casting spells, bewitching others, and transforming themselves into animals or various objects. The *diablo* conducted classes in a cave in Peña Blanca. Some were fated at birth to become witches, so families carefully watched a newborn for signs of strange or deviant behavior. A baby so afflicted must be cured before the following Friday, or it would surely die. A mother who feared that apparent admirers harbored evil designs against her child would touch the infant's forehead and whisper, "*Dios te guarde tan linda* (God keep you, pretty baby)." One category of *brujas* was composed of individuals who had made a *pactado con el diablo* (pact with the devil). These *diablos* banded together in groups to enhance the power of their magic and dispensed services for fees. Colonial emigrants brought this tradition intact from Spain.

The missionaries, sometimes as credulous as lay people, strove to stamp out Pueblo sorcery, and kept voluminous records of witchcraft trials. No official court of Inquisition existed on the Río Grande, but friars had a special commission from the tribunal in Mexico City to gather evidence on heresy, apostasy, and witchcraft. Although official trial records confirmed the presence of sorcerers in the pueblos, and regarded them as an ever-present threat to the community to be dealt with harshly, the Spanish church and state insisted on the use of legal forms in the investigation, trial, and sentencing of witches. This policy helped to avert the development of the witch-hunts that sent so many hapless women to their deaths in New England and Europe. Most alleged to be witches, it should be noted, were women.

The Christian cross was the most potent protection against a *bruja*.

Witches are afraid of the symbol of crossed pine needles, twisted yucca fibers, open scissors, or a crucifix. A pair of scissors displayed with blades open replicates a cross hanging over the door in the Manuel de Baca House *cocina* at Las Golondrinas.

Bruja repellant hangs above the Baca cocina door (also shown on page 150)

Docents report no sighting of witches has occurred for years. Another prophylactic against witchcraft was the use of pious phrases and formulas in moments of danger. Exclaiming *"Madre de Dios* (Mother of God)" or *"Alabados sean los dulces nombres de Jesús, María, y José* (Praised be the sweet names of Jesus, Mary, and Joseph)"* would make a *bruja* powerless. Wearing a San Benito medal also helped protect the wearer, for the saint's name means "blessed." It was well known that Christians of doubtful faith were the most likely victims of a spell.

By the last quarter of the nineteenth century, officials no longer accepted claims of witchcraft. Accordingly, victims of alleged black magic sometimes took matters into their own hands. A case in point occurred in Tierra Amarilla in

1882. Here an individual, having broken off a love affair after many years, was attacked by a loathsome disease. Convinced his former lover had bewitched him, he sought to force her to free him from the spell by whipping her severely. Near death from this mistreatment, she managed to escape by claiming she must travel to Abiquiú to obtain ointments and medicines. The offending lover was brought to trial and fined $150 and costs.

Herbs with extraordinary properties were used to banish spells and hexes. Magical decoctions were sold to those willing to pay. Some plants, carried by a person or hidden in the home, gave protection against evil design. The *calabacilla* (wild gourd) toted in a pocket or purse had this power. The frequently cultivated marijuana could be smoked, drunk in a decoction, or chewed each morning to keep *brujas* at bay. An amulet of rank-smelling garlic also protected against witchcraft. *Gente de chusma* (flying demons), who sailed on the winds, were unable to enter a home marked by a cross of ground mustard seed. A broth made from dried *datura* (jimson weed) and the fangs of a rattlesnake caused a faithless lover to repent. (Of course, it might also kill him.) Were-animals, when coaxed into circles drawn in the soil with the call "¡Venga bruja! (Come, witch!)," were captured and exposed. The innumerable persons named Juan were especially skilled at catching *brujas* in these circles. Witches believed a common *piedra imán* (lode-stone), possessed special powers that required it to be fed iron filings, steel particles, needles and water every Friday. If the stone was neglected, the owner could lose his mind and turn into a skeleton. The *piedra imán* gave superior knowledge to its owner, and helped him to perform various transformations. Some householders kept a *piedra imán* to protect against witchcraft, or for use as a love amulet.

The *cachana* root (blazing star or gayfeather, also known as "witch root") protected the wearer from evil when carried in a little bag sewn inside a *camisc* (shirt). No doubt Pueblo Indian servants brought this tradition into Hispanic households. Zía medicine men supplied the potent safeguard to Hispanics, but cautioned against its abuse. Today, Zía Indians closely guard their secret location of *cachana*.

A notorious *bruja* and herb doctor, Dolores la Penca, had been abandoned as an infant. About 1900 she lived in a small abandoned *adobe* house, the last dwelling in Santa Fé on the way to Agua Fria. It was filled with the materials of her bizarre craft. Dolores roamed the Sangre de Cristo Mountains collecting herbs and plants, causing much concern among her neighbors. Eventually her evil arts were turned against her. A young bride-to-be had accepted a gift of sweet-smelling soap from the *bruja,* and broke out in a frightful rash; she was certain a spell had been cast upon her upcoming marriage. On the day of the nuptials, the bride's brother and cousin were working some distance away from her home. They observed an owl hooting in a piñon tree. The cousin was sure the owl was Dolores, come to make mischief. He marked a bullet with a cross, loaded his rifle, and shot the bird in the eye, mangling the owl's wing in the process. Returning home, the two men found the witch's *adobe* vacant, and the bride's complexion free of blemish. They later learned that Dolores had been slain mysteriously on the night of the wedding. A bullet had pierced her right eye and her body mangled. Many tales of the evil nature of owls are to be found in New Mexican folklore.

As late as the 1930s, stories of *brujas* flourished in the northern foothills of the Sandía Mountains at La Madera. In 1939, a resident of Las Placitas was a target of witchcraft. Given a bowl of hominy she suspected had been doctored, she added additional ingredients to disguise it, and returned the gift to its sender. The supposed witch succumbed at the feast of San Antonio after eating the concoction.

Fiestas, Folk Dramas, and Morality Plays

The spirit of community is most happily conveyed through its celebrations, its *fiestas,* folk dramas, and morality plays. *Fiestas* occur throughout Catholic Latin America and are marked by the celebration of Masses, and processions of revered patron saints of the village communities. In the Catholic religious calendar and in Pueblo tribal ceremonies, the tradition of the *fiesta* is deeply rooted in the history of both the Hispanic villages and the Indian pueblos. Not all, however, continue to celebrate *fiesta* in the old traditional ways, and some of the following descriptions are reconstructions based on accounts that have come down to them.

In the Hispanic colonial village, a *mayordomo (fiesta* councilor) took charge of preparations for this special event. He was responsible for raising funds to cover expenses, and if the money raised did not cover costs, he and his fellow councilors were expected to make up the deficit. The *mayordomos* were also responsible for keeping the village church clean and in good repair. *Santos* were dressed in fine attire, altar clothes cleaned and mended, and faded and worn paper flowers replaced with bright new ones. If there was no resident priest, the visiting cleric and his party were welcomed to the home of the *mayordomo*. Vespers were held in the chapel the evening before the *fiesta* with *luminarias* set ablaze just before the service began. After the service, all went to confession in order to be ready to receive communion at Mass the following day. After Mass, a *fiesta* dinner was served to the refrains of a *cantador* (singer) who sang *corridos* (old ballads) that told of feats of love and war.

Men held *carreras de caballos* (horse races) or a *corrida de gallo*. During the latter, an unlucky fowl, its head greased, was hung from a limb of a tree barely within the reach of a man on horseback, ready to be snatched by a horseman galloping at full speed. The slippery rooster often slid from the competitor's grip only to be stolen by another. On other occasions, the hapless bird was buried alive with only its head above the ground. When the rider managed to pull the ill-fated fowl loose, others pursued him attempting to wrest the prize, pulling and tugging, until the poor bird was torn asunder. If the rider managed to hang onto the trophy, he took what was left of it home for supper. Another pastime required horsemen to grab the tail of a running bull and whirl it topsy-turvy, a feat that caused great amusement. Josiah Gregg observed such bull baiting on special occasions in Santa Fé as late as 1844.

Even into the early 20th century, women and children in the village of Arroyo Hondo still bathed in the river or in *acequias* on *El Día de San Juan*, St. John's Day, June 24. They believed the waters were holy because Saint John had blessed them when he baptized Jesus in the Jordan River. San Ysidro, patron saint of farmers, is honored nowadays with the Spring and Fall Festivals at El Rancho de las Golondrinas as its patron saint.

During the early June Spring Festival, and after Mass held on the performance stage or in the shade of the concession stand, a visiting priest blesses the fields, *acequias*, and animals during the procession of San Ysidro. Led by the Caballeros de Vargas, an all male religious civic organization, bearing colorful banners representing colonial families, the procession escorts a *bulto* of San Ysidro on its *andita* to the *Oratorio de San Ysidro* (Saint Isidore Chapel). There the saint watches over the fields from high on the hill above the Sierra Village. Villages, such as the mountain hamlet of Cordova, traditionally celebrate the saint's May 15 feast day with a *velorio* that begins after vespers the eve before. Again, an image of San Ysidro is taken through the fields, and the procession, chanting prayers and singing the hymn for San Ysidro, proceeds to Las Joyas, some three miles away, where a bower is already prepared to host the wake. The following *alabado* in honor of San Ysidro was collected in the village of Valdez by Loren W. Brown for his Federal Writer's Project.

San Ysidro and blessing of the waters

San Ysidro Labrador Saint Isidore, Husbandman,
Patrón de los labradores, Saintly patron of the farmer,
Que nos libre tu favor May your favor grant us protection
De langostas y temblores. From locusts and temblors dread.

Por la gran misericordia By virtue of the mercy shown
Con que te ayudó el Señor, By the Lord to you of yore,
Derrama paz y concordia Grant the peace and sweet accord
Entre todo labrador. Dwell with the farmers evermore.

Pues que fuiste designado Since 'tis you who has been chosen
Por patrón de la labor, As saintly patron of the farmer,
Siempre serás adorado Hymns of praise shall e'er by them
Del devoto labrador. Be sung in honor of your name.

Cuando el Señor por castigo When our Lord as punishment
Nos manda mal temporal, Sends adverse winds and hail,
Con tu bondadoso abrigo We on your kind protecting grace
Nos vemos libre de mal. Rely to save our crops from harm.

Del ladrón acotumbrado From the arrant thief who steals
Que nunca teme al Señor, With no fear of God's wrath,
Nos libres nuestro sembrado, Oh grant protection for our fields,
Te pedimos por favor. We ask it for your grace.

El granizo destructo, Hail, our most destructive foe,
Que no nos cause su daño, Oft lays our harvests flat,
Te pedimos con favor Its wrath withhold, and grant to us
Tener cosecha este año. A bounteous harvest this coming year.

En tus bondades confiado Confiding in your kindly heart
Te pido de corazón I ask with all my own
Le mandes a mi sembrado That you will deign to bless
Favores y benedición. And grant fair weather to my fields.

Adios, Oh Santo glorioso, Farewell, Oh blessed saint,
Escogido del Señor, Until the coming year,
Hasta del año venidero, Thou chosen one of the Lord,
San Ysidro Labrador. Saint Isidore, the Husbandman.

During the *velorio* at Arroyo Hondo, the dark of night is broken by the row of blazing candles surrounding the image. *Rezadores,* prayer leaders and readers in a *morada,* sing the many stanzas of the *alabados.* The people join in singing the chorus, and a communal repast is served at midnight. The *velorio* ends when the first rays of the morning sun fall on the face of San Ysidro and the village of Cordova. The procession again forms, and the *buito* of San Ysidro is escorted back down the trail through valley and field until it is placed once again in the *capilla.* The devotees disperse and gather again in the evening for a night filled with song and dance. The *velorio* brings the villagers together to manifest their faith and their wish for a good harvest.

San Gerónimo Day, celebrating St. Jerome, a major celebration throughout northern New Mexico. On his September 13 feast day at the Taos Pueblo, special events were held with its mirror festivities in the village of Taos. The young women of Taos were known far and wide for their beauty, and the *fiesta* was an occasion for the display of their new and colorful wearing apparel. From their western reservation, the Apache arrived several days before the event, clad in their fancy beaded leather vests, multicolored shirts, braided hair bound by bands of multi-colored beads and high-crowned Mexican sombreros. On the morning of the festivities, the dusty roads that led to Taos were choked with wagons, buggies, and people on horseback for at least ten miles. Presently, painted runners emerged from their kivas and took their places for the famous relay race that decided who would be the governor for the upcoming year, and who would serve on his council. The sound of the *tombé,* chanting, and dancing marked the finish of the race, and then everyone made their ways to the village of Taos where the festivities continued.

The annual Santa Fe procession of the statue of La Conquistadora still honors a promise made by Don Diego de Vargas. The sacred image returned with Vargas to inspire his military to take back the City of Holy Faith. Vargas vowed after 1693 to hold a Mass and a *fiesta* each year in honor of the sacred image should she help him make a non-violent return to Santa Fé. In point of fact, Vargas's return was not without bloodshed. In 1712, Vargas' friend, Lieutenant Governor Captain General Juan Páez Hurtado, officially confirmed the annual celebration of La Cofradía de la Conquistadora. A replica of the thirty-one inch statue is still taken in procession by the Caballeros de Vargas from her sanctuary in the north chapel of the Cathedral Basilica of St. Francis, and paraded through the streets of historic Santa Fe to the Rosario Shrine, originally built in 1807 at the old Vargas encampment site next to the Rosario Cemetery. There she resides for nine days before being returned in procession to the cathedral. Today's *fiesta* is a romantic re-enactment of the founding of the ancient City of the Holy Faith, La Villa de Santa Fé, and it provides an excuse for many festivities. The archbishop crowns the *fiesta* queen, *La Reina*, and she and her court that now includes an Indian princess, reign during the festivities.

Don Juan Oñate introduced religious folk drama to New Mexico in 1598 when he stopped his advance at the Rió Grande to rest and give thanks, and to lay claim to the land beyond for God and King. His dramatic re-enactment of *Los Moros y los Cristianos* was a mock battle featuring horses, steel swords, and firearms. Most likely originating in Aragón in the twelfth century, the pageant still performed today in New Mexico's Santa Cruz and elsewhere begins at a castle held by the Moors during the Christian re-conquest of Spain. The sultan sends a spy into the Christian camp with an ample supply of wine where he gets a sentry tipsy and steals the *Santa Cruz* (Holy Cross). King Alfonso refuses to pay the ransom demanded by the sultan for the return of the priceless relic, and a pitched battle follows. The infidel is vanquished and pardoned after he converts to the Holy Faith and embraces the sacred symbol. The drama features an intervention by Santiago Matamoros, Saint James the Moor Killer, the same Santiago that helped turn the fateful battle in at Ácoma Pueblo in 1599 according to Gaspar Pérez de Villagrá, Juan de Oñate's chronicler.

Los Matachines is a dance reportedly rooted in Aztec traditions that portrays the spiritual conquest of Mexico; it is still an indispensable symbol of worship in some villages of New Mexico. Moorish elements are evident in masks and costumes, complete with rainbow colored ribbons that flutter from crowns and shoulders. Pueblo legend holds that Moctezuma flew north in the shape of a bird with the grave news that bearded foreigners were on their way, putting all in great peril. But he promised that if the Indians learned the dance of the strangers, they would be spared, and the two peoples would become as brothers. Both Hispanics and Indians dance *Los Matachines*, but with a difference.

Matachine dance has traditions from the Moors

In one Spanish version, a make-believe Spanish *toro* (bull) runs wild through the lines of dancers who use three-pronged *palmas* (trident swords) to split the air and invoke the Trinity. The sound of *tombés*, rattles, guitars and violins helps to calm the chaos of battle, softening the defeat and surrender theme. In the middle of the pageant, the great king, Monarca, most likely Moctezuma, seeks the council of Malinche, the mistress of Hernan Cortés, the conquistador of Mexico, and is converted to Christianity. He identifies Malinche as the Virgin. She takes up the king's rattle and *palma,* and weaves through the lines of dancers. Her role is performed by a pre-pubescent girl dressed in white. Carnivalesque *abuelos,* mythical grandparents of the mountains, make fun of people, ridicule the new order, and control the dancers. These "grandfathers of the mountains" subdue the bull, kill and castrate him, and throw his seed to the happy crowd. Hispanics perform the play, with its conversion theme, as an act of devotion to the saints and La Virgen de Guadalupe. On special occasions, a Hispanic troupe performs a modified *Los Matachines* dance at El Rancho de las Golondrinas.

Indians tend to view the dance as a parody, a satirical secular celebration. They ridicule Malinche, and the play becomes in part a re-enactment of the sexual conquest of Mexico. Dancers at Ohkay Owingeh Pueblo perform the pageant each year on December 24 and 25.

When the December 27 performance of *Los Matachines* concludes in the village of Alcalde, the heroic play of *Los Comanches* begins. It is performed on horseback, and commemorates the death of Cuerno Verde, the great Comanche chieftain. Cuerno Verde and his warriors attacked Alcalde in the 1770s, and it is the only community where the dance is still performed. The action depicts the Anza military campaigns of 1774 and 1779 that ended with the death of Cuerno Verde. In the play, dramatic tension erupts between the protagonists, the aged but wise Spanish Don Carlos and a brash young Cuerno Verde. They dispute the fate of two children who have been taken captive by the Indians. In the older, traditional version, Don Carlos calls upon Santiago and the Virgin to ensure a Spanish victory, and the play culminates with the death of the Comanche chief. In the modern play, denying history, Cuerno Verde lives and rides off with the other role players.

January 1 finds Hispanics of Los Ranchos de Taos playing the role of Comanche dancers who sing to the beat of the *tombés*, moving from house to house in nearby northern villages, while their children dance at the church of San Francisco de Asís. The actors pay homage to Comanche elders who are no longer able to dance with the group. Youngsters dance to honor all Manuels and Manuelas named after the Holy Child, Emmanuel. Dressed in fanciful costumes, they re-enact the dramas of *genízaro* captivity and redemption. A troupe of dancers, moving from house to house, may visit as many as twenty homes. The songs are a fusion of Plains, Navajo, and Pueblo songs, using vocables, words whose meanings have been lost. Emotions run high in the depiction of battles, captivity, and redemption. *El desempeño* (captive's ransom) may be a drink of water for the child dancers and whiskey for the adult singers. A lunch, a simple thank you, or a full tank of gasoline will see the parties home.

The November feast of Santo Tomás, the Apostle, honors the *genízaro* heritage of Abiquiú. Almost every Hispanic family there recalls an ancestor who was taken captive or was redeemed from captivity. The children dance with Tewa-style face paint, and are costumed in buckskin, ribbons, feathers and scarves. After Mass, little *cautivos* dance back and forth in rows holding a feather in each hand. The *Nanillé* dance is sung with vocables; the meaning of the name has been lost. A pantomime of captivity and redemption is performed, and when a *cautivo* is presented to the people with "¿Quién lo conoce?" (Who knows this person?), someone may come forward and pay the *desempeño* to the singers. If not claimed, the poor captive becomes the property of the singers. After the ransom is paid, *el borracho* (drunk) performs a burlesque dance while singers circle each other, pretend to fall down drunk, and one waves an empty whiskey bottle. Both sexes utter war cries during the dance. In reality, the performance is a satire intended to minimize the pain of unhappy historical memories. Spanish colonial policy used alcohol as a means of pacifying the natives, making them more dependent on the government. Neighborhood participants now celebrate victory and community through the symbolic sharing of alcohol.

A drama still performed today at Christmas time is *Los Pastores* (The Shepherds), a morality play used by missionaries to expose the flawed human condition. Shepherds, journeying to see the Christ Child, are tempted and taunted by Lucifer. Other actors in the play include the Archangel Michael, who announces the birth of the Christ Child, and invites the shepherds to travel to Bethlehem to present Him with gifts. Bartolo, a lazy shepherd provides comic relief, the attractive shepherdess Gilita, and a hermit accompany the party. As the party rests for the night, Lucifer appears and attempts to prevent the shepherds from reaching Bethlehem. The Archangel appears and awakens the hermit to warn him against the temptations of sin. Even so, Lucifer entices the hermit to steal the gifts intended for the Christ Child from the shepherds, and to carry off the fair Gilita. The shepherds waken as Lucifer continues to create mischief. Saint Michael enters the fray to defeat the Devil, and the hermit ultimately shoves the Devil into the mouth of hell. We should note that the introduction of sheep and other domesticated animals to the New World profoundly changed Indian lifeways, and the symbolic association of domestic animals with the infant Jesus came to play an important role in the process of conversion that the Franciscans may not have anticipated.

A week before Christmas, many communities perform *Las Posadas* (The Lodgings), a short pageant performed either in or out-of-doors, tells the biblical story of Mary and Joseph as they traveled from inn to inn seeking shelter, only to be turned away. Singers accompany Mary and Joseph as the couple visits different homes representing the inhospitable inns of Bethlehem. The drama culminates on Christmas Eve when the party finds refuge in a church, community center, or a host's home with its symbolic stable, and the celebration of the birth of Christ commences. *Las Posadas* is festive and gay, a time for communal coming together, sharing of food, and bringing together friends with gifts of bizcochitos.

About Christmas time, children were cautioned, "*Si no te sosiegas, llamo el abuelo*" (if you don't behave, I'll call in the Grandfather) to keep children on their good behavior. The *abuelo,* who appeared about a week before Christmas, was a fearsome being in his frightening mask, grotesque costume and his rawhide whip. The apparition let out a blood-curdling cry as he approached the door of the home where a group of children cowered behind the skirts of their mothers. With a crack of his whip and a bellow, he would demand of the parents, "¿Han sido buenos muchachos estos?" The frightened brood looked to the faces of their parents beseeching them to intervene. The parents would vouch for the children saying that, indeed, they were *buenos niños* (good children), and knew how to say their prayers. The *abuelo* would listen to quivering voices recite prayers, and then send the children to bed. After the youngsters were out of hearing with bedcovers pulled tightly over their heads, the parents would offer the *abuelo* food and drink. The *abuelo* may very well have been another family member assuming the role of the family disciplinarian, thus freeing parents from the responsibility.

The clergy used *Los Pastores* and other morality plays to teach basic religious concepts including religious themes, lessons in which good triumphs over evil, the Biblical stories of Adam and Eve, and El Niño Perdido, the story of the Virgin Mary's search for the child Jesus that became lost in Jerusalem during a feast celebrating the Jewish Passover. Many are performed in pantomime, and are accompanied by *alcbados* and Gregorian chants. Included in the repertoire is the non-Biblical "Four Apparitions of Our Lady of Guadalupe."

12

Rites of Passage

The Early Years—The Sacrament of Marriage—The End of Life

The Early Years

New Mexican Hispanic communities had long been self-reliant and cohesive, and their rites of passage were and are the celebrations of key events of a lifetime. They are the bond that holds the community together, creating social harmony and stability, and transmits culture from one generation to the next. In communities where life was often fragile, the needs of the whole take precedence over that of the individual. Rituals are still an important instrument for reinforcing the cohesiveness so necessary to the survival of a culture.

Social historian Adrian Bustamante tells us specific values gave meaning to New Mexican rituals and customs. Family members were required to show *respeto* (respect) for others, and exhibit behavior that did not bring shame on the community. Parents were responsible for rearing their children according to the community's standards and mores, and for ensuring that the rites of passage were performed as children came of age. Much importance was placed on *pundonor* (family honor) that required all members of the family to act in a principled and honorable manner. Children were to guard against bringing any shame or scandal to the family, and were expected to show *respeto* for their elders. When a member of the family died, a certain protocol was to be observed, proper prayers said, a burial ceremony conducted with dignity, and a respectable mourning period observed. *Compadrazgo* (ritual co-parenthood) required future kin to assist the family in observance of the rites of passage, and served as a cohesive factor in village life.

Birth was a most important event, and everything possible was done to ensure a safe birthing. There were no doctors in colonial New Mexico, and the fate of the mother and her infant were in the hands of the *curandera* and the *partera* (midwife). Herbs were prescribed and advice and directions given. A cord or band tightly bound around the waist of a mother in labor kept the upper organs in place. A rope suspended from a *viga* provided the mother with a means to suspend herself, and help push out the baby. Upon a successful delivery of a girl, siblings of the baby went from door to door with the news, "Mother says that you have a new handmaiden at your service." The neighbor would respond saying, "May God lend her to your parents for many years." The birth of a boy was honored in a similar manner.

Sick people were expected to avoid a pregnant woman, for they might give her the *mal de ojo* (evil eye). To test to see if the infant was infected with the evil eye, an egg was broken into a bowl of water, and the color and condition of the egg studied to determine the presence of the dreaded condition. If the evil eye appeared, the infant was at risk, and someone with the name of Juan had to spit into the face of the newborn before the upcoming Friday. An expectant mother dared not sleep in moonshine, or the baby might be "eaten by the moon" and born without limbs, The moon was held responsible for many problems with newborns. Prayers to San Ramón Nonnatus, a thirteenth-century Spanish saint who had been born by Caesarean, helped with a safe delivery, and a *bulto* of the Christ Child in a cradle near the bed provided protection for the newborn. The placenta was to be buried outside near the house, insuring that a child, once grown, would always return home. A cord of colored yarn, blessed by the priest and tied around the baby's throat, summoning San Blas to guard against diseases of the throat.

Padrinos de pila (baptismal godparents) regarded their appointment an honor, and assumed responsibility for promoting the godchildren's moral development. *Padrinos* became intimate members of the family, and were especially cherished by their godchildren. The baptism, often conducted after Mass, was set for forty days after the baby's birth. The *ahijado* (godchild) was dressed in special finery by the *madrina* (godmother). At Mass, the *padrinos* informed the priest of the baby's name, or rather a series of names that included those of saints and family members. After Mass, the *madrina* offered the child to the mother saying, 'Receive this precious gift that comes from the church, having received the holy sacraments and holy water." The mother then repeated the phrase in the first person, "I receive this precious gift . . ." The ceremony concluded with the recital of other prescribed phrases. A family reception followed where each child received *la arras* (gold coins) and the godfather gave the baby a coin. By the sixteenth century, *criados* were baptized and received Christian first names. At the baptismal font, the friars reminded *criados'* owners of their religious duties towards their wards.

If the child was sickly, baptism could occur at any time. Baptized children who died at an early age were considered blessed, being *angelitos* (angels), and those christened who died without sin were believed to go directly to heaven. The body of a deceased child, clothed in a long white dress, was placed in its little coffin decorated with ribbons and flowers. An *alabado* of the Santo Niño was sung. Angels were believed to carry the tiny soul to heaven, and the funeral was an occasion for celebration.

Because New Mexico was a missionary field, Hispanic children initially were confirmed in the Catholic Church at the time of their baptisms. Later, and after due instruction, the rite was performed when the child reached twelve or thirteen years of age. *Padrinos* were required to attend the instructions and the ceremony, and the bishop reminded the young person, with a light slap on the cheek, that he or she must be prepared to suffer for the child's religion. The first communion was and still is a special occasion. The child attended Catechism classes and, with the help of the family and *padrinos*, learned the requisite lessons and prayers. The seven-year-old youngster received a prayer book, communion clothes, went to confession for the first time, and received his or her first absolution. Kneeling before the elders, the communicant received the blessing, "May God, the Father, the Son, and the Holy Spirit, bless you now and forever." The child accepted gifts from family and friends, and the day was the occasion for a family dinner.

More popular today than in former times, is a rite of passage for girls, a tradition recently borrowed from Mexico. The event occurs when a daughter passes from adolescence to adulthood at age fifteen. At times the *quinceañera* is celebrated with an elaborate celebration. A church ceremony attests to her religious faith and family values, and her godparents present her with traditional gifts of a ring, a symbol of her responsibilities to community and church, and a cross or religious medal. After Mass, a *fiesta* follows with toasting, dancing, and feasting. At other times, if the family so chooses, the *quinceañera* may be the simple act of repeating her baptismal vows during Mass.

The religious support system, Jesus, Mary, the angels, and the saints complement the human support system. *Familia y fé*, family and faith, are the most important influences in the lives of Hispanic New Mexicans. Children are named for the saints who serve as their protectors, and the saints are treated as revered members of the family. Supplications to the saints take the form of prayers, devotions, and pilgrimages. If the saints do not respond, they may be punished with temporary banishment from the bosom of the family. As recounted earlier the expulsion of an offending saint into a drawer, a cupboard specially prepared for that purpose, a closet, or turning its image to the wall, can be the tools of chastisement. One guest in the *capilla* at Las Golondrinas reported, "We throw a pillow slip over ours." Once the saint is again in favor, he/she is returned to his place of honor and devotion.

The Sacrament of Marriage

In former days, some wealthy families arranged their children's marriages while they were still quite young in order to maintain alliances and their upper-class status. Such arrangements discouraged other families from proposing a match, and assured the children's future. A good marriage by the eldest son protected the family's standing. Upper class daughters were married off as early as possible to minimize the possibility of a fatal error, the loss of virginity. A bride who had been deflowered was second-hand goods, and the dowry demanded by a prospective suitor increased correspondingly. It was the bride's responsibility to make the marriage work regardless of whether she liked her spouse or not. If the couple was not compatible, they still had to carry on.

In some households, the young suitor's parents broached the offer of marriage in a letter delivered to the parents of the prospective bride. A rejected suitor was notified and hopefully mollified by a gift. Tender regard for the feelings of others required the rejection be handled tactfully so as not to bring shame on the disappointed suitor. Acceptance might require the young man work for the prospective father-in-law for a brief period. Banns, the public notice of the proposed marriage, were read at the church on three successive Sundays.

The formal agreement was followed by the filing of a *diligencia matrimonial* (pre-nuptial investigations) that recorded the marriage contract with the church. Some days before the wedding at the *prendorio* (engagement ceremony), the intended's father introduced the prospective groom to her family, and the young woman received *memorias* (gifts), e.g. gold inter-twined puzzle rings or jeweled rosaries. The couple knelt before the eldest male in the bride's household as he placed a rosary over the young woman's head and another over the suitor's head. Sometimes *lazos* (double rosaries) were used instead of engagement rings. Families with Sephardic roots often clandestinely substituted wreaths of vines and other greenery. The godfather then gave the bride a box containing thirteen *arras,* a gift from the groom as a pledge to support her. As mentioned earlier, after introductions and gift giving, the feasting and *baile de prendorio* (engagement ceremony) commenced. Couples of modest or no means would often enter into a state of concubinage until enough wealth was saved, and the services of an itinerant priest obtained.

Most Hispanic marriages occurred after harvest when more money and time was available. Indians who married sacramentally did so from May through September, as the summer solstice was the most favored time. Traditional weddings of substance had three parts: the bride's departure from her natal dwelling with her retinue, the ceremony itself, and the procession from the church to the groom's home. Ceremonies took place in the church where the bride entered on the arms of her parents, followed by the groom, matron of honor, and guests. The sacrament of marriage was set within the celebration of Mass where the priest explained the responsibilities of matrimony to the bride, groom, and to the community at large. After the words *"ego vos in matrimonium conjugo,"* (I join you in matrimony) were spoken by the priest, the groom placed a ring on the bride's left thumb with the words, "In the name of the Father, and of the Son, and the Holy Spirit, Amen." The ring was moved to the next finger with each successive pronouncement, coming to rest permanently on the ring finger. If the groom was too poor to present a ring of gold or silver, none at all would suffice.

As the newlyweds left the church, celebratory gun salutes and music sent packing any evil spirits waiting to prey on the nuptial couple. Merriment followed as musicians led the wedding party to the home of the groom's parents where the passage to conjugal life was celebrated. Sometimes, the bridal couple might proceed to the bride's home after Mass. The pair received well wishers in the *sala* (living room), visitors slipped coins into the bride's hand, and guests were offered refreshments.

Circuit-riding priests would solemnize weddings in remote communities after couples were "married" in the eyes of their neighbors. The practice had its roots during the time when the service of a priest was not available to conduct the service, and communities had to take charge of such matters. The wedding party often chose to follow musicians directly to a home or a reception hall where invited guests were served dinner. There a well-to-do groom presented to his bride and to those assembled the *donas,* personal gifts of a handmade chest for the trousseau and Spanish combs, bolts of silk, gold and silver jewelry, gold coins and other sundries. The bride was expected to make two or three changes of her gown during the wedding dance. As the dance extended into the early morning, the *entriega de los novios,* the return of *novios* to *padrinos,* was performed where the newlyweds were surrendered by the *padrinos* to their parents for a final blessing.

A performance of *La Entriega de los Novios* by a notable New Mexican folk musician, Cipriano Vigil, is found in *La Música de los Viejitos: Hispanic Folk Music of the Río Grande del Norte* by Jack Loeffler.

"Ave María," dijo el ave The bird says, "Ave María,"
para empezar a volar, to begin its flight.
"Ave María," digo yo I say, "Ave María,"
para empezar a cantar. to begin to sing.

A Dios le pido licencia, From God I ask license,
memoria y sabiduría, memory, and wisdom,
para formar el estado to form the state
que se ha formado este día. which has been formed today.

Esta mañana salieron This morning emerged
cuatro flores a la iglesia, four flowers from the church,
el padrino y la madrina, the godparents,
el novio y sus princesa. The groom and his princess.

¿Qué significan las arras What do the coins signify
cuando las van a usar? When they are used?
significa el mismo cuerpo They symbolize the same body
que allí se van a juntar. that there will be joined.

Cristo nos dio a conocer Christ made it known to us
que él padeció en su morada that He suffered in his dwelling place,
llevó la cruz con esmero He carried his cross with great care
como a su esposa adorada. like a beloved wife.

El matrimonio es legal Marriage is legal
con la voluntad de dos, with the consent of both partners,
el matrimonio es bonito marriage is beautiful
con la voluntad de Dios. with the will of God.

El matrimonio es delicado Marriage is delicate
como un vaso de cristal, like a crystal glass,
no más una vez se rompe if it is broken even once,
ya no se puede juntar. it cannot be mended.

Óigame usted, el esposado, Listen to me, new husband,
lo que le voy a decir: to what I have to tell you:
Tiene a su princesa a su lado, You have your princess at your side,
Dios la saber bendecir. God knows how to bless her.

Óigame usted, la esposada Listen to me, new wife,
lo que le voy a cantar: to what I have to sing to you:
Tiene a su novio a su lado, You have your husband at your side,
no lo vaya a abandonar. do not abandon him."

Este versito que canto This little verse that I sing
se lo dedico al padrino I dedicate to the godfather,
el estado en que se encuentra the state that you are in
es un estado divino is a divine state.

Por este río para abajo Downstream in this river
corre el agua cristalina flows the crystalline water
donde se lavan las manos where the godparents
el padrino y la madrina. wash their hands.

Del cielo bajó un pintor An artist descended from heaven
para pintar tu hermosura to paint your beauty,
Señora Eufrasia Romero Señora Eufrasia Romero
se esto está usted segura. Of this you can be certain.

Y con este me despido, And with this I bid you farewell,
dispensen lo mal trovado. please pardon the singing.
Aquí tienen sus hijitos Here you have your children
están ellos entregados. They are now delivered.

The ceremony, conducted by the *entregador/a* (a skilled vocalist), was sung in verse before the entire party, and could include as many as fifty *coplas* (stanzas). Some verses, prepared or improvised, solemn or humorous, alluded to certain of the wedding party and guests. The *entregador* advised the couple, blessed them, offered advice regarding marital commitments and other duties, returned them to their parents, and sent them on their way. The rite had five parts: *La invocación* (invocation), *Los versos de la Santa Escritura* (Holy Scriptures), *Los versos de la iglesia, Los consejos o parabienes* (advice), and *Los verses de la gente* (verses for the people).

The End of Life

When someone died or was near death, all hurried to the church to learn who was stricken. A single toll gave notice of an infant's death—a double toll signified the death of an adult. At the ringing of the bells, everyone would bow to the Blessed Sacrament carried by the priest as he hurried to the bedside of the mortally ill to administer the *extremaunción* (extreme unction). Close relatives dressed the deceased's body in its best clothes. The body was then wrapped in a shroud, and placed in a coffin surrounded by lighted tapers, or on a *palajuela* (ladder) that served as a litter. If the departed was a member of the 3rd Order of St. Francis, the deceased would have decreed in his will that his body be "shrouded with the habit of Our Father, St. Francis, whose tertiary son I am, although unworthy." A large dish of chopped onion was often placed under the deceased's body in an effort to mask its odor, for embalming was not practiced. The scapular, two small pieces of cloth bearing the likenesses of saints, joined by strings and worn around the neck under clothing, was fastened to the shroud. The scapular was a sign of religious devotion. It protected the wearer from the fires of hell. *Angelitos* were exempt from eternal damnation.

We are fortunate to have the eighteenth century will of an affluent Las Golondrinas Baca family member. Marina de Jesús Baca had the document executed before witnesses less than a month before she died. In her April 16, 1784 will, she declared her Catholic faith, asked the intercession of her patron saint, the Virgin Mary, directed her body be shrouded in the habit of St. Francis, and requested a funeral Mass be said. After small monetary bequests, she ordered two novenas, and another "for the repose of the soul of my deceased husband, Juan Tafoya." The High Mass and vigils for Doña Marina de Jesus Baca were paid for with two cows and calves, one ox, one bull, one old female burro, ten varas of cloth, ten varas of wide unbleached muslin, and a rebozo. Fray Juan Bermijo, chaplain of the Santa Fé garrison, said the Mass in 1822. She left her property, consisting of a dwelling of four rooms, a ranch in the Pueblo Quemado, and 25 head of cattle to her one surviving child, Polonia.

The *velorio* (religious wake) ensured that the body of the deceased would not be left unattended the night before the funeral. Members of the community gathered to keep vigil and weep over the body, pray, sing and visit. The men made the coffin, dug the grave, and provided firewood, while the women prepared food for all. At the *velorio*, the rosary was said, and a *rezador* sang *alabados* accompanied by the weeping and wailing of mourners. Supper was served, and although many visitors went home before midnight, selected individuals stayed the night to pray, sing, tend the *luminarias* and visit. If the deceased was a Penitente, fellow members led the *velorio* procession from the *morada* to the home.

The next day, the body was taken to the *capilla* or *iglesia*, and the *eulogio* (eulogy) given. Then the men and boys, chanting *alabados*, accompanied the body to the *camposanto* with its elaborately decorated markers, many homemade. Whenever the funeral party stopped to rest, *sudarios* for the departed soul were said, and rocks and a small wooden *descanso* were added to a cairn. The markers told silent stories of life in the villages, of epidemics, bad winters, death at childbirth or mining disasters. After the interment, another meal was served at the family home. The household of the deceased mourned for one year with shutters closed and mirrors draped with black. Women wore mourning black and the traditional *tápolo* (black woolen shawl), and life went on.

13

The Day of the Yankee

The Republic of Texas—The Mexican American War—The American Civil War—Post American Civil War

The Republic of Texas

Almost from the day she achieved her independence from Spain in 1821, the new nation of Mexico was torn asunder by political and ideological differences. Lacking the means to control or develop its distant, sparsely populated northern provinces, the Mexican government signed a contract with Stephen F. Austin to colonize the area east of the Río Grande in order to create a buffer between the United States and Mexican territories. In 1821, Austin led the first group of three hundred Anglo families along the Lower Río Grande and Colorado Rivers to settle a grant of twenty thousand acres. By 1832, Austin's colonists numbered eight thousand, and by 1835, the number had grown to thirty-five thousand. Native Mexicans in Texas were outnumbered seven to one. The requirement that immigrants must be Catholic or convert to Catholicism was ignored. The growing number of Anglo slave owners paid no heed to Mexican laws that abolished slavery and the slave trade.

Then in 1834, conservative Antonio López de Santa Anna became president of Mexico, and imposed a centralist regime that deprived the Mexican states of virtually all rights to self-government, and revolts flared in California and Texas. On March 2, 1836, Sam Houston, leading an anti-Mexican faction, seized the provincial capital of San Antonio de Bejar, and declared Texas an independent republic. The Republic of Texas was born with Houston as president and Stephen Austin as secretary of state. But Mexico would not recognize Texan independence, and the new nation had ten stressful years of life before it was annexed to the United States in 1845, a move that disappointed zealots for the Texas Republic. When the United States Congress annexed Texas, the Mexican government broke off diplomatic relations with the United States.

The Mexican-American War

Two nations now faced each other across a disputed boundary. In the United States, a growing number of politicians and journalists proclaimed it was America's manifest destiny to expand over the entire continent. But Mexico's leaders were determined to defend their honor and territory. The boundary between Texas and Mexico had always been the Nueces River in Texas territory, but it served American expansionist policy to claim that the boundary farther west was the Río Grande. When newly elected President James K. Polk tried to buy California and to secure Mexican acceptance of the Río Grande River boundary, the Mexican government rejected his offer. Then, in a move clearly designed to provoke a Mexican military response, Polk ordered United States troops into the territory between the two rivers. The ploy worked. In response a small Mexican cavalry patrol crossed the lower Río Grande and attacked American forces. On May 13, 1846 President Polk signed a congressional declaration of war against Mexico, claiming that American territory had been invaded. The war enjoyed significant support in Congress although Abraham Lincoln, then a young congressman, openly disapproved. Southerners expected that land taken from Mexico would be open for slavery. For the Confederate mercantile community, the Santa Fe Trail had immense commercial significance. Silver and furs were transported eastward, and manufactured goods traveling west on the Santa Fe Trail were coveted assets.

President Polk ordered a two-pronged offensive attack into the heart of Mexico under the commands of Generals Zachary Taylor and Winfield Scott. He also sent orders to Colonel Stephen Watts Kearny to seize the New Mexican territory with as little disruption of life and the lucrative Santa Fe Trail trade as possible. Kearny sent out a call for volunteers to expand his force of three hundred army regulars, and before long he had ready some sixteen hundred eager men with artillery and a train of supplies. His Army of the West proceeded down the north route of the Santa Fe Trail, followed by Missouri merchants determined not to miss a season of trade.

The New Mexican three-time governor, Manuel Armijo, was in a quandary. Anglos had long resided in New Mexico, and there had been little conflict between the two peoples. But now Anglos were attacking Mexican national honor. The governor and his staff attempted to prepare panicky New Mexicans for the American onslaught. He enlisted four thousand volunteers, and announced plans to make a stand against the invaders at Apache Canyon, some fifteen miles east of Santa Fé. But after setting up camp and ordering his men to build defenses at the mouth of the canyon, Armijo precipitously called off the operation and fled south toward El Paso. Manuel Armijo has been accused of cowardice for fleeing an encounter with Colonel Kearny. In his defense, it must be observed that his militiamen were equipped with antiquated weapons, and were expected to confront an American force with modern weaponry; perhaps some informed the governor that they could not and would not fight, while others were bitter at not being well enough outfitted to fight. It is known that James Magoffin, a Santa Fe trader, acting as an emissary of the American government, met with Armijo in secret, but we have no record of what was said there. Magoffin may have convinced Armijo to abandon his defense of New Mexico, and perhaps offered the governor a bribe. In any case, his departure left Santa Fé undefended, and on August 18, 1846 La Villa de Santa Fé surrendered to the Army of the West.

Colonel Kearny was sorely in need of finding suitable pasturage in New Mexico for his livestock—horses, mules, and oxen. Where Missouri offered rich grazing, little suitable forage was to be found along the Santa Fe Trail. He dispersed his starving animals to feed throughout the Santa Fe region to Galisteo, San Miguel and Bernal Springs to the east, and then west to the "Delgado Ranch" in La Ciénega.

The first troops in La Ciénega Valley were assigned to K Company of the 2nd Missouri, regulars in the Army of the West under the command of Major "Bull" Sumner. Before long, their animals overgrazed the area. Next to come were the men of Major Meriwether Lewis Clark's Light Artillery with their emaciated dragoon horses and mules. All were cold and hungry. Foraging to feed the mounts and draft animals, and the low compensation to valley's inhabitants for damages generated many complaints. They had been assured by Kearny that nothing would be taken without payment. The camp was removed to Bent's Fort.

Complying with his mandate to take over New Mexico with as little disruption to life and trade as possible, Kearny, shortly to be promoted to the rank of Brigadier General, oversaw a smooth transition from Mexican to American rule. The American forces did not pillage or rape the local population, or attack

Catholic institutions as some had feared. To help inspire trust and confidence, Kearny attended Sunday Mass regularly. Within six weeks, he created a new political system to insure New Mexico's security and stability. Kearny appointed trader Charles Bent, resident of Taos and proprietor of Bent's Fort on the Río Napeste (Arkansas River), to the post of governor, designated other civil officials, and had lawyers compose a set of laws for the new American territory. The resultant Kearny Code was printed in Spanish and English, and widely distributed along with the United States Constitution. Then Kearny, believing all was well, moved across the Southwest to the Los Angeles basin where he, Kit Carson, and others were later to defeat the Californio Angelinos in the Battle of San Pascual, and Southern California was secured for the United States. In short order, U. S. naval Commander John Sloat, with seven frigates carrying marines, sailed into San Francisco Bay and annexed Northern California.

A visitor to the ranch of Manuel Baca y Delgado, Las Golondrinas, was Captain Philip S. George Cook, in command of General Kearny's Mormon Battalion. He recorded camping "at the picturesque rancho of Señor Vaca y Delgado, my old acquaintance."

On the monument in Santa Fe's plaza, dedicated to Steven Watts Kearny are inscribed these words: "In this plaza Gen. S. W. Kearny, U.S.A., proclaimed the peaceable annexation of New Mexico, Aug. 19, 1846." Spain had been the culturally powerful presence in New Mexico for more than two centuries when Mexico, along with the rest of Central and South America, successfully revolted. Then, for twenty-five years, New Mexico was part of the new nation of Mexico. When Colonel Sterling Price arrived in Santa Fe with reinforcements from Missouri, he found growing discontent with American rule. Proud New Mexicans resented the imposition of an alien power that too often made plain its contempt for them who were deemed indolent, fanatical and degenerate because of race mixing. New Mexican Indians, aware of the scornful Anglo attitude towards them, also had reason to reject American rule. Even so, some realized benefits were to be had by accepting reality.

Becoming aware of the mounting ferment, Colonel Price arrested some suspected rebel leaders in the capital, but could not avert the coming storm that came to be known as the Taos Rebellion of 1847. After Governor Bent returned home to Taos for Christmas, a force of Hispanics and Indians broke into his house early on the morning of January 9, 1847. There he was scalped alive, and his body riddled with bullets and arrows as his family escaped into an adjacent room through a hole frantically dug through the dirt wall with a fireplace poker and metal spoon.

> It was reported by Anita Thomas of Santa Fe, a descendant of slave owner José Francisco Baca y Terrus, that while Baca was a member of the Mexican legislature, he met in the home of her great-great-grandmother with a group to plot against Kearny and his occupation forces. Fiercely proud of his Mexican heritage, Baca y Terrus foresaw the whittling away of New Mexico's hard-won independence along with her wealth. When the coup d'état failed, and Baca y Terrus was not jailed or imprisoned, he withdrew from public life. When he left his position as alcalde of Santa Fe, he moved his entire household to his country home at Las Golondrinas. never relinquishing his Mexican citizenship. He eventually came to terms with being an American citizen, and was buried beneath the floor of El Santuario de Guadalupe along with other prominent leaders. Baca y Terrus was the grandson of rabble-rouser, Diego Manuel Baca, and the great-grandson of Old Miguel.

Another Anglo merchant and Bent's friend, Simeon Turley, the trader and entrepreneur who distilled the famous Taos Lightning whiskey, did not flee with other Americans, trusting that friendly relations with his Hispanic and Indian neighbors to keep him safe. A mob of three hundred men besieged his flourmill and distillery in Arroyo Hondo. Three Americans, including Turley, managed to escape in the swirling smoke of the fire set by the invaders. As Turley fled from his burning compound, an old-time friend persuaded him to hide in an abandoned *ranchito* until help arrived. There he was met with a deadly hail of bullets and arrows. More Americans in the region met with the same fate. When Colonel Price in Santa Fe heard of the death of Bent and other Americans, he swiftly marched north from Santa Fe with 353 soldiers and some mountain men, defeated rebel forces in Santa Cruz and Embudo, and encircled Taos Pueblo. The insurgent leaders took refuge inside the fortified mission church of San Geronimo de las Taos. On February 4, 1847 American troops, using howitzers positioned within sixty yards of the church to achieve crossfire, breached the three-foot thick *adobe* walls, and fired several rounds of grape shot into the hole at point blank range. The furious assault destroyed the church and inflicted a heavy loss of life on those seeking safety inside. Within two months, some 102 Americans and 318 Mexican and Indian allies were killed or wounded. The ruins of the mission church remain a mute testimony to the tragedy that took place behind the Taos Pueblo cemetery.

On February 6, Colonel Price convened a military court to try insurgents, and one, Pablo Montoya, quickly convicted of rebellion, was hanged the next day in the Taos Plaza. A civil trial then convened to try six men who were singled out and charged with the Bent murder, with George Bent, brother of Charles Bent, serving as foreman of the jury. The jury debated less than fifteen minutes before returning guilty verdicts for all six prisoners. Parish priest Antonio José Martínez, who strongly protested the verdicts, buried five on the day of the hanging.

Company K of Price's Regiment occupied La Ciénega after the Taos Insurrection. Private John Dunlop, a hospital steward assigned to the camp, found it "lovely." He "found it a great relief to be freed from the vices and debaucheries . . . of Santa Fe."

Lieutenant James Simpson, U. S. Army, observed that Manuel Baca y Delgado's ranch was an exception to the overgrazing in La Ciénega Valley. He wrote, "The face of the country today has presented, with some trifling exceptions—along the Río Grande, at Delgado's and between Agua Fria and Santa Fe—one extended barren waste of uncultivable soil."

Lieutenant James W. Abert, United States Topographical Army surveyor, surveyed the La Ciénega Valley while traveling in 1846 to record the many water sources, and the abundance of plant and animal life. He described La Ciénega as a thriving community. Passing again through the valley at Christmas time, he and his mule became mired in mud, and had to be extracted from their unfortunate situation. He almost missed the Christmas festivities in Santa Fe.

The word "treason" does not appear in the record of the first trial. But on March 8, a grand jury convened in Santa Fe to hear charges and returned indictments against four other men, the first being Antonio María Trujillo. He was summarily tried and sentenced to hang for "high treason against the government under which you are a citizen." He was hanged on April 16, 1847. For unknown reasons, the death sentences and the charges against the other three were dropped. Perhaps the court was influenced by Trujillo's attorney's eloquent defense that questioned the authority of the American court to try a Mexican citizen for treason. Trials of others continued, and by the end of April, four more New Mexicans and five Indian insurgents were hanged, bringing the total number of executions to fifteen. Meanwhile, Padre Martínez pleaded for a stop to what he called a vendetta. If the executions continued, he complained, no one would be left to plant the fields for the next harvest. Padre Martínez and other leading Hispanics signed a proclamation of loyalty to the United States in December, 1847. In tune with the changing times, the politically astute Martínez wisely chose to work for conciliation, and to act as intermediary between the warring factions.

A dissenting comment on the Taos Revolt by Robert Tórrez, former state historian, suggests a view of the 1847 events that differs sharply from the traditional interpretation. Rather than revolutionaries and traitors, he argues, the rebels can be regarded as Mexican patriots and martyrs who had fought in defense of their country.

> Governor William Carr Lane visited the estancia of Las Golondrinas in 1847. In his journal he recorded: "Halted at Las Golondrinas (The Swallows), the ranch of José Francisco Baca four leagues from Santa Fe and a good road, 12 miles, where we were hospitably entertained until the next day. The old general is seventy years of age and declines to marry again for fear his wife might injure him . . . . I ate and slept for the first time in a Mexican house. The old gentleman is very active—rides to Santa Fe always in an hour, and once did it in 26 minutes on a Mexican horse which he killed. I saw very fine cattle at his ranch and was told he kept stock winter and summer in the mountains."

The Mexican American War did not conclude until 1848 with the Treaty of Guadalupe Hidalgo, doubtless the most important document in the history of the modern Southwest. With the stroke of a pen, Mexican citizens became citizens of the United States. The treaty confirmed American claims to Texas, and ceded to the United States all the territory in the present states of New Mexico, Arizona, California, Nevada, Utah, and portions of Colorado and Wyoming. It also guaranteed the pre-existing rights of Mexican citizens, promising ". . . they shall be maintained, and protected in the free enjoyment of the liberty, property, and religion which they profess." In return, the United States paid Mexico

$15 million, and assumed $3,250,000 in claims of its citizens against Mexico. The treaty was ratified on March 10, 1848, but only after "a fair standard for adjudicating land grants" text was dropped from the text. This omission was later to cause any number of problems.

There remained the disputed boundary between Texas and New Mexico. In the Compromise of 1850, Texas received $10 million from the United States to surrender its claims to territory west to the Río Grande River in New Mexico, and to abandon other claims that stretched into Oklahoma, Kansas, and Wyoming. Three years later, the Gadsden Purchase of 1853 acquired for the United States another thirty thousand square miles of land in southern New Mexico and Arizona in return for payment of $10 million to cash-strapped Mexico. The need for a practical route for a projected southern transcontinental railroad was the primary motive for this acquisition. Thus did the United States reach from sea-to-sea.

New Mexican fears of United States mistreatment of the newly acquired territory and its former Mexican citizens were soon justified. When Congress voted to make New Mexico a territory, it stipulated Congress must approve all laws enacted by the territorial legislature, a condition never imposed on any other territory. The civil and military governor, Colonel Munroe, argued that ". . . unstable elements of the Mexican character, the general ignorance of the people, . . . and the strong sympathies a large number entertain for Mexican institutions and its government as opposed to that of the United States . . . ," rendered the territory unfit for self-governance and statehood. By contrast, California was admitted as a state in 1850. The majority of California's Hispanics were overwhelmed by twelve times their number when Americans rushed to the Sacramento gold fields seeking fortunes.

Now subject to American law, Hispanic women lost rights they had enjoyed under Spanish and Mexican rule including the right to inherit property, to retain property brought to a marriage, to serve as guardians for their children, and to control their own earnings. New Mexican men were denied voting rights until January 6, 1912 when New Mexico was finally admitted as the 47th state to the Union. Arizona, which had been part of the New Mexico Territory, was admitted one month later on February 14 as the 48th state. New Mexico's women were franchised to vote in 1920. New Mexico's Indians were declared citizens of the United States in 1924, but were not granted suffrage until 1948, although under Mexican rule they had enjoyed the rights of Mexican citizenship since 1824.

The major grievance of Hispanics concerned their land rights, rights that were specifically guaranteed by the Treaty of Guadalupe Hidalgo. Claiming these titles were "imperfect," U. S. courts ruled that the U. S. government had the right to adjudicate them. In effect, New Mexican residents were assumed to be guilty of land fraud until they could prove otherwise. Anglo squatters, sometimes acting on behalf of moneyed interests, used the disorder to surreptitiously occupy Hispanic properties. The limited understanding by Hispanics of the new legal system and the high cost of litigation played into the hands of a fraternity of predatory lawyers, speculators, and politicians known as the Santa Fe Ring, who soon forced many off their lands. Thomas B. Catron, Missouri lawyer, Confederate army veteran, and protégé of business man Stephen B. Elkins, was one of the apparent leaders of the Santa Fe Ring. Catron became New Mexico's first United States senator. His vast holdings included 593,000 acres of the Tierra Amarilla Grant in northern New Mexico and Southern Colorado, and 240,000 acres of the Mora Grant on the eastern flank of the Sangre de Cristo mountain range. By the 1880s, Catron owned more land than anyone else in the United States. The struggle of Hispanics to regain their ancestral lands continues to this day. Title fights fester, and other disputes over water and mineral rights remain unresolved.

The Kearny Code, enacted in 1848, introduced new concepts of jurisprudence, many of them punitive. The code provided for the establishment of the jury system, and for capital punishment. New Mexico jails were now meant for detention while cases were being tried, and wrongdoers were subject to jail sentences. Previously, there were no jails capable of incarcerating prisoners with the exception of a small detention facility in the Palace of the Governors in Santa Fe prior to the American invasion. They were considered a waste of public money. "A prisoner in an *adobe* jail, with a spoon and time on his hands would be out of there in no time," says Robert Tórrez. As an alternative to jail sentences, prisoners were often let out for wages, and the earnings paid off fines or compensated victims. Corporal punishment, and sometimes exile, had been the preferred means of dealing with serious offenders.

Between 1852 and 1928, reflecting a new punitive and vengeful spirit, one hundred and forty-four lynchings took place. There were so many hangings in the quarrelsome town of Las Vegas that the windmill used as the favorite hanging site was torn down, not because of opposition to public executions, but because it had become a "public nuisance." Citizens complained the sight of so many dangling bodies created a bad image, threatening capital investment. Contrary to tradition, there is no case on record of anyone being hanged for the crime of stealing horses or other livestock. The execution of Black Jack Ketchum for train robbery was the only incidence of hanging for an offense other than first-degree murder. However, there were many extra-legal lynchings at the hands of vigilante groups that resulted in hanging. Most legal hangings took place between 1876 and 1885. Legal executions were public spectacles, and trains were charted to bring in the curious.

Western Justice Player measures gunslinger for his coffin

The American Civil War

The issue of slavery that polarized Americans in both the North and South, and caused the Civil War, aroused little interest in New Mexico. Although the Confederacy dreamed of creating a slaveholding empire that expanded from Texas to the Pacific, New Mexico had few black slaves. In fact, slavery of blacks was not viable in a region with so little agriculture and plenty of cheap native labor. Most of the Southern sympathizers were ranchers from Texas who had settled in the Mesilla Valley in the south of New Mexican territory. Confederate military planners were deluded in thinking that New Mexicans would support secession, that a Confederate army could live off of the land, that the common border between Texas and New Mexico made their union inevitable, and that the region was so remote that the Union could offer little or no military assistance. The Confederacy coveted the rich gold fields in California, the gold and silver mines in Colorado, and needed New Mexico as a transit route to Lower California's harbors and ports, making the Confederacy a sea-to-sea power. Unlike the Atlantic and Gulf of Mexico ports, they were not under Union blockade.

In what was truly a quixotic venture, a regiment of the Texas Mounted Volunteers with 350 recruits under the command of Lieutenant Colonel John R. Baylor marched on El Paso in 1862 and occupied Fort Bliss. Soon, near present-day Las Cruces, Baylor forced an outnumbered company of Union troops to surrender. Meanwhile, Confederate President Jefferson Davis authorized the West Pointer Henry H. Sibley to raise an army of Texans in order to seize the Union forts in upper New Mexico and the gold fields of Colorado. Sibley managed to attract twenty-six hundred men to form three regiments. The plans were to move north from El Paso and Mesilla, attracting sympathetic volunteers along the way, take the Union-held forts in Northern New Mexico, seize the Colorado gold fields, and then pursue the gold in California. The Confederates did not realize that New Mexicans had long memories. New Mexicans had not forgiven the Texan invasion of 1841, nor had they forgotten more recent incursions. *Tejano* (Texan) was a detested word. The Confederates assumed that the Indians would become their allies. In fact, the Plains Tribes took note of the fact that Americans were fighting amongst themselves, took no sides in the conflict, moved to settle old grudges, and pursued their own interests.

Meanwhile, Union commander Colonel Edward R. S. Canby prepared to repel the Confederate menace, and with outnumbered, poorly trained regular troops and dispirited native militia, he headquartered at Fort Craig just below Socorro on the Rio Grande. With him was Colonel Kit Carson, who had traveled from his home in Taos to join in the fight. Confederate General Sibley forced Union commander Canby to leave the safety of Fort Craig and engage his troops at the Valverde Ford. A fierce battle ensued, but Sibley failed to carry the day. Canby held the fort, and the Confederates were forced to bypass the enemy as they pressed on toward Albuquerque, planning to return later to finish off Fort Craig.

Rebel charge, Battle of Glorieta Pass re-enactors

Historian Marc Simmons relates in his *New Mexico: An Interpretive History* an incident that occurred in the bloody battle at the Valverde Ford. A Union officer selected two sorry old mules, loaded them with wooden crates filled of howitzer shells, and with three men under cover of darkness, slipped across the river toward the Confederate camp. There they lit the fuses, slapped the mules on their rumps intending to send them through the sleeping enemy, and beat a hasty retreat. The party did not reckon with the homing instinct of mules, and the surprised saboteurs found themselves being followed by the combustible pair. The panicked foursome raced for camp, and was barely out of range when the ensuing blast woke every man on both sides of the river. The casualty count was two dead mules.

Federal troops in Albuquerque's supply depot, hearing of the impending Confederate onslaught, burned what military stores they could not carry north with them. The Rebels captured the Cubero military post west on the Navajo frontier where supplies intended for an Indian campaign were stored. With seized Union supplies, the rebels moved northward. Meanwhile local citizens, responding to a plea by New Mexican Governor Henry Connelly, provided him with volunteers, mules, supplies, and money.

What Sibley did not know was that the Colorado Volunteers had traversed Ratón Pass with two batteries of artillery, and had arrived at Fort Union on the Santa Fe Trail. The fort housed thirteen hundred Federal troops under the command of Colonel John Slough. There they were joined by a nervous Governor Henry Connelly, other territorial officials, and the small garrison from Fort Marcy. Despite these reinforcements, the situation did not look rosy for the Union.

After hearing of the Confederate offensive threatening Albuquerque, on March 10, 1862 Governor Henry Connelly evacuated his staff and the Union troops at Fort Marcy, and relocated all at Las Vegas. Supplies and equipment were taken to Ft. Union. The Confederates marched into undefended Santa Fe, and for more than two weeks, the Confederate flag flew over the Palace of the Governors.

The turning point in the campaign to conquer the Southwest, and a major setback for the Confederate cause, came at Glorieta Pass. The battle, known as the Gettysburg of the West, was the death knell for Confederate ambitions in the Southwest. The pass lies three miles east of Apache Canyon, the same corridor left undefended by General Armijo when Colonel Kearny came down the Santa Fe Trail a decade and a half before. Confederate forces intended to take Fort Union, and open up the way to Colorado and its gold fields. Slough was ordered by Colonel Canby to protect Fort Union at all costs, but not to initiate a major battle. Slough decided that the best spot from which to defend the fort would be on the Santa Fe Trail. He dispatched an advance party of 430 Colorado Volunteers under the command of Major John M. Chivington. There on March 26, 1862 Chivington confronted Major Charles Pyron and four hundred Confederates scouting the western end of Glorieta Pass at Apache Canyon. Chivington attacked and drove the Confederates back down the canyon, but then withdrew to Kozlowski's Ranch near the Pecos

Pueblo Ruins out of concern that the entire Confederate brigade was near at hand at Pigeon's Ranch. It was not long before two battalions of Confederates from Galisteo, under the command of Lieutenant Colonel William "Dirty Shirt" Scurry, marched through a bitter night to reinforce Major Pyron. Meanwhile, Slough and Chivington planned their assault at Kozlowski's Ranch. The strategy called for Slough on March 28 to take two-thirds of the Union troops and its artillery west toward Santa Fe. Meanwhile Chivington would lead his men over Glorieta Mesa, and charge the Confederate rear guard.

Scurry proceeded with his force eastward along the Santa Fe Trail. He left his supply wagons at Johnson's Ranch at the junction of Glorieta Pass and Apache Canyon, now known as Cañoncito, and moved onward to engage Slough's forces at Pigeon's Ranch. The brutal conflict, known as The Battle of Glorieta Pass, lasted for six hours before Slough forsook his position.

Casualties of war, Battle of Glorieta Pass re-enactors

The Confederates won the day, but victory turned into defeat when Chivington and his Colorado Volunteers located the poorly defended Confederate supply train at Cañoncito. Chivington's men surprised the Confederate guard, burned sixty-four wagons, and slaughtered hundreds of horses and mules. Now Sibley and his Texas Volunteers confronted the problem of being faced with the Colorado Volunteers and the other Union troops with their troop supplies destroyed.

He could do nothing but retreat through Galisteo and on to Albuquerque, where the rebels once again engaged Canby and his Union troops, this time in a half-hearted scuffle. As the Sibley Brigade fled New Mexico, foraging off the land and seizing whatever foodstuffs they could find, their dreams of glorious victory and an empire in the West turned into smoke.

The only remaining building at Pigeon's Ranch has a bit of poetry scribbled on the interior wall of the main house. It reads:

"Where men live raw in the desert maw
And death was nothing to shun
Where they buried 'em neat
without preacher or sheet but sweet
And writ on their tombstone crude
This Jasper was slow with his gun."

In 1987, Kip Siler discovered a Civil War graveyard on his Cañoncito property. Authorities exhumed thirty-one bodies of Confederate Soldiers killed in battle, and most were re-interred at the National Cemetery in Santa Fe. The Battle of Glorieta Pass site, now part of Pecos National Historical Park, is open to the public.

The Battle of Glorieta Pass is again staged at El Rancho de las Golondrinas every May when The New Mexico Civil War Commemorative Congress re-enactors stage artillery and marching demonstrations, replicate camp life, and hold mock Union and Confederate skirmishes.

Nazario Gonzáles, of one of New Mexico's oldest families and a member of the successful mercantile firm, Perea Company, married María Rita Baca y Terrus. María was born at Las Golondrinas and was listed in the 1821 census of La Ciénega. Nazario held several political offices, served in the American Civil War, and rose to the rank of lieutenant colonel in New Mexico's territorial militia.

A little known incident of Taos history still resonates today. Shortly after Fort Sumter surrendered to Confederate forces in April, 1861 Colonel Kit Carson, Captain Smith H. Simpson, and several others stood guard around-the-clock to prevent Confederate sympathizers from tearing down the Union flag flying over the Taos plaza, intending to raise the Confederate banner in its stead. Carson commanded the First New Mexico Cavalry Volunteers at that time. Out of respect for what happened there so long ago, the U. S. Congress later granted permission to fly the flag in the Taos plaza day and night without benefit of illumination.

Post American Civil War

The end of the Civil War did not bring peace to the Southwest. In 1848, the United States annexed the Mexican Cessions, the territory of present-day California, Nevada, Utah, Arizona, New Mexico, and part of Colorado. The Plains Indians' way of life, based on hunting and raiding, came into direct conflict with white settlers. In 1862, Brigadier General James Carlton replaced Colonel Edward Canby as commander of the Military Department of New Mexico. He was to wage relentless wars against all hostile tribes to force them onto reservations where they were to be Christianized and taught to farm. Because his first attempts at relocating the Navajo were not successful, Carlton came to determine that total war was necessary to bring the pastoral but hostile Navajo under control. The devastating Navajo raids on New Mexican settlements had to be stopped.

Soon a policy was implemented to relocate the Apache and the Navajo. Under orders from Carlton, the Mescalero Apache, in the southeast quarter of New Mexico, were the first to be forcibly relocated by Lieutenant Colonel Kit Carson. When Kit Carson was assigned the task, he asked several times to be relieved. He did not agree with Carlson's policy of unconditional surrender or annihilation. He accepted the assignment, however, hoping that his involvement might help mitigate the state of affairs. Carson's troops criss-crossed the Navajo territory, and relentlessly destroyed the Navajo economy, with its livestock, gardens and orchards. Many Navajo, starving and exhausted, retreated into the canyons of Canyon de Chelly, and there in bitter cold, found themselves facing Carson's troops. Convinced by Carson that it was better to surrender than face annihilation, the Navajo capitulated. He brought some four hundred warriors and their families to the Bosque Redondo Reservation on the lower Pecos River in 1863. The captives made the "Long Walk" to an inhospitable place where they were forced to live side by side with the Apache, their traditional enemies. Carson resigned his post in disgust after seeing the appalling conditions that developed in the concentration camp.

When Bishop Lamy visited, hoping to open a parochial school, he was equally appalled by the squalor and disease he witnessed. The agony, known by the Navajo as the *hweeldi* (Navajo suffering), ended in 1868 when they were allowed to return to their homeland, now a reservation. One-third of the nine thousand Navajos held captive died, in part because of the nine hundred mile roundtrip they were forced to march. The Mescalero Apache resumed the old pattern of raiding, but were eventually confined to a Sacramento Mountains reservation in Southeastern New Mexico in 1879. The Plains Indians, the Comanche, Kiowa, Cheyenne and Arapahoe, continued to threaten the Santa Fe Trail until 1874, when the United States cavalry units converged in the Texas Panhandle to harass the Indians into submission. There the nomads agreed to be confined to reservations in the Indian Territory of Oklahoma.

Once the Great Plains region was safe, an eastern New Mexican ranching economy began to supplant the traditional sheep industry. The great cattle drives of Charles Goodnight and Oliver Loving blazed the famous Goodnight-Loving Trail through New Mexico, the first herd of longhorns being driven north in 1866. The pair made a round-up of Texas beef cattle that had roamed free during the American Civil War, and drove their herds from Texas to New Mexico to feed military post personnel. What stock was not sold was trailed north into Colorado where gold miners provided a lucrative market. The remainder was driven to Montana to stock rangeland. Disputed land titles allowed Texas cattlemen to lay claim to vast areas of New Mexican territory and control the water supply, provoking conflict with settlers who wanted to farm on small plots with water rights. Some large Anglo ranches extended for thirty to forty square miles. The opportunity to rustle cattle appealed to Eastern migrants fearing prosecution back home for a variety of offences, and Hispanics enjoyed taking a few head now and then from the detested *Tejanos*. Cattle rustling became a growth industry, adding to the problems caused by Indians raiding for horses to use in trade.

Apache bands under Chief Victorio bolted from their reservation in 1879, and waged war across from the Río Grande into Arizona until his death in 1881. Nana, Geronimo's near blind and crippled son-in-law, continued to war in Victorio's place. Nana won eight battles before he and his warriors surrendered at the eastern Arizona San Carlos Reservation. Geronimo, the quintessential Apache War Chief and his warriors, had one last hurrah in 1885—they raided until forced to surrender the following year. Geronimo and 498 Chiricahua men, women, and children were forced into exile in the swamps of Florida to live out the rest of their lives. Geronimo was returned to Fort Sill, Oklahoma where he died in 1909 as a United States prisoner of war. The Indian Wars came to an end in 1886 and the eastern plains of New Mexico were thrown open to settlement.

The great herds of buffalo that roamed the Great Plains were soon decimated. Anglos indiscriminately hunted the great beasts to take hides and choice parts, leaving the rest of the carcasses to rot. Deliberate slaughter by the U. S. military, intended to destroy the economy of the Plains nomads, contributed to the destruction of the herds. The last Comanche buffalo hunt took place in 1879 when the Comanches faced starvation. Provisions promised by the U. S. government failed to arrive. No herds were found, and a battalion of Texans killed and scalped one hunter. The amity New Mexicans and Comanche had enjoyed since the days of Governor Juan Bautista de Anza was shattered, and the *comanchero* trade was dead.

14

The Long and Painful Road to Statehood

**Padre Martínez and Bishop Lamy—The Coming of the Railroad
—Cultural and Emotional Ties—El Rancho de las Golondrinas
—A Living History Museum**

Padre Martínez and Bishop Lamy

The life of the celebrated Padre Antonio José Martínez of Taos, whose role in the Taos Rebellion of 1847 was mentioned earlier, spanned the Spanish, Mexican, and American periods of New Mexico's history. Padre Martínez was a champion of Hispanic interests in the troubled period after the Mexican-American War. Born in Abiquiú in 1792, he learned "to read correctly, write, and do some arithmetic" by age five. Little else is known of his early schooling. At age nineteen, Don Severino, Antonio's father, arranged for his marriage to María de la Luz Martín of Abiquiú. María died in childbirth fourteen months later, leaving a daughter who died at the age of twelve. At age twenty-four, Antonio José entered the Tridentine Monastery in Durango, Mexico on a scholarship, a stroke of luck since financial help was beyond the means of most families. Martínez returned to New Mexico as an ordained *cura* (clergy), and a well-educated and widely read priest who excelled in canon law. He traveled to Taos where his parents then lived, and commenced his ministry.

Active in politics, he exhorted Mexican President Santa Anna to implement a humane, enlightened policy for the Southwest's nomadic Indians. The Chimayó Rebellion of 1837 may have contributed to the foundation of his liberal political views. Padre Martínez worked to meet the religious needs of the community through the institutional church, and through the grass roots lay organization, La Hermandad de Nuestro Padre Jesús Nazareno, the Brotherhood of Our Lord Jesus Christ the Nazarene. At his death, these Penitentes gave Martínez a hero's funeral.

Devoted to the promotion of education and learning, Padre Martínez took advantage of a recently arrived printing press, the first in New Mexico, to publish religious and educational materials for his school that enrolled both sexes, a rare practice. The small hand press was imported from Durango, Mexico by Santiago Baca y Ortiz at the request of Ramón Abreú. Padre Martínez brought the son of Baca y Ortiz, Jesús María Baca, to Taos to operate the press. The prelate published the first provincial newspaper, *El Crepúsculo de la Libertad,* The Dawn of Liberty. It had fifty subscribers and survived but one month, most likely because there were too few persons who could read. Martínez subsequently published primers and catechisms for use in primary education.

In his capacity as priest and public man, Padre Martínez confronted two sets of problems. One arose from the new political, economic, and social order in New Mexico following the Mexican-American and American Civil Wars. Another was linked to the arrival of the young French cleric, Jean Baptise Lamy, modern, zealous, and strict in matters of the Faith. He was the first cleric to be appointed by the American Catholic Church rather than by the Spanish or Mexican Church in Durango, Mexico. The two clergymen differed radically on the proper role and rights of native clergy, the interpretation of canon law, and the issue of imposed tithing which Martínez wished to be voluntary. These differences may have been compounded by Lamy's less than adequate Spanish because he had to learn the language upon arrival at his post. Lamy was appointed by the Vatican as the first Bishop of Santa Fe in 1851, and became Archbishop in 1875. The strife between the two adversaries became so heated that Lamy excommunicated Martínez in 1857. But Padre Martínez placidly ignored the Bishop's act, and continued to serve as the priest of Taos until his death in 1867.

Padre Martínez had other bitter enemies. They included Governor Charles Bent, the trader's brothers George and William, and the influential French traders, Charles Beaubien and Céran St. Vrain. Martínez' defense of his parishioners against what he saw as grasping business practices of some Americans undoubtedly contributed to those enmities. Bent and his colleagues, Beaubien and Guadalupe Miranda, acquired the huge Maxwell Land Grant along the Cimarron and Canadian Rivers by means that Martínez considered illegal. Martínez suspected Bent for aiding American smugglers on the Santa Fe Trail, of conspiring to promote Texas claims to New Mexican territory, and of selling guns and alcohol to the Indians from his fort on the Arkansas River. Resentment provoked by these issues no doubt contributed to the January 18, 1847 Taos massacre of Governor Bent and other Americans.

Bishop Lamy's dislike of Martínez carried over to the French priests he brought to assist in his campaign to reform the New Mexican Catholic Church. Like Lamy, they denounced the threats to the church and public morality that Padre Martínez supposedly posed. Their most serious charges against the Taos priest alleged he had violated his vow of celibacy. When Severino Martínez's valuable Taos estate was settled a decade after the priest's death, many purported Martínez heirs filed claims professing to be his direct descendants. The archives of the Archdiocese, however, which recorded other charges of Martínez's alleged failures and transgressions, often in great detail, do not contain a single reference to his alleged immoral conduct. The rumors, charges, and circumstantial evidence gathered from questionable baptismal records, suggesting he had fathered one or more natural child, sufficed to cast an enduring cloud over his historical image.

In her 1927 novel, *Death Comes for the Archbishop*, Pulitzer prize-winning author Willa Cather contributed to the making of Padre Martín's negative image. The novel portrays Lamy in the person of its fictional hero, Father Latour, as an introverted, private man, hardly the energetic, serious, and goal-oriented person he was in reality. Father Martínez, on the other hand, is depicted as the embodiment of evil. In her opening chapter Cather assigns to Latour the comment that "He [Father Vaillant, Lamy's real life vicar apostolic, Joseph Machebeuf] will be called upon for every sacrifice, quite possibly martyrdom. Only last year the Indian pueblo of San Fernandez de Taos murdered and scalped the American Governor and some dozen other whites. The reason they did not scalp their Padre, was that their Padre was one of the leaders of the rebellion and [he] himself planned the massacre. This is how things stand in New Mexico!" Another character in the novel volunteers, "Our Padre Martínez of Taos is an old scapegrace, if ever there was one; he's got children and grandchildren in almost every settlement around here." Unfortunately the novel, so well written and persuasive, leaves many readers ignorant of its weak factual base. As a result, they are left with distorted images of both Lamy and Martínez, and of their legacies.

What are the facts in the Martínez-Lamy dispute? The puritanical bishop had hardly arrived in Santa Fe when he set about imposing a strict discipline on the local priests. The cheerful convivial lifestyle of some native clergy scandalized Lamy and many Americans in New Mexico. Lamy, moreover, was convinced that the rustic architecture and iconography of the medieval Hispanic church was archaic and unsuited to the times. He wanted to replace the revered old edifices and religious art with European Romanesque architecture and baroque plaster images of the saints. On the other hand, many Hispanics regarded Lamy's religious reforms as an attack on New Mexico's unique, deeply rooted Catholicism. Undoubtedly Padre Martínez was a leading critic of Lamy's efforts at reform and reconstruction. Due to his tenacity, the permissive attitude of Hispanics and that of their priests underwent a change. Eventually, the energetic, resolute bishop was successful in introducing many reforms.

> José Vieira, who emigrated from the Azores, built the Vieira house at what is now Sunrise Springs Inn and Retreat, a parcel once in part owned by John Lamy, a nephew of the Archbishop. John planted fruit trees imported from France which helped the agricultural economy of the Cienega Valley. José married Carmelita Gonzáles Pino, daughter of Cleofita and Germán Pino; the couple was John Lamy's next door neighbors.

Archbishop Michael Sheehan arrives to say Mass

The old *adobe parroquía* at Santa Fé, which had served Santa Fé parishioners since 1717, was deemed by Lamy unsuitable for an Episcopal residence. In 1869, Lamy began constructing a new cathedral around the ancient *parroquía*; the new edifice was of native limestone in the Romanesque-Revival architectural tradition of Byzantium and ancient Rome. Lamy imported European tradespeople as local artisans had no experience with new building materials and technology. The facade was to support two towers, each one hundred feet in height, but they were never finished, most likely because money was scarce. The dome was to reach a height of eighty-five feet, and the nave to measure two hundred feet in length. The only part of the old *adobe* structure that remains is the ancient Our Lady Chapel where the revered image of La Conquistadora resides. The Diocese of Santa Fe was elevated to an archdiocese in 1875 with Bishop Lamy as its first Archbishop. He died in 1888, and was interred under the sanctuary floor of his new cathedral. The impressive edifice was renamed the Cathedral Basilica of Saint Francis of Assisi by Pope Benedict XVI on October 4, 2005.

Education and Statehood

In 1855, W.W.H. Davis estimated that 40 percent of the sixty thousand residents in New Mexico could not read or write. Earlier private subscription schools existed, and were financed and administrated by concerned families with negligible impact. Some became the religious schools of the 1850s and 1860s. Most New Mexicans of the time had little use for formal education. Reading and writing was considered the limited province of officials, their clerks, and the priests. A referendum put to qualified voters in 1856 proposed a per capita tax of one dollar per year to fund public education. The assessment was soundly defeated with seventeen voting in favor and 5,038 persons opposed. Franciscan schools, placed under secular management after the Order's departure, were short of income, and their educational facilities deteriorated. New Mexicans doubtless feared a secular public school system would threaten their own parochial instruction, and priests campaigned against such a move. Not least of the concerns was the increased emphasis on the English language. There was a decline in literacy after the Mexican American War until about 1870.

Bishop Lamy may be credited with introducing the first true system of religious education in New Mexico. Considering the sorry state of education when Lamy began his campaign of reform, one must conclude amelioration was needed, and that his endeavors met with success. In a few years Bishop Lamy established a working system of parochial schools. Before long, the Bishop had five hundred pupils enrolled in Santa Fe. Established in 1853, the Loretto Academy of Our Lady of Light was staffed by nuns from St. Louis, and soon had to expand its facilities. Lamy went on to found St. Michael the Archangel's College at Santa Fe, now Santa Fe University of Art and Design, and St. Michael's High School, employing the newly arrived Christian Brothers as staff. Its curriculum was oriented to the culture and language of the new American territory.

Between 1850 and 1891, New Mexican Catholics and Anglo-Americans disagreed over the issue of public education. Catholics wanted to preserve their culture, language, and the status quo. Before long, Lamy obtained the services of the Society of Jesus (Jesuits), another teaching order. Jesuits continued to teach in public schools in New Mexico and Colorado with Catholic textbooks since no others were available; public funding of sectarian schools was rejected.

An article appeared in the June 7, 1877 issue of the *Daily New Mexican*. The reporter relates that some sixty students, along with faculty from St. Michael's College, were off "for a frolic" to Las Golondrinas. The wagon train, laden with students, merry-making provisions with an ample supply of beer, two clergy, and a reporter, arrived in time for supper. All were to spend the night in bedrolls under the stars. Nazario Gonzáles arrived to invite the two chaperons and the reporter to the comfort of his home, a more commodious accommodation. The morning 6 o'clock toll of the bell of the Church of St. Joseph in La Ciénega called the party to Mass. Returning to camp, the boys appeared to have lost considerable sleep after their "Roman howl," blankets serving for togas the evening before. A spirited game of football and other "youthful" sports finished off the holiday at Las Golondrinas.

Anglos viewed the American common school as the primary means of promoting their democratic institutions. Protestant denominations developed missionary programs to create parochial schools that taught children to read and write in English so they could study the Bible; missionaries used this wedge to convert Catholic students to Protestantism. The Presbyterians alone had some fifty "plaza schools" from Colorado south to Socorro, New Mexico. Education became a pawn in the struggle for cultural and political power in New Mexico.

The endeavor intensified in 1872 and again in 1888 when constitutional conventions were held to consider statehood. The proposed constitution, nonsectarian public education, and statehood were all rejected. Finally, in February of 1891, the legislature approved "An Act Establishing Common Schools in the Territory of New Mexico." Public schools were to be free and nonsectarian, and English the official language. When Congress enacted the Cyber-Morrell Act of 1887, the western Homestead Act that opened territories to settlement, it stipulated two sections out of each township be reserved to fund public education. The Ferguson Act of 1891 endowed each state with a land grant college. The number of public school students increased from 29,312 in 1870 to 54,820 and in 1890, the number doubled. Today's New Mexico public education system is partly financed from revenue earned by leasing the public lands set aside by the Act of 1887, and from oil revenues generated from these lands.

The coming of the railroad, and the resulting growth of commerce, gave a stimulus to public education. When men came to work on the railroad, they brought children who needed to be educated. After the Atchison, Topeka, and Santa Fe Railroad came over Ratón Pass in 1878, the one-room cabin on the corner of Savage Avenue and North Forth Street in Ratón became La Escuela de Ratón (Ratón School), a subscription school operated by Miss Belle McArthur to teach children in the growing community. Two years later when a public school was built, the one-room school house became a private residence with another room added to increase living space. Eventually the school fell into disrepair, and the owner, Delores Noel, donated the building to El Rancho de las Golondrinas in honor of her mother, Ida Atwater. Today, visiting children are invited to sit in the diminutive desks with slate board and chalk to learn how education was dispensed in a one-room school. There is a small library in one corner, and a stool with a dunce cap awaits a reluctant learner. Across the lane, the visitor will find willow bushes, the kind used to provide switches to punish youngsters for infractions of school rules.

One of the first owners, and possibly the builder, of the cabin later converted to the Ratón School House was Buck Foster, a gunslinger, stage coach driver and gambler. Foster was shot and killed by a farmer with whom he was quarreling. Belle McArthur, 1881–1882, was the teacher for the subscription school in Ratón. The building was abandoned two years later when the public school was built.

Ratón subscription school

The Coming of the Railroad

From 1849 until the arrival of the railroads in 1879, stagecoaches were the only regular means of public transportation. Before the coming of the railroad, travel on the Santa Fe Trail from Missouri to Santa Fe was possible only seasonally, and would take from thirteen days to a month. But after the railroad arrived, a few days travel any time of year sufficed. Passengers bought one-way tickets from Independence, Missouri to Santa Fe for $250. After the railroad tracks were laid and service begun, stagecoaches continued in use as feeder lines to meet passenger and freight trains. The coaches carried mail to points the railroads could not reach, and delivered express packages to the frontier. As late as 1882, thirty-eight New Mexican stage lines brought passengers from remote areas to rail towns until the arrival of the automobile.

María Cleofas Gonzáles and Germán Pino, whose combined properties made them some of the wealthiest citizens of the Ciénega Valley, were noted for their generous hospitality and gracious parties given at the former paraje, El Alamo. Nicolas de Jesús Pino, Germán's father, once operated a stagecoach station on Bonanza Creek.

A sister of Cleofas, Elvina, was persuaded to marry widower Andres C' de Baca in order to help raise his five motherless children. Although of modest means initially, through his two marriages, Andres acquired a portion of the Gonzáles estate that included land and forty thousand sheep.

The U. S. military continued to rely on commercial stage lines for communication and transport between its remote posts. They also supplied cavalry units that protected the routes. But change could not be denied; traditional patterns of settlement that restricted life and economic activity to the Rio Grande River valley gave way to denser populations along railroad tracks. Ratón, Deming, Gallup, and Las Vegas came into their own.

The Atchison, Topeka and Santa Fe Railroad (AT&SF) was the first to lay tracks into New Mexico, and became the primary carrier. The now venerable railroad was not only responsible for a wave of immigrants, inexpensive freight, and new opportunities, it was accountable for the rise of art colonies in Santa Fe and Taos. In an effort to promote the yet untapped tourist travel, William Haskell Simpson, the advertizing genius for the AT&SF, began sponsoring artists for three-to-four week expense-paid excursions to the Southwest to capture the region's grandeur and unique cultures on canvas. In return, Simpson retained the rights to reproduce selected art works for promotional use on calendars, in eastern hotel vestibules, rail stations, bank lobbies, and other venues. Many artists determined to stay in the West once they experienced New Mexico's majestic skies and vistas.

The story of the race between the Atchison, Topeka, and Santa Fe and the Denver and Rio Grande (D&RG) railroads is the stuff of Wild West legends; the D&RG originated in Colorado, the AT&SF from Kansas. The most direct route for the rail lines to come into New Mexico was by way of Ratón Pass in the northeastern part of the state. The first railroad to begin construction through the pass would own the right-of-way. Because of natural and man-made disasters, violence and intrigue, the AT&SF found the going slow. As the construction crew neared the pass, it observed the rival D&RG rapidly gaining on them. An AT&SF engineer, disguised as a shepherd, explored the pass under the very noses of the D&RG surveyors. The two railroad companies were in a dead heat when on March 1, 1878 just hours ahead of the rival crew, the AT&SF team crashed a community dance party at midnight, and pressed partygoers into service. The D&RG team, arriving at daylight to lay track, was dumfounded to find men and women, clad in festive clothes, swinging picks and shovels. The first AT&SF locomotive crossed over the summit of Ratón Pass on the bright December 7, 1878 afternoon.

> Amiel Weeks Whipple, Union army officer, was chosen by the United States War Department to direct the survey of a possible transcontinental railroad route along the thirty-fifth parallel from Fort Smith, Arkansas, to Los Angeles. He visited La Ciénega in 1853 where he recorded a tranquil village set in a valley with well watered and manicured fields, houses, a church, and a torreón. He noted a wagon trail referred to by villagers as El Camino Real de Tierra Adentro.

When the railroad came, the hamlet of Willow Springs was transformed into the bustling railroad center of Ratón, complete with a roundhouse. The rail yards became the center of commercial activity, and many small rail lines connected at Ratón to transport coal. The rails replaced the Chisholm, Texas, and the Goodnight-Loving Trails along which cattle had been driven to markets. Cattle and sheep ranches were commercially linked to markets back East. The town of East Las Vegas soon provided the necessary repair facilities for the railroad. An eighteen mile spur to the southeast connected Santa Fe to the mainline at the hamlet of Lamy.

Other railroads soon crisscrossed New Mexico. The D & RG laid track south along the Rio Grande, past Isleta Pueblo, and on to Los Lunas, where the D&RG built a southern plantation style mansion for Solomon Luna in return for a right-of-way through his vast family holdings. He was the largest individual sheep baron in the Southwest, and one of New Mexico's richest citizens. The railroad continued on the old Chihuahua Trail south with a link to the Southern Pacific Railroad at Deming. Soon a second transcontinental rail line connected the AT&SF with the Southern Pacific at Deming. Communications expanded with the installation of the telegraph that accompanied railroad construction. Telephone service soon followed. Las Vegas had the first telephone exchange installed in 1881, and Santa Fe followed in 1894, but long-distance service was not available until 1905.

Montgomery Ward printed the world's first mail order catalog in 1875-1876, a new way of marketing in New Mexico. Sears-Roebuck, with its own catalog, soon began shipping mail order goods to the underserved market. Prefabricated buildings were freighted in by railroad and constructed on site. New building materials were imported to construct splendid homes; the Victorian architecture of old Las Vegas and Ratón reflects the trend. Professional and business people saw the economic potential in New Mexico, and came in increasing numbers to the territory. They included Jewish businessmen sometimes looking for opportunities, some fleeing persecution in Europe. The scenery, the climate, and the romance of the western frontier attracted growing numbers of tourists. Fascinated New Mexicans watched the rapid changes brought by the railroads, and some were appalled by the passing of the old ways.

The Twentieth Century

The twentieth century brought New Mexico a flood of cultural changes that appeared to many of its Hispanic and Indian people as a threat to their traditional ways of life. The railroad, whose significance we have already mentioned, was a major instrument of change. It transformed the state's economic base, primarily reliant on husbandry, to include tourism and the export of coal, other minerals, oil, and beef. It also provided easy access to the area for jaded Easterners in search of romance and adventure, for artists who had discovered the peculiar charm of New Mexico's light and skies, and for intellectuals who sought refuge from a capitalist technological society. They were convinced of the moral superiority of primitive native peoples past and present. Artist Georgia O'Keeffe is quoted as saying, "If you ever go to New Mexico, it will itch you for the rest of your life."

Native New Mexicans, both Indians and Hispanics, worried their ways of life would be irretrievably transformed, and that Anglo economic drives, institutions, and lifestyles would threaten their own rich and treasured cultures. They feared the loss of their unique folk religion and language, and viewed with suspicion a public education system dominated by Protestant Anglos. Conservative Easterners had their own doubts about integrating their new Spanish-speaking neighbors into the larger American community. Their misgivings and fears had deep historical roots in the Anglo psyche, going back even before the first contact with Hispanics by way of the Santa Fe Trail. Anglos tended to view New

Mexicans as an ignorant race of dubious morality, and some even questioned if this alien mixed-blood people could ever be assimilated into existing American society.

During the turbulent post-Civil War years, New Mexico was widely regarded as a haven for outlaws. In 1880, General William Tecumseh Sherman humorously proposed declaring war on Mexico in order to force it to take back New Mexico. The general public thought the predominantly Hispanic and Indian peoples of New Mexico were too foreign and too Catholic, with their medieval Penitente practices, to be granted statehood, and besides that, they did not even speak English. No doubt these and other prejudices contributed to the delay of six decades in admitting New Mexico as a state on January 6, 1912.

La Ciénega valley of today retains much of its uniqueness in spite of the encroachments of Santa Fe and the ever sprawling subdivisions. Recent to the landscape is the non-operating pari-mutuel racetrack, Santa Fe Downs, currently owned by Pojoaque Pueblo. Farther south is the upscale real estate development of Las Lagunitas with its private lake, the former holding ponds for the historic Guicú ditch.

To the west of Interstate 25 traffic and the mass transit Rail Runner Express, where passengers using wireless Internet service whiz by without a thought to what went on in La Ciénega Valley through generations, lie the villages of La Ciénega, the hamlet of Cieneguilla, the fashionable subdivision of Las Lagunitas, and El Rancho de las Golondrinas, neighbor to the upscale retreat and spa, Sunrise Springs. Many home sites, some which date from the days of the reconquest, accommodate modest dwellings. Often overlooked in the valley is a flourishing art colony.

The Living History Museum

New Mexican research archives reveal La Ciénega Valley residents divided the land repeatedly throughout the Spanish colonial period which would appear to negate the claim that one family owned El Rancho de las Golondrinas until the 1930s. Documents do reveal that most Ciénega Valley land owners were related by birth, marriage, or some other social relationship. The Baca, the Pino, and the Gonzales families, all part of the mosaic, were reported to be the wealthiest landowners in the Valley in the late 19th century.

In the depth of the Great Depression, the four hundred acres of Las Golondrinas property was sold. The deed is dated ". . . the 17th day of October, 1933, by and between Elfego Pino, party of the first part, and Leonora F. Curtin and Leonora S. M. Curtin, parties of the second part . . . ."

The purchase price of $15,000 was satisfied with $13,500 in cash and two hundred sheep. The *rancho* had been in the Vega y Coca/Baca/Pino families for some 220 years; the Pino family line descended from Pedro Baptista Pino, New Mexico's representative to Spanish parliament in 1812. It was Elfego Pino who married Ymelda Baca, great-granddaughter of Baca y Terrus. Prior to the sale, Pino had set about to consolidate ownership of the lands now known as Las Golondrinas by registering quitclaims to titles to several parcels, and by outright purchases of others. In 1950, Leonora S. M. Curtin deeded her half of the ranch to Y. A. Paloheimo, her son-in-law. The Paloheimos purchased and combined other adjacent La Ciénega properties that resulted in some eight hundred acres that included the two hundred acre El Rancho de las Golondrinas Living History Museum.

Unflattering stories have been repeated about the supposed avarice of certain Pino family members. It seems that a search for fabled wealth is inevitable. One account hints that rawhide baskets, filled with gold by José Francisco Baca y Terrus and his son, were hidden within the *terrones* walls of the Baca house. The ancient building was reportedly all but destroyed by Elfego Pino in a vain attempt to find treasure. This may explain why but two rooms remain today. Another story claims that Elfego used coercion and intimidation to acquire portions of the property to add to his already considerable estate.

Fruit peddler Luis Baca made a living by growing and selling produce from the Las Golondrinas orchards. A license dated September 26, 1890 was granted for a "peddler with one animal" to sell fruits and vegetables in Los Cerrillos and Madrid. Luis had ordered fruit tree seedlings from a Chicago nursery that arrived on the AT&SF in May, 1888 just in time for the growing season. It is rumored that Elfego Pino coerced Luis into signing away his portion of the ranch property while his family was away at church.

The 1884 Survey identified "one of the finest houses around," a one story large *adobe* home estimated at $200 in value. Sometime in the early 1900s, Elfego Pino, using milled lumber, remodeled the *adobe* structure by adding a second story, and incorporated a gas light system. This Victorian style building is known today as the Pino House.

The Curtin women stocked their small working ranch with sheep, cows and horses, with Parley Blackwelder their first manager. Shortly after Blackwelder left for other employment, The Curtin women leased the ranch to Jesse Bonner who fled the Texas dust-bowl with his wife and five children. A corrugated sheet metal pitched roof was installed to store hay over the original 16th century structure that had seen untold uses. Bonner owned two hundred dairy cows and supplied milk to a Santa Fe dairy, and the venerable old building served as a dairy barn for Bonner's enterprise. The *vigas* were sawn off, and the roof literally raised and fitted with corrugated tin to store hay for his milk cows.

Today it houses the *capilla* exhibit at the museum. Jesse's daughter, Glenna Bonner Duff of Albuquerque, reported the following anecdote about life at Las Golondrinas from 1934 to 1947: "Mrs. Curtin said we could have any of the fruit, apples, pears, etc. that had fallen to the ground. Well, we kids were there early every morning picking up the fruit that had fallen in the night. Mama canned and preserved every morsel, and as the weather got cooler, we wrapped the apples in papers and stored them in a cool place so we could have fresh fruit all winter. . ... There was a spring bubbling up from the ground a little ways from the house, with huge cottonwood trees surrounding it. We hand-carried all the water we used for drinking, cooking and bathing from that spring. . .. Daddy got a herd of two hundred dairy cows and would have half of them 'fresh' at one time. These cows had to be milked twice a day. In addition to the milking there were corn and alfalfa fields to tend . . ., we had horses, pigs, goats, chickens, turkeys and ducks. . . . Mama had a large vegetable garden every year and that took a lot of attention. . . . We were the only 'Gringos' in the whole community but we never felt different . . . because we were all struggling and didn't have the time or energy to feel sorry for ourselves. . . Daddy also dug and made an in-ground silo. One time during the making of the silage, after it had fermented, some of the calves got into it and were stumbling and wobbling around. They were 'drunk' from drinking the water from the fermented corn. Even a couple of roosters got into it and when they tried to crow that was even funnier." After World War II, Jesse Bonner sold his cattle and moved to Santa Fe. Facundo and María Pino then assumed the management of the ranch.

During the 1950s as the restoration of the ranch began, Y. A. and Leonora F. Paloheimo began searching throughout Northern New Mexico and Southern

Colorado for old barns, mills, corrals and other artifacts that suited the purposes of creating and furnishing a "working" ranch. The structures were disassembled; each piece was marked with metal archaeological tabs, and re-assembled carefully in selected landscapes throughout the ranch. Where such practices were sometimes criticized by those who saw their patrimony being moved elsewhere, old timers can now appreciate that historic structures have been preserved at El Rancho de las Golondrinas. One might have to search far and wide, possibly to Northern Spain and the Pyrenees, to find examples of the log notching style using only gravity to keep buildings in place.

Molino Grande with its overshot water wheel

243

The discovery of El Molino Grande de Sapelló (big mill) was a singular find. The Paloheimos were driving from Las Vegas to Sapelló when they saw an *adobe molino* in disrepair, but sound. Leonora recalled that, "We stopped and saw the owner at a distance working on the property. My husband climbed the hill and spoke to him, and in no time seemed to win his confidence because he said, 'Many people have asked me to sell it but you can have it!" Mr. Paloheimo had the original Sapelló building remodeled into a small apartment for its owner, and the *molino's* mechanism was moved and installed at El Rancho de las Golondrinas in a new structure of *adobe* and wood near the Sierra Village complex. Equipped with a new overshot water wheel, it mills flour during festival weekends. The machinery was manufactured in Buffalo, New York, and transported by rail and freight wagon to its Las Vegas site in the 1880s. The Pacheco family milled as many as 150,000 pounds of flour annually for the military at Fort Union and elsewhere, and for the Navajo who had been incarcerated on the reservation at Bosque Redondo.

Power to run the *molino* is supplied by the weight of water falling into cups on the water wheel that yields twelve hundred pounds of force (equal to 25.0 horsepower), and drives the sophisticated system of shafts, gears and pulleys. The millstones moved from Sapelló are made from French chert brought to the United States as ship ballast. Visitors to Las Golondrinas will find the Molino Grande de Sapelló in operation during Festival times along with the diminutive Molino Barela de Truchas that represents the *molinos* favored by New Mexican villagers. A caution to researchers—El Molino Grande should not be considered an historic structure in the academic sense. Another exhibit at the living history museum, the non-operational Molino Viejo de las Golondrinas (Old Las Golondrinas Mill), recorded in the Manual Francisco Delgado will, was rebuilt on the site.

As might be suspected, the motion picture industry has discovered La Ciénega Valley and El Rancho de las Golondrinas. One movie set constructed at Las Golondrinas has survived and remains in place. La Casa de Madrid (Madrid House) near the Molino Grande de Sapelló was used in the 1978 20th Century Fox filming of *Butch and Sundance: The Early Years*. Others sets are constructed, filmed, and dismantled after use.

The Shepherd's Cabin below the Sierra Village complex was at one time a Southern Colorado ranch shelter for fence riders.

The log building, now known as The Shepherd's Cabin, was initially moved from the San Luis Valley in southern Colorado in the 1950s to a site near the New Mexico Supreme Court in Santa Fe. The structure was used as a utility shed during the construction of the Cider Press Gift Shop on the Santa Fe River. No longer in use, it was deemed a public nuisance after it was repeatedly vandalized. Mr. Paloheimo received a phone call from its owner to determine if he would be interested in moving the old cabin to El Rancho de las Golondrinas. The structure was torn down in 1985, logs numbered with archaeological tags, and reassembled where it is today.

Sierra Village complex

In the Sierra Village at Las Golondrinas we find several structures collected elsewhere, disassembled, transported, and reassembled on the hillside. The buildings represent an evolutionary span of from about 1750 to 1912, the year of statehood; they typify the lifestyles many Hispanics lived in the northern mountains. The earliest is the Casita Primitiva (Primitive House/Grandfather's

House) with its flat dirt roof, two small rooms, packed earth floor, and tiny fireplace. It was collected in the mountain village of Truchas. The dwelling exemplifies the simple home that was constructed by villagers with no tools other than an axe and an adze. Pine logs were plastered with *adobe* to stop drafts and to keep the home warm in winter and cool in summer. The small *adobe* fireplace radiated an amazing amount of heat. The house displays only a few pieces of crude furniture as families slept and ate on the floor.

The adjacent *corrales y cobertizos* (corrals and sheds) and *trochiles y gallineros* (pigpens and chicken coops) represent similar structures still in use today in remote New Mexican villages. The *chiquero* (pen for newborn animals) was covered to protect against birds of prey and other predators.

The diminutive Casa de la Abuelita (Grandmother's House) is a favorite of children who visit the museum, and was also collected in the village of Truchas. It is a simple, tight, one-room house with a peaked roof, a wood plank floor, and is furnished with a black cast-iron *estufa* (stove), spool beds and handmade wooden furniture.

Casa de la Abuelita in Sierra Village

There is a small pantry for foods and herbs. An occasional visitor fondly recalls the time when he or she was the grandchild who lived with Grandma who sometimes needed assistance. In return, the grandchild learned domestic skills and traditions, sometimes that of a *curandera*. One guest visiting the Sierra Village observed, "I was that grandchild and I loved being the one who lived with my grandmother." On the same day another exclaimed, "I hated it. I had to milk the cow and everything." The construction and furnishings of the house testify to the arrival of the railroad to the territory. Sawmills that cut the planking for the pitched roof and wooden floor, and the *estufa*, with its metal utensils, were all imported from the East along the Santa Fe Trail or by rail.

Between Grandmother's House and the Casona de Mora (Mora House) next door, the visitor finds a replica well house, firewood stacked like a teepee to dry, and an iron kettle and wooden slat table used to wash wool fleece prior to carding and spinning. During Las Golondrinas festivals, docents have demonstrated the use of fine suds obtained by swishing crushed *amole* root in warm water to launder wool fleeces, while others bake *bizcochitos* (anise flavored sugar cookies) in the *horno*.

The Mora House is representative of a large classic house of *adobe*, and is roofed with the milled lumber favored by New Mexican mountain villagers in the late 1800s. It is an example of a rural "territorial" architectural style, and showcases the uniformity of building materials that became available: mass produced door casings, double hung sash windows, metal hinges, door handles, locks and trims. Traveling salesmen took orders and placed requisitions with manufacturers in Missouri, the merchandise to be delivered by rail, and then freighted to the building site. Pitched plank roofs found favor in the mountains because they shed winter snows. Many Sierra Village visitors fondly confide that they, or other family members, lived or still live in homes similar to the Mora house. The two large, airy and rooms, simply furnished by museum staff, are entered through an enclosed entrance from a grand porch covered by a *portal*. In the living room is a *rinconera* (corner cupboard) where treasured china dinnerware is displayed. The much admired sleigh bed served for seating and sleeping, and the well-laden wood slab table and benches could accommodate many fine meals. Of special interest are the bedroom furnishings including a swinging *cuna* (cradle) of steamed and bent wooden slats suspended from a two-wheeled wooden frame. The walls in all three homes in the Sierra Village display cheerful designs of hydrated *tierra amarilla,* applied with pads of sheep's wool dipped in the buff-colored solution and a stencil.

The New Mexico territorial buildings seen in New Mexico today use an architectural style made possible by the introduction of sawmills, mass produced hardware, and brick-kilns; brick coping capped the *adobe* parapets helped retard erosion. Some Santa Fe Plaza facades and the Laboratory of Anthropology are examples of a territorial style introduced by architect John Gaw Meem and his associates.

The Sierra Village *dispensa de cueros y zaleas* (storeroom for skins and hides) was used to warehouse skins of sheep and hides of other livestock, and the *soterrano de comida* (root cellar) stored foods, potatoes, carrots, squash and apples, packed in sand for use during the harsh winter months. Throughout the village, a visitor finds other memories of the past: an *arado*, a *vagón* (wagon to haul logs for *vigas*), a *criba* (grain sifter) and the *jardín de hierbas* (herb garden). High above the Sierra Village is the recently constructed Oratorio de San Ysidro, or Saint Isadore Chapel. Here the *bulto* of San Ysidro resides throughout the summer, watching over the fields.

Procession from Oratorio de San Ysidro

The Mora House, a replica of a 1900 pitched roof *adobe* mountain home with its nearby herb garden and apple orchard, and built on an old foundation, represent the latest time period to be interpreted at El Rancho de las Golondrinas.

Special Programming

Festival and special weekend programs provide a variety of experiences throughout the season. In mid-May, "Battlefield New Mexico: The Civil War and More" finds the New Mexico Civil War Commemorative Congress re-enactors staging artillery and marching demonstrations, replicating camp life, and holding mock Union and Confederate skirmishes. "Spring Festival and Children's Fair," held in early June, finds costumed villagers shearing sheep, baking bread, introducing children to ranch animals, plus games and other hands-on activities. "Fiber Arts Festival: From Sheep to Blanket" is held later in June, the process of turning fleece of the churros to the finished textile is demonstrated by expert weavers.

July's "Santa Fe Wine Festival" offers the visitor a chance to taste and purchase some of New Mexico's finest fruit of the vine. Later, with the "¡Viva México!" celebration, guests can enjoy *música, arte and más* from our colorful neighbor to the south, Mexico.

Danza de la Pluma from Oaxaca, Mexico

Later in the month, the "Herb and Lavender Fair" encourages visitors to tour the herb garden, meet lavender and herb product vendors, and attend lectures on cultivating lavender, plus hands-on activities. "Summer Festival, Frontier Days and Horses of the West" is held in early August. Mountain men and women demonstrate their skills and spin tales of the past. Peruvian Paso horses are put through their paces. Later in August, "Fiesta de Los Niños: A Children's Celebration" invites children to ¡Ven a jugar con nosotros!, come out and play with us! Games, crafts and entertainment for the whole family with children under thirteen admitted for free.

The "Santa Fe Renaissance Fair" is held in mid-September, a lovely time at Las Golondrinas. In residence is Clan Tynker with live steel combat, jugglers and dancers, kid's games, and food with wine and mead available for the adults. "Harvest Festival" held early in October is the most popular community celebration at Las Golondrinas. Children have their feet hosed off prior to stepping in a cowhide vat where they crush wine grapes. Docents press apples for cider, volunteers string chile ristras, wheat is threshed, and sorghum cane is squeezed to free juice that is reduced by boiling in vats to yield molasses. Guests are treated to samples of cuisine made using harvest produce.

Renaissance Fair pirates

"Adventures in the Past" is a summer day camp at El Rancho de las Golondrinas for children ages 9-12. They have *aventuras* (adventures) that include hide tanning, adobe making, blacksmithing, hiking, tortilla making, baking in hornos, weaving, candle and rope making, and tinsmithing. They also learn about horses, sheep, burros and how to shoot a bow and arrow.

The museum is open for self-guided tours June through September on Wednesdays through Sundays from 10am to 4pm. Before the season opens to the general public, school groups arrive to tour and picnic at Las Golondrinas. About 1500 little feet kick up the dust on each of the eight "Spanish Colonial Days" hosted by El Rancho de las Golondrinas. Guided tours are available other times of the year. Special tours are available for Josefina® aficionados and for those who care to tour "Hollywood on the Ranch."

Bread baking in the horno

La Ciénega Valley Cultural and Emotional Ties

A prominent member of the C'de Baca family, and author of *The Eden of Ciénega*, is George C'de Baca. His sensitive discussion of life in the valley tells of struggles to keep his Hispanic culture alive and yet adapt to modern ways. Below is his conclusion:

"I guess one could rationalize this revolution by arguing that this is progress. La Ciénega, and all the old villages, are moving into the next century as all things must do. The *viejitos* must move over for the new generation to make its mark on this earth. The old set of values has been superseded by a new set of values. New technology, new lifestyles, and new agendas supplant the old. Destroy the old and build a new world is today's natural order of things. That is progress by today's standards. Never mind the destruction of an ancient heritage and the damage done to Mother Earth. Those things no longer sustain us. The *cosechas* (harvests) have been replaced by the supermarkets and the fast food places. *La Fé* has been replaced by corporate America and the financial institutions, and the *diablos* and *bultos* have been replaced by the entertainment industry. Those are the new gods: *la fé nueva y la cultura nueva*—the new faith and new culture.

"The Eden of La Ciénega has gone the way of the Eden of Genesis into the pages of history and into the memory of those who were touched by it."

Families are bonded to their parcels of land accumulated through sales, exchanges, inheritance and disputes. Boundaries had to be adjudicated when, although the Treaty of Guadalupe Hidalgo guaranteed old land rights would be honored, confusion, and occasional skullduggery muddied titles. Traditional ways of identifying and recording boundaries, such as natural features and ephemeral landmarks, left many a parcel in legal limbo.

La Ciénega holds its heritage dear and cherishes histories and stories. For generations, old timers told of La Mina Colorada, and searched in vain for its hidden wealth. The late Ricardo C'de Baca quoted as saying, "I love this land. I'm proud to have been born and raised here. This is the richest place in the whole world. We have water, rich red soil, and somewhere is hidden La Mina Colorada. Mines were filled in after the Pueblo Revolt to hide all traces of their location." Josiah Gregg's journal told of Indian elders who cautioned their people not to engage in mining, but to pursue

agriculture for fear former abuses would recur should old mines be reopened.

Agriculture was no longer a viable source of income by the end of the Great Depression, but many valley residents remained tied to the land but sought employment elsewhere in the mines, industry, and the military, bringing cash into the barter economy. Commercial forces, new home building, and the increasing number of factory built and mobile homes installed in the valley, each with a newly drilled well and septic system, decreased the agricultural acreage, and lowered the water table. Having inherited the job from his father, Reynaldo Romero has been *mayordomo* of the *acequia* association for more than 40 years. With deep concern, he faults the weather, the drought, and "too many straws in the aquifer" for the disappearance of the water table which fed the valley's springs so generously. There may come a time when the living history museum of Las Golondrinas will have to pipe water in from elsewhere in order to irrigate its small acreage of demonstration crops, and to run its *molinos* on festival days.

Facundo Pino and his wife, María, never knew of the covert escapades that took place at the ranch. Facundo was manager of El Rancho de las Golondrinas after the Bonner family moved away, and he and his family occupied the Pino house. Nick, Facundo's son, and his friend, Ignacio Urban, found the valley their clandestine playground. After Nick's parents were asleep, the boys would slip out of an upstairs Pino House bedroom window, shinny down the trunk of a nearby tree, bridle some horses, and have a great time riding about their valley surroundings.

Josephine Tondre, a widow with three sons, imported French wine grapes and developed a winery six miles south of Isleta Pueblo. She used native labor that earned fifty cents a day. The winery produced one hundred thousand gallons of wine sold to churches and bars from Fort Wingate to the west, and up the Rio Grande Valley to Santa Fe. In the 1870s, the family planned to spend the night at the Las Golondrinas paraje, but took heed of a warning given by a man riding a donkey. The traveler warned them that robbers knew cash from the sales was in gold and hidden in the hubs of the wagon. Needless to say, Josephine and her party did not stay the night. The family still wonders—was the stranger on the donkey St. Joseph?

The tranquility and pastoral setting of the valley spawned an art colony that has labored in the village since its first studio tour in 1979 with sixteen artists participating. Craftspeople and artists, some descendents of the original Hispanic settlers and the Anglos who found their sense of place in the valley, sought to market their wares at home rather than make frequent trips to arts and crafts shows. On occasion, old fashioned barter found craftsmen trading pottery, woodworked pieces, vegetable and fruit produce, butter and eggs, a chicken or two, or a turn of the plow in a garden patch. A visit today to La Ciénega's Art Tour will find many talented sculptors who work in different media, woodworkers and furniture makers, printmakers, and fiber, and mixed media artists along with ceramicists.

> During the Great Depression, the Works Progress Administration fostered a furniture, pottery, and leather working industry in La Ciénega. Henry Gonzáles came from Albuquerque to administer the local program, and remained to marry Melinda C'de Baca, a local girl. Her brother, Tomás, taught furniture making; his son David is now a furniture maker in the village.

The residents of the centuries old community have seen threats to their traditional way of life. A proposed 1985 development project planned a "country store" off exit 271 on Interstate 25 frontage road with a forty-four room motel, restaurant, gas station, and convenience store, and forty condominiums. Area residents rose up in unity to defeat the proposal.

Then in 1991, a developer proposed a subdivision to be called "At Santa Fe" on 265 acres with a five-star hotel, two hundred plus homes and townhomes, a championship golf course, and forty thousand square feet of retail space. The $20 million dollar development was met with stiff opposition by the neighbors. A concerned grass-roots movement, not to be intimidated by well funded developers and their lawyers, used community meetings, the media, competent legal counsel, and the *corrido* composed by folklorist, Roberto Mondragon, *El Corrido de La Ciénega,* a powerful weapon against the despoiling of their beloved valley. Mondragon was Lieutenant Governor of New Mexico from 1971–1974, and again from 1979 to 1982.

A verse from the ballad reads:

Ahi van poner un golf course They're going to build a golf course
donde vengan los turistas, where tourists will play,
alla encontrarán los ricos there you will find all the rich ones
corriendo ligeros tras de sus bolitas. chasing around their little balls.

Richard C' de Baca, former cabinet secretary of New Mexico's Department of Public Safety, spent a lifetime watching over the old petroglyphs and the pictographs on his 250 year old family farm. To ensure they would be protected after his death, he and his wife, Juanita, donated nineteen acres to the Bureau of Land Management in 1933. For their generous gift, the C' de Bacas received the BLM Partners in Public Spirit Award.

Emotions run high over perceived assaults on land and water use in the Valley, and New Mexico's Hispanic families resolve to maintain their presence in the face of change. Jerry Ortiz y Pino, columnist for *The Santa Fe New Mexican* wrote in reply to an insensitive observation by a journalist, "I simply want to mark in some way that which is being erased. It was a rich network of beliefs and values that sustained us. In the future, I hope people of many different ethnic origins will continue to tap into that tradition. We may not endure as a separate people, but our values can. . . . For us Hispanics who have loved and stubbornly stayed on this land for hundreds of years, there is no migration, no place to go, no other choices. This is our land and our home."

La Ciénega and La Cieneguilla have pursued official designations as Traditional Historic Communities in a quest to preserve their lifestyle, and to control development. Santa Fe County Commissioners granted the designations as provided by state law. The intent is to protect the communities from being annexed by a larger municipality unless voters decide otherwise.

Alonso Rael holds that the family was fortunate to be able to keep its original land within the La Cieneguilla Grant. Because of family connections, the 240 acres escaped being sold for back taxes. The Rael family treasured their ancient heritage, and conveyed the undeveloped land to the Bureau of Land Management where it will be maintained as open space in perpetuity. It lies near the prehistoric La Cieneguilla Pueblo and the over four thousand petroglyphs pecked into the basalt boulders, also owned by the Federal Bureau of Land Management.

Alonso's quiet valley home remains a gathering place for the Raels for holiday parties and reunions. In 1947, across the river Alonso painted a huge white cross on the hillside, the only sign that this refuge exists.

Historian Marc Simmons reminds us of the strong cultural and emotional ties that still link New Mexico with its Spanish *patria* (native land). As the government of Spain was preparing for the Columbian Quincentenario of 1992, a small group of Spanish diplomats, dignitaries, and anthropologist Professor José Antonio Jáuregui came to New Mexico to invite a delegation to travel to Spain and take part in the activities. While on tour, they arrived at Las Golondrinas during the Spring Festival, and were met at the flagpole by a Spanish militia re-enactor group, all in brilliant red coats, hats with plumes, and with Spanish muskets. As the guests arrived, the honor guard snapped the Spanish flag onto the pole, ran it up, and fired a volley; the soldiers removed their hats and cried, "*Viva España, Viva el Rey, Viva el Rey de España!*" Overcome with emotion, the visiting professor could not hold back his tears and said, "*Señor Simmons, tu sabes, nosotros los españoles somos una gente emocioñal*—We are a very emotional people, we Spaniards. You can't imagine," the professor continued, "what it means to us to come here to the United States and to see our flag honored, to see it raised on the flagpole and to hear the huzzahs and the *vivas* (live long) to the king and our country."

After the flag ceremony, the party was given a tour. Professor Jáuregui reported, "My grandfather was a *molinero* in Catalonia, and he died long before I was born. I never knew my grandfather, but I was always so interested in what he did because older members of the family would talk about, as children, going into his mill, and he would sing the milling songs as he ground the wheat. He was the last miller in the area, and by the time he died, the old mill had been torn down, and I never even saw it. I was taken into what you call the Truchas mill, and for the first time in my life I saw a part of my life, a heritage I had not known. And I had to come halfway around the world to Las Golondrinas to recapture this fragment of my personal history."

One wonders what any one of the old timers would think of the valley today, and of the resolute attempts to hold tradition near and dear. Will this unique community retain its traditional identity and cohesiveness into the twenty-first century? El Rancho de las Golondrinas hopes to help secure the legacy for generations to come.

Epilogue

The many beneficiaries of the Las Golondrinas legacy, and indeed the preservation of the Hispanic colonial culture in northern New Mexico, might look to a remarkable couple who had the vision to save the ancient *estancia* and bring it to life once again, Leonora F. Curtin and her husband Y. A. Paloheimo.

The Curtin family of New Mexico consisted of two dynamic women, Leonora Scott Muse Curtin and Leonora Frances Curtin, mother and daughter, who had ties to Pasadena, California. Eva Scott Feynes, Leonora F. Curtain's grandmother, built a Beaux Arts mansion in 1905 that is now the home of the Pasadena Historical Museum of History, a private, nonprofit community-based institution. There she hosted a salon for distinguished visitors. One was Charles Lummis of the Landmark Association who encouraged Eva to paint historic *adobes* before they were demolished. Leonora S. M. Curtin was living in Pasadena where she met and married Thomas E. Curtin, who then died at the onset of World War I.

From the time of her first visit to New Mexico in 1889 with Eva Feynes, her mother, in search of a dry climate, Leonora S. M. Curtain had an engrossing interest in the region's culture. In 1948 she published a book that is still in use today, *The Healing Herbs of the Northern Rio Grande*. The volume has been reprinted by several publishers: The Laboratory of Anthropology, Mountain Press Publishing, the Southwest Museum, and the Western Edge Press.

Recognizing Leonora S. M. Curtin's dedication to the preservation of cultural heritage, The Leonora Curtin Wetland Preserve, a thirty five acre parcel adjacent to El Rancho de las Golondrinas, was established by the Santa Fe Botanical Garden (SFBG) in 1987. The Botanical Garden executed a long term lease in 1993 with Las Golondrinas trustees to develop educational programming on environmentally responsible garden design, plant selection and care, and water catchment and harvesting techniques.

Born in 1903 in Colorado Springs, Colorado and educated privately in the United States and abroad, Leonora F. Curtin was fluent in several languages, including Spanish. She collaborated with ethnographer John P. Harrington to record Native American languages, and proposed the publication of a Navajo primer for use in Navajo schools. In 1931, Leonora traveled to Morocco to research

Arabic origins of Spanish words and traditions. She was an accomplished artist in her own right, and especially favored watercolors.

Leonora F. Curtin came to Santa Fe in the winter of 1916 with her now widowed mother, Leonora S. M. Curtin. A decade later, Eva Scott Muse Fenyes, her daughter and granddaughter, all skilled in investments and business, saw the value of building a home on a three acre parcel of land on historic Acequia Madre in the then pastoral section east of the plaza in Santa Fe. In 1928–1929, the three women designed and had constructed the elegant 614 Acequia Madre Territorial-style structure, using handcrafted *adobes* laid two abreast. The mansion soon hosted a salon for artists, preservationists, and promoters of culture. Artist Gerald Cassidy, ethnographer John P. Harrington, writer Mary Austin, anthropologist Adolph Bandelier, director of the School of American Archaeology (School of American Research in 1917) Edgar Lee Hewitt, and others were part of the intellectual mix. Leonora F. Curtin Paloheimo lived there until her death. Now known as the Curtin-Paloheimo House, the historic residence and gardens are available to rent for special occasions.

After the purchase of Las Golondrinas from Elfego Pino in 1933, mother and daughter made their country home in long neglected La Loma, an *adobe* house high on a bluff overlooking the developed part of Las Golondrinas. They oversaw reclamation of the decades-old residence, but kept modernization to a minimum in order to maintain it in harmony with its immediate environment, indoor plumbing, and electrical wiring were the only concessions.

Becoming deeply involved in the Hispanic Colonial culture, the two Curtin women, along with members of the Spanish Colonial Arts Society, Inc., saw the need to preserve Hispanic crafts, and to encourage their revival. They founded and operated Spanish Market in the patio of the Museum of Fine Arts from 1925 to 1932. Six months later, Leonora F. Curtin opened "Native Market," a shop on Palace Avenue with a furniture-finishing operation in the basement. On opening day in 1934, the shop sold out its entire inventory. Santa Fe's Native Market provided an outlet to train craftsmen to design and create traditional Hispanic crafts of high quality, textiles, furniture, and religious art for use in contemporary living. The shop closed its doors in 1940. Today's thriving Spanish Market sprang from these roots.

Leonora was and is remembered for her ardent interest in and support of the New Mexican Spanish Colonial crafts revival. In Sarah Nestor's 1978 book, *The Native Market,* Leonora F. Curtin was quoted as saying, "I talked craft revival, teaching, marketing, and every aspect to all who would listen." With the onset of World War II, New Mexican Hispanics were able to find jobs in a strengthening economy. Native Market was no longer necessary and was discontinued. Leonora never stopped promoting and collecting Hispanic crafts.

In October of 1981, Leonora and Y. A. Paloheimo received the Governor's Award for Excellence and Achievement in the Arts for the founding and development of El Rancho de las Golondrinas, and for Leonora's pioneering work in the creation of the 1930s Native Market in Santa Fe. Then on a bright September afternoon in 1995, after a lifetime of dedication to cultural and charitable causes, Leonora F. Curtin Paloheimo, wearing a bright red felt sombrero and silver Navajo jewelry, received Spain's highest honor for foreigners, a medal inducting her into the Order of Isabela la Católica. The presenter was Gonzalo de Benito, Spain's consul general and representative of King Juan Carlos. The award, made to non-Spanish persons who advance Spanish culture in their own countries, is one of only six ever granted to New Mexicans. Four other recipients were humanist Fray Angélico Chávez, scholar John Kessell, historian Marc Simmons and María Benitez, flamenco dance master. The consul general called the ranch the "most comprehensive example of Spain's presence" in the Southwest. Marc Simmons commented that the ranch was "the only Hispanic heritage museum in the United States, probably the only one in the world."

Remembered by her family as strong-willed, nurturing, gracious, witty, cheerful, and practical, her son, George, recalls that his mother cut the children's hair while they were growing up in order to save money. Leonora followed her husband in death in 1999. She saw two hundred developed acres of the Ranch of the Swallows buffered by an additional seven hundred acres come under the management of the Rancho de las Golondrinas Charitable Trust. Leonora continued serving as a financial patron. Subsequent parcels have been sold by the Trust, and the current figure stands at four hundred acres.

Yrjö (Yrko) Alfred, better known to his friends as "Y. A," a naturalized citizen came to the United States from Finland in the mid-1920s. A wealthy man in his own right, he combined philanthropic and broad cultural interests, and in 1948, assumed the post of Finnish Vice Consul of Southern California, Arizona and New Mexico where he served a seventeen-year tenure. Y. A. was made an honorary citizen of New York City while acting as dean of the 1939–1940 New York World Fair's forty-eight foreign commissioners. Leonora Curtin toured the Finnish Pavilion during the 1939–1940 New York World Fair, but did not meet

Y.A. until later while attending a dinner given by a mutual friend. The couple was wed in New York City in 1946. The newlyweds divided their time between Santa Fe and Pasadena and the Feynes Mansion that became the home of the Finnish Consulate of the United States.

From 1952 to 1965, Y. A. and Leonora visited Finland often where they established a school for orphans on the Paloheimo family estate in Jarvenpaa, Finland. There they adopted four children, George, born 1946, Nina (Paloheimo Bovio) in 1946, Eric in 1947 and Eva in 1949. The Paloheimo estate bordered that of the great Finnish composer Jean Sibelius. Y. A., who knew him well, liked to recall, "His oldest daughter married my oldest brother."

Paloheimo was the founder of the Finlandia Foundation of Pasadena, California, dedicated to strengthening cultural ties between the United States and Finland. Paloheimo's Finnish Folk Art collection is housed in his *tupa* (farmhouse), a replica built by Y.A. on the grounds of the former home of Eva Feynes, Leonora S. M. Curtin, and Leonora F. Curtin. Before the elder Curtin died, the compound was donated to the Pasadena Historical Society and Museum.

The notion of establishing a "living history museum" was Y.A. Paloheimo's happy idea, for he had seen the Viking culture in Scandinavia revered and interpreted through such an "open-air" concept. He played a leading role in the creation of the Colonial New Mexico Historical Society, one of his and Leonora's many cultural contributions that won them the Governor's Award in 1981 for "their major contributions to the arts in New Mexico." Y. A. held a master's degree in agriculture and forestry from the University of Helsinki earned in 1923, and was a founding member of the Association of Living Historical Farms and Agricultural Museums (ALHFAM), the organization was sponsored by the Smithsonian Institution, and dedicated to the preservation of old ways of life. El Rancho de las Golondrinas is a charter affiliate member.

The couple, along with their four adopted Finnish children, spent summers at Las Golondrinas with its ancient, long-neglected hacienda. One of the ranch's original structures, built in the 18th century, was still in use as a barn, but others were in ruins. Struck by the beauty and historical interest of the place, and encouraged by architect John Gaw Meem, the Paloheimos began the long process of its restoration. According to Earl Porter of the Las Golondrinas Master Planning Committee, Y. A. was "a man of vision of what might be, went looking for things that could be, and put them where they looked like they should be."

Old Ciénega Village Museum opened for limited days each summer beginning in 1972. In 1976, Governor Juan Batista Anza re-enactors from Arizona traveled to Las Golondrinas to present a pageant, and to take part in the nation's bi-centernial celebrations. Over time, and as development proceeded, the museum was deeded by the Paloheimos to El Rancho de las Golondrinas Charitable Trust in 1986. In 1990, the museum was opened for school tours in April and October, and for public admission Wednesdays through Sundays from June through September. The Trust's mission statement specifies that the museum be dedicated to education, especially that of children, of New Mexican Hispanic colonial cultural heritage. Spanish Colonial Days school tours help to satisfy the mandate.

Leonora Paloheimo continued with restoration and stewardship of the museum site after her husband's death in 1986 at eighty-six years of age, the same year that the museum was deeded to the Trust. Y. A. was interred in Kallio-Kuninkala, Finland. Leonora followed her husband in death in 1999, and her ashes lie by Las Golondrinas Mill Pond, a favorite place of hers. Their son, George Paloheimo, served as a trustee and as the museum's director.

Leonora Paloheimo memorial

Help me to know that the eagle
And the toad and I
Are brothers of the grass and the rain.
O, heart in my heart, humble me now,
Our song is the same.
Leonora Curtin Paloheimo
December 7th, 1903, November 27th, 1999

Appendix I

Provenance of Las Golondrinas Historic Buildings

Pino House
    Adobe structure extensively remodeled in Victorian architectural style by Elfego Pino that added a 2nd story of milled lumber about 1904. Gas light system installed.

Las Golondrinas Placita (Casa Mayor)
    Reconstructed on original site. Built by the family of Miguel Vega y Coca early 18th century.
    Building that houses the Capilla and Founder's Room (so called because the inaugural meeting of the Colonial New Mexico Historical Foundation was held there) is original.

La Cocina Con Fagón De Pastor (Kitchen with Shepherd's Bed Fireplace)
    Shepherd's Kitchen is partly original, the balance reconstructed. The remaining eight rooms were rebuilt on original foundations.

Sheep Pens (Baca Placita)
    Trampas, New Mexico. Acquired from Jose Romero.

La Casa de Manuel de Baca (The House of Manuel de Baca) (Baca Placita)
    Built by Manuel de Baca in 1835. Was once a larger home. Made of *terrones* and *adobe*.

La Tiendita (Country Store) (Baca Placita)
    Trampas, New Mexico. Acquired from José Martinez in 1969. José's grandfather's house and later a country store/post office.

La Hojalateria (The Delgado Tinshop) (Baca Placita)

El Taller De Cuero (The Leatherworking Shop)
    Constructed on site by Las Golondrinas docents in 2000.

Carretería Wheelwright Shop (Historic Fields)
    Truchas, New Mexico. Built in the mid-1800s. Acquired from Mrs. Bonifacio Dominguez.

Woodworking Shop (Historic Fields)
    Constructed by a Las Golondrinas docent in 2007.

El Molino Viejo De Talpa (The Old Talpa Mill)
    Talpa, New Mexico. Built in early 1800s.

La Herreria Manuel Apodaca (The Manuel Apodaca Blacksmith Shop)
    Building acquired from Max Martinez, part of log barn from El Guique near Ohkay Owingeh Pueblo.
    Contents purchased from Manuel Apodaca. Bellows obtained from Casia's Blacksmith Shop in Ohkay Owingeh Pueblo.

El Molino Viejo De Las Golondrinas (The Old Golondrinas Mill)
    Truchas, New Mexico. Structure acquired from the Padilla family.

El Molino Barela de Truchas (The Barela Mill from Truchas)
    Built in 1873 by José de la Luz Barela. Structure acquired from Barela family of Truchas, Installed by the historic acequia. Restored 1989–1992.

La Escuela De Ratón (The Ratón School House)
    Built at 300 North 4th St., Raton, New Mexico. in 1878. Harvey Applegate added bedroom addition. Ida Atwater owned the property in 1934. Donated by Delores Noel of Tesuque, New Mexico, 1979.

La Casa Del Pastor (The Sheepherder's Cabin)
    Santa Fe, New Mexico. Donated by Betty Caldwell.
    Moved from the San Luis Valley, Colorado in 1950. Installed by Jimmy Caldwell by State Supreme Court on the Santa Fe River for use as a construction shed. Moved to Las Golondrinas in 1984.

La Morada de la Conquistadora (The Penitente Meeting House)
>   Replica (2/3 scale) of South Morada in Abiquiú, New Mexico.
>   Built in 1972 by Elias Sena, ranch foreman. Used 2,640 *adobe* bricks.

Cemetery markers collected in Truchas by State Highway Department.

La Casa de Madrid (Madrid House)
>   Built as a set for the filming of *Butch Cassidy and the Sundance Kid: the Early Years,* by 20th Century Fox in 1978.

El Molino Grande de Sapelló (The Big Mill from Sapelló)
>   Building constructed on site in 1972. Acquired from the Leger Family. Machinery manufactured in Buffalo, N.Y. Shipped over the Santa Fe Trail in 1870. Installed in Sapelló Molino, Sapelló, N.M. Mill stones of French chert used as ship's ballast.

Trochiles y Gallineros (Pigpen and Chickencoop) (Sierra Village)
>   Trampas, New Mexico. Acquired from the Lopez Family.

La Casita Primitiva (Grandfather's House) (Sierra Village)
>   Truchas, New Mexico. Acquired from Suzie Barela.
>   Built in 1850 by Juan Augustin Sandoval, the great grandfather of Suzie Barela. Juan's son, Demecio Sandoval, was the last to live in the house.

La Casa de la Abuelita (Grandmother's House) (SierraVillage)
>   Truchas, New Mexico. Acquired from the family of Isabel Sandoval Quintana, grandmother of Suzie Barela.

La Casona de Mora (Mora House) (Sierra Village)
>   Building reconstructed on original foundation. Represents the architecture in Mora, New Mexico.

El Oratorio de San Ysidro (Saint Isidore Chapel) (SierraVillage)
>   Constructed on site.

Appendix II

Motion Pictures Filmed at Las Golondrinas

Information from the New Mexico Film Museum website: www.nmfilmmuseum.org

2010
    MacGruber
    Tiger Eyes

2008
    Comanche Moon
    Kit Carson

2007
    Seraphim Falls
    Shoot First and Pray You Live

2005
    Into the West: Episode 2 "Manifest Destiny"
    Into the West: Episode 4 "Hell on Wheels"
    Into the West: Episode 5 "Casualties of War"

2004
    Investigating History: Billy the Kid

2003
    The Missing

1999
    All the Pretty Horses
    Gunfighters of the West

1998
> John Carpenter's Vampires
> The Staircase

1997
> Walker, Texas Ranger: Last of a Breed

1996
> Fools Rush In
> The Lazarus Man

1994
> Wyatt Earp

1988
> Young Guns

1987
> The Gambler Part III: The Legend Continues

1980
> Wild Times

1979
> Butch & Sundance: The Early Days

Glossary

Many Spanish words have more than one meaning, but those listed here are translated for use in the context of this document. A few non-Spanish words are included.

A

abogado (lawyer)
abajo (lower)
abuelita (grandmother)
abuelo(a) (grandparent)
abuelos (magical grandparents of the mountains)
acequia (lateral irrigation ditch)
acequia madre (mother ditch)
adelantado (governor, captain general)
adobe (sundried brick)
aguaciles (sheriffs)
ahijado (godchild)
ajo (garlic)
alabado (song of praise)
alacena (wall cupboard)
alba (song of praise)
alcalde mayor (governor)
alcoba de huéspedes (guest bedroom)
alegría (cockscomb blossom)
alférez (ensign)
amole (yucca root)
amor (love)
andita (litter)
angelitos (baptized children who died without sin)
arado (plow)
araña (spider)
arbolarias (herb healers)
armarios (armoires)
armas de pelo (shaggy goatskin chaps)
arras (gold coins)
arriba (upper)
audiencia (council of magistrates)
aventuras (adventures)
aves de corral (chickens)
ayuntamiento (local assembly building)

B

baile (dance)
baile de prendorio (engagement dance)
bajada (hill or descent)
banco de pared (adobe bench)
borracho (a drunk)
botas (wineskins)
bruja (witch)
buey (ox)
bueyes (oxen)
bulto (sacred statue)
burro (donkey)

C

caballos (horses)
caballos de silla (saddle horses)
cabildo (town council)
cabras (goats)

cachana (blazing star or gay-feather)
caja (box)
caja de madera (wooden chest)
calabacilla (wild gourd)
calidad (social status)
cama (bed)
camino (road)
camisa (shirt)
camposanto (cemetery)
canoa (wooden trough)
cantador (singer)
capilla vieja (old chapel)
capitán (captain)
careo (confrontation)
carga (cargo)
Carmelitas (Carmelites)
carreras de caballos (horse races)
carreta (cart)
Carreta de Muerte (Death Cart)
carretería (wheelwright shop)
carretero (wheelwright)
carro (cart)
casta (caste)
caudillo (leader)
cautivos (captives)
cecinas (jerky)
cena (supper)
chamiso blanco (rabbit bush)
charolitas (small bowls)
chile verde (green chile pepper)
chiquero (pen for newborn animals)
chispa (strike-a-light tool)
chorizo (sausage)
churro (breed of sheep)
chuza (game similar to roulette)
ciboleros (Hispanic buffalo hunters)
ciénegas (marshlands)

cigarrillos (cigarettes)
ciudad (city)
cobertizos (sheds)
coches de paseo (carriages)
cocina (kitchen)
colador (strainer)
colcha (bedspread, also embroidery)
colcheras (embroiders)
comales (flat sheets of iron)
comancheros (mixed blood traders)
cómo le va (how are you)
compadrazgo (ritual co-parenthood)
compadre (ritual co-parent, godfather)
conde (count)
conducta (caravan)
confradía (confraternity)
contra acequias (lateral ditches)
contraventanas (shutters)
convento (missionary living quarters)
conversos (converted Jews and descendants)
copla (stanza)
corrales (corrals)
corrida de gallo (rooster pull or rooster race)
corrido (ballad)
cosechas (harvests)
cota (aster family)
coyote (Indo-Hispanic)
criado (Indian servant)
criba (sifter)
criollo (a person of Spanish blood born in the New World)
cuarto de recibo (living room)
cuchara (spoon)

cuento (story)
cuna (cradle)
cura (clergy)
curandera/o (healer)
custos (ranking prelate)

D

datura (jimson weed)
depósito (repository)
descanso (memorial or resting place)
desempeño, (captive's ransom)
diablo (devil)
dicho (proverb)
dieciocheno (cloth of 1800 threads in the warp)
diligencia matrimonial (pre-nuptial investigations)
dispensa (storage room)
doctrinario (educated mission Indians)
donas (gifts of a handmade chest and goods)
donative voluntario (voluntary gift)

E

efectos del país (local products)
encomendero (had right to Indian tribute)
encomienda (grants for Indian tribute and labor)
entrada (formal entry, expedition)
entregado-/a (vocalist who conducted the wedding ceremony)
entriega de los novios (return of wedding couple to parents)
era de trillar (threshing floor)
escuela primara (primary school)
españoles (Spanish)
estancia (small ranch)

estudiante (student)
estufa (stove)
eulogio (eulogy)
extremaunción (extreme unction)

F

familia y fé (family and faith)
fandango (dance)
fanega (2.57 bushels)
fiesta (feast and entertainment)
fiestecitas (parties)
fiscal (church warden)
fiscales (church wardens)
fogón (fireplace)
fogón de esquina (corner fireplace)
fragua (forge)
frenos (bits for bridles)
fuelle or bofes (bellows)
fueros (judicial jurisdictions)
fuerte (secured storage)

G

gallinas (hens or fowl)
gallineros (chicken coop)
genízaros (hispanicized Plains Indian captives)
gente de chusma (flying demons)
gente fina (high class people)
golondrinas (swallows)
guerra a fuego y sangre (war by fire and blood)
guitarra (guitar)

H

herrador (farrier, one who shoes horses)
herraduras (horseshoes)
herrero (blacksmith)
hidalgo (minor nobleman)
hidalguía (upper-class status)

hijuela (inventory of bequeathed belongings)
hojalatería (tin shop)
hojalatero (blacksmith)
hombre bueno (arbitrador)
horno (beehive shaped outdoor oven)
hoz (sickle)
hweeldi (Navajo suffering)

I

iglesia (church)
invocación (invocation)

J

jabón de lejía (soft lye soap)
jardín de hierbas (herb garden)
jerga de lana (woolen rug)
jueces (judges)
juez (judge)

K

kachina (beneficent spirits)

L

lancero (lancer)
lanzaderas (shuttles)
latía (small dressed pole)
lazos (double rosaries)
legua (l league = 2.68 miles)
limpieza de sangre (purity of blood)
lingua franca (main language)
lisos (heddles)
luminarias (small bonfires)

M

Madre de Dios (Mother of God)
madrina (godmother)
maestro (primary school teacher)

majolica (glazed pottery)
mal de ojo (evil eye)
malacate (hoist)
malva (mallow)
manda (religious vow)
mano y metate (grind-stones)
manzanilla (camomile)
mariguana (marijuana)
mariola (aster family)
matanza de animales (butchering area)
matanza del cerdo (pig slaughter)
matracas (clackers)
mayorazgo (entailed estate)
mayordomo (overseer, also fiesta councilor)
memoria (gift)
mestizo (offspring of Indian and Spanish parents)
milagro (miracle)
milpas (crop fields)
molinero (miller)
molinillo (wooden whisk)
molino (grist mill)
moradas (sacred praying places)
morcilla (blood sausage)
mula blanca (white mule)
mulatero (muleteer)
mulos (mules)

N

nicho (niche)
nopal (prickly pear cactus)
novenas (prayers over nine days)

O

obraje (workshop)
ojos (springs)
oración (prayer)
oratorio (private chapel)

oshá (parsley family)
ovejas (sheep)

P

padre (father or priest)
padrinos (godparents)
paisano (compatriot)
palajuela (ladder)
paraje (campsite)
parroquia (parish church)
partera (midwife)
partidarios (sharecropper)
partido system (system of shares)
pastor (shepherd)
pastora (shepherdess)
patria (native land)
patria potestad (paternal authority)
patria potestad (supreme authority)
patrón (proprietor)
peine (comb beater)
peninsulares (persons born in Spain)
peones (laborers)
peso de plata (silver coins)
petaquilla de piel (leather chest)
piedra imán (lode-stone)
pieza pequeña de indios (small Indian)
piezas de indios (individual Indians)
placita (little plaza)
plumajillo (yarrow)
poblador (colonist)
pobre (poor individual)
poleo (penny royal)
portal (covered porch)
posada (inn)
pósito (pit)
pozo (water well)
praqué (field marigold)
prendorio (engagement ceremony)

prensa de lagar (grape press)
presbítero (clergy)
presidio (military headquarters)
procurador-general (attorney general)
protector de indios (protector of the Indians)
pueblo (town)
puerta de zambullo (pedestrian door)
puertón (large door)
punche (native tobacco)
punchón (wooly mullein)
pundonor (family honor)
punta de buey (ox goad)
puntas de pies (toes, not foot)

Q

quinceañera (young women's celebration of 15th birthday)

R

raja (cedar strip)
rebozo (large shawl)
reconquista (re-conquest)
reconquistador (reconqueror)
regidor (councilman)
reina (fiesta queen)
rejas (wooden bars)
repartimiento (labor system)
requerimiento (formal statement)
reredo (altar screen)
resguardo (safeguard)
residencia (judicial review)
respeto (respect)
retablo (line painting of sacred figure)
rezadores (prayer leaders)
rico (wealthy individual, land owner)

rinconera (corner cupboard)
rodezno (horizontal water wheel)

S

sabanilla (all-purpose white textile)
sala (large room, hall)
salea (sheepskin)
sálvamos (save us)
Santa Cruz (Holy Cross)
Santa Fé (Holy Christian Faith)
santero (creators of religious art)
santo (image or statue of holy person)
santuario (sanctuary)
sarape (blanket)
selenita (selenite)
señorita (unmarried woman)
siesta (afternoon rest)
silleta (chair)
sombrero (wide brimmed, low crowned hat)
soterrano (root cellar)
suertes ("ribbon" or "long-lot" platting)

T

talco (mica)
talleres de tejer (weaving workrooms)
tanques (springs/ponds)
tápalo (black woolen shawl)
tarabilla (dancing damsel)
tejano (Texan)
tela (warp threads)
telars (looms)
terrones (blocks of sod)
tewas (moccasins)
tiendita (little country store)
tienebre (branched candelabrum)
tierra amarilla (yellow clay)
tombé (small Indian drum)
torreón defensivo (watchtower)
trastero (cupboard)
trochiles (pigpens)
tuna (fruit of the prickly pear cactus)
tupa (Finnish farmhouse)
tziguma (cottonwood tree)

V

vagón (wagon to haul heavy loads)
vales (licenses)
vaquero (cowboy)
vara (1 vara = 2.8 feet)
velorio (religious wake)
viga (log beams)
vinatero (vintner)
visita (visit)
vivas (live long)

W X Y Z

yerba de tusa (coneflower)
yeso (gesso)
yugo (ox yoke)
yunques (anvils)
zaguán (covered entry or gate)

Bibliography

Alberts, D. *The Battle of Glorieta: Union Victory in the West.* College Station (TX): Texas A & M University Press, 1998.

Aranda, Charles. *Dichos, Proverbs and Sayings from the Spanish.* Santa Fe: Sunstone Press, 1977.

Atilano, C., Reid, A., Reyes, R. "An Ethno Historical Study of La Ciénega New Mexico." [thesis] Colorado Springs: Colorado College, 1980.

Awalt, B., Rhetts, P. *Charlie Carrillo: Tradition & Soul.* Albuquerque: LPD Press, 1995.

Baxter, J. O. "Livestock on the Camino Real." *El Camino Real de Tierra Adentro.* BLM Cultural Resources, New Mexico State Office, Santa Fe: 1993, 11:101-111.

Beck, W. A., Haase, Y.D. *Historical Atlas of New Mexico.* Norman (OK): University of Oklahoma Press, 1969.

Beerman, E. "The Death of an Old Conquistador: New Light on Juan de Onate." *New Mexico Historical Review*, 1979, 54(4)305-319.

Boyd, E. *Saint & Saint Makers of New Mexico.* Santa Fe: Western Edge Press, 1998.

Brooks, J. F. *Captives & Cousins: Slavery, Kinship, and Community in the Southwest Borderlands.* Williamsburg (VA): University of North Carolina Press, 2002.

Brown, L.W. *Hispano Folklife of New Mexico.* Albuquerque: University of New Mexico Press, 1978.

Brugge, D. M. "Captives and Slaves on the Camino Real." *El Camino Real de Tierra Adentro 2.* BLM Cultural Resources. New Mexico State Office, Santa Fe: 1999, 13:103-109.

Bunting, B. *Early Architecture in New Mexico.* Albuquerque: University of New Mexico Press, 1976.

Bunting, B. *John Gaw Meem: Southwest Architect.* Albuquerque: University of New Mexico Press, 1989.

C' de Baca, G. *The Eden of La Cienega.* Kearny (NE): Morris Publishing, 1998.

Campa, A. L. *Treasure of the Sangre de Cristos.* Norman (OK): University of Oklahoma Press, 1963.

Castillo, R., Griswold, D. *The Treaty of Guadalupe Hidalgo: A Legacy of Conflict.* Norman (OK): University of Oklahoma Press, 1990.

Chávez, Fray Angélico. *But Time and Chance: The Story of Padre Martinez of Taos, 1793-1867.* Santa Fe: Sunstone Press, 1981.

Chávez, Fray Angélico. *Chávez, A Distinctive American Clan of New Mexico.* New Edition. Santa Fe: Sunstone Press, 2009.

Chávez, Fray Angélico. *La Conquistadora: The Autobiography of an Ancient Statue.* Santa Fe: Sunstone Press, 1983.

Chávez, Fray Angélico and Adams, Eleanor B., Translators and Annotators. *The Missions of New Mexico, 1776.* New Edition. Santa Fe: Sunstone Press, 2012.

Chávez, Fray Angélico. *My Penitente Land.* New Edition. Santa Fe: Sunstone Press, 2012.

Chávez, Fray Angélico. *Origins of New Mexico Families.* Albuquerque: University of New Mexico Press, 1992.

Chávez, Fray Angélico. *Our Lady of the Conquest.* New Edition. Santa Fe: Sunstone Press, 2009.

Chávez, Fray Angélico. "The Penitentes of New Mexico." *New Mexico Historical Review,* 1954, 29:97-123.

Chávez, Fray Angélico. "Phoe-Yemo's Representative and the Pueblo Revolt of 1680." *New Mexican Historical Review,* 1967, 48(2):85-126.

Chávez, T.E. *New Mexico Past and Future.* Albuquerque: University of New Mexico Press, 2006.

Cobos, R. A. *Dictionary of New Mexico and Southern Colorado Spanish.* Santa Fe: Museum of New Mexico Press, 1983.

Cook, M. J. "Daughters of the Camino Real." *El Camino Real de Tierra Adentro.* BLM Cultural Resources. New Mexico State Office, Santa Fe: 1993; 11: 47-156.

Curtin, L. S. *Healing Herbs of the upper Rio Grande.* Santa Fe: Laboratory of Anthropology, 1947.

Cutter, D. C. "The Legacy of the Treaty of Guadalupe Hidalgo." *New Mexico Historical Review,* 1978; 53(4): 305-315.

Davis, W.W. *El Gringo: New Mexico and Her People.* Lincoln (NE): University of Nebraska Press; 1982.

De Aragón, Ray John. *The Legend of La Llorona.* Santa Fe: Sunstone Press, 2006

De Aragón, Ray John. *Padre Martínez and Bishop Lamy.* Santa Fe: Sunstone Press, 2006.

De Aragón, Ray John. *The Penitentes of New Mexico, Brothers of Light.* Santa Fe: Sunstone Press, 2006.

De Aragón, Ray John, translator. *Recollections of the Life of the Priest Don Antonio José Martínez* by Pedro Sanchez. Santa Fe: Sunstone Press, 2006.

Dickey, R. F. *New Mexico Village Arts.* Albuquerque: University of New Mexico Press; 1990.

Dunnington, J. O. *Guadalupe, Our Lady of New Mexico.* Santa Fe: Museum of New Mexico Press; 1999.

Ellis, Florence H., Jenkins, Myra E., Ford, Richard. *When Cultures Meet: Remembering San Gabriel Del Yunge Oweenge.* Santa Fe: Sunstone Press, 1987.

Esquibel, J. A., Colligan, J. B. *The Spanish Recolonization of New Mexico: An Account of the Families Recruited in Mexico City in 1693.* Albuquerque: Hispanic Geneological Research Center of New Mexico, 1999.

Everett, D. "The Public School Debate in New Mexico, 1850–1891." *Arizona & the West, A Quarterly Journal of History*, 1984, 26(2):107-134.

Forrest, S. *The Preservation of the Village*. Albuquerque: University of New Mexico Press, 1989.

Francis, E. K. "Padre Martinez: A New Mexican Myth." *New Mexican Historical Review*, 1956, 31:4: 265-289.

Gallegos, B. P. *Literacy, Education, and Society in New Mexico 1693–1821*. Albuquerque: University of New Mexico Press, 1992.

Grant, Blanche Chloe. *Doña Lona*. New Edition. Santa Fe: Sunstone Press, 2007.

Gregg, J. *Commerce of the Prairies*. Norman (OK): University of Oklahoma Press, 1954.

Gutierrez, R. A. *When Jesus Came, the Corn Mothers Went Away*. Stanford (CA): Stanford University Press, 1991.

Hayes, J., editor. *The Day It Snowed Tortillas: Tales from Spanish New Mexico*. Santa Fe: Mariposa Publishing, 1982.

Hendricks, R. "Road to Rebellion Road to Re-conquest." *El Camino Real de Tierra Adentro*. BLM Cultural Resources. New Mexico State Office, Santa Fe: 1993, 1:77-83.

Hernandez, M., Morga, E., Trujillo, G. "Vega y Coca/De la Vega/Laso de la Vega y Vique/Coca 1693–1800 Pt. 1." *Herencia: The Quarterly Journal of the Hispanic Geneological Research Center of New Mexico*, January 2004; 12(1): 2-16.

Hordes, S. M. "The Sephardic Legacy in New Mexico: A History of the Crypto-Jews." *Journal of the West*, 1996, 35(4):82-90.

Horgan, P. *Great River: The Rio Grande in North American History*. New York: Rinehart & Company, Inc., 1954.

Ivey, J. E. "Seventeenth-Century Mission Trade on the Camino Real." *El Camino Real de Tierra Adentro*. BLM Cultural Resources. New Mexico State Office, Santa Fe: 1993, 11:41-67.

Jordan, L. *Spanish Colonial Life in New Mexico*. Santa Fe: Colonial New Mexico Foundation, 1983.

Keleher, William A. *The Fabulous Frontier, 1846–1912*. New Edition. Santa Fe: Sunstone Press, 2008.

Keleher, William A. *Memoirs, Episodes in New Mexico History 1892–1969*. New Edition. Santa Fe: Sunstone Press, 2008.

Keleher, William A. *Turmoil in New Mexico, 1846–1868*. New Edition. Santa Fe: Sunstone Press, 2007.

Kessell, John L. "Diego de Vargas: Another Look." *New Mexico Historical Review*, 1985, 60(1):11-28.

Kessell, John L. and Hendricks, R., Dodge, M.D. *To the Royal Crown Restored: The Journals of Don Diego de Vargas, New Mexico, 1692–1694*. Albuquerque: University of New Mexico Press, 1995.

Kessell, John L. *Kiva, Cross and Crown*. Albuquerque: University of New Mexico Press, 1987.

Kessell, John L., editor. *Letters From the New World: Selected Correspondence of Don Diego de Vargas to his Family 1675–1706*. Albuquerque: University of New Mexico Press, 1992.

Kessell, John L. *The Missions of New Mexico Since 1776*. New Edition. Santa Fe: Sunstone Press. 2012.

Kessell, John L., editor. *Remote Beyond Compare: Letters of Don Diego de Vargas to His Family from New Spain and New Mexico, 1695–1705*. Albuquerque: University of New Mexico Press, 1989.

Knaut, A. L. *The Pueblo Revolt of 1680*. Norman (OK): University of Oklahoma Press, 1995.

Lacy, Ann and Valley-Fox, Anne. *Stories from Hispano New Mexico, A New Mexico Federal Writers' Project Book*. Santa Fe: Sunstone Press, 2012

Lamadrid, E. *Tesoros del Espiritu: A Portrait in Sound of Hispanic New Mexico*. Embudo (NM): El Norte Academia Publications, 1994.

La Farge, Oliver. *Behind the Mountains*. New Edition. Santa Fe: Sunstone Press, 2008.

Lange, Y. "Santo Nino de Atocha: A Mexican Cult is Transplanted to Spain." *El Palacio*, 1978, 12(1):3-8.

Laughlin, Ruth. *Caballeros*. New Edition. Santa Fe: Sunstone Press, 2007.

Lecompte, J. "The Independent Women of Hispanic New Mexico, 1821–1846." *Western Historical Quarterly*, 1981, 12(1):17-35.

Loeffler, J., Loeffler, K., Lamadrid, E. *La Musica de los Viejitos*. Albuquerque: University of New Mexico Press, 1999.

Lummis, C. F. *The Land of Poco Tiempo*. Albuquerque: University of New Mexico Press, 1952.

Maestas, J. G., Anaya, R. A. *Cuentos: Tales from the Hispanic Southwest*. Albuquerque: Museum of New Mexico Press, 1980.

Magoffin, S. *Down the Santa Fe Trail into Mexico*. Lincoln (NE): University of Nebraska Press, 1962.

Mares, E. A., Weigman, B. S., Steele, S. T., Smith, P. C., de Aragon, R. J., editors. *Padre Martinez: New Perspectives from Taos*. Taos: Millicent Rogers Museum, 1988.

Marquez, R. S. *New Mexico: A Brief Multi-History*. Albuquerque: Cosmic House, 1999.

Martinez, W. O. *Anza and Cuerno Verde: Decisive Battle*. Pueblo (CO): El Escritorio, 2004.

Miller, D. A. "Hispanos and the Civil War in New Mexico." *New Mexico Historical Review*, 1979, 54(2):105-119.

Montaño, M. *Tradiciones Nuevomexicanos: Hispano Arts and Culture of New Mexico*. Albuquerque: University of New Mexico Press, 2001.

Moorhead, M. L. *New Mexico's Royal Road: Trade and Travel on the Chihuahua Trail.* Norman (OK): University of Oklahoma Press, 1958.

Nestor, Sarah. *The Native Market of the Spanish New Mexican Craftsman, 1933-1940.* New Edition. Santa Fe: Sunstone Press, 2009.

Norstrand, R. L. *The Hispano Homeland.* Norman (OK): University of Oklahoma Press, 1992.

Nuevo Mexico Profundo: Rituals of an Indo-Hispano Homeland. Santa Fe: Museum of New Mexico Press, National Hispanic Cultural Center of New Mexico, 2000.

Olsen, M. L. "Old Ruts and New: The History of the Santa Fe Trail." *Kansas History, A Journal of the Central Plains,* 1996-1997, 19(4), 228-241.

Otero, Miguel Antonio. *My Life on the Frontier, 1864-1882.* New Edition. Santa Fe: Sunstone Press, 2007.

Otero, Miguel Antonio. *My Life on the Frontier, 1882-1897.* New Edition. Santa Fe: Sunstone Press, 2007.

Otero, Miguel Antonio. *My Nine Years as Governor of the Territory of New Mexico, 1897-1906.* New Edition. Santa Fe: Sunstone Press, 2007.

Otero-Warren, Nina. *Old Spain in Our Southwest.* New Edition. Santa Fe: Sunstone Press, 2006.

Padilla, C., editor. *Conexiones: Connections in Spanish Colonial Art.* Santa Fe: Museum of Spanish Colonial Art, 2002.

Pescador, J. J. *Crossing Borders with the Santo Niño de Atocha.* Albuquerque: University of New Mexico Press, 2009.

Peterson, K. "New Faces of the Penitentes." *El Palacio,* Spring/Summer 1992, 17-20, 52.

Preston, D., Esquibel, J. A. *The Royal Road: El Camino Real from Mexico City to Santa Fe.* Albuquerque: University of New Mexico Press, 1998.

Pino, P. B., Bustamante, A., Simmons, M., translators. *The Exposition of the Province of New Mexico, 1812.* Albuquerque: University of New Mexico Press, 1995.

Prince, L. Bradford. *New Mexico's Struggle for Statehood.* New Edition. Santa Fe: Sunstone Press 2010.

Prince, L. Bradford. *The Student's History of New Mexico.* New Edition. Santa Fe: Sunstone Press, 2008.

Riley, C. L. *Rio de' Norte: People of the Upper Rio Grande from Earliest Times to the Pueblo Revolt.* Salt Lake City: University of Utah Press, 1995.

Schackel, S. K. "Resurrected Rancho: Old Cienega Village Museum." [thesis] Albuquerque: University of New Mexico, 1982.

Sides, H. *Blood and Thunder: An Epic of the American West.* New York: Doubleday, 2006.

Simmons, Marc. *Coronado's Land: Daily Life in Colonial New Mexico.* Albuquerque: University of New Mexico Press, 1991.

Simmons, Marc. *New Mexico: An Interpretive History.* Albuquerque: University of New Mexico Press, 1977.

Simmons, Marc and Turley, Frank. *Southwestern Colonial Ironwork:The Spanish Blacksmithing Tradition from Texas to California*. New Edition. Santa Fe: Sunstone Press, 2007.

Simmons, Marc. *Spanish Pathways: Readings in the History of Hispanic New Mexico*. Albuquerque: University of New Mexico Press, 2001.

Simmons, Marc. *The Last Conquistador: Juan de Onate and the Settling of the Far Southwest*. Norman (OK): University of Oklahoma Press, 1991.

Simmons, Marc. *Witchcraft in the Southwest*. Lincoln (NE): University of Nebraska Press, 1974.

Simmons, Marc, translator. *Father Juan Augustin de Morfi's Account of Disorders in New Mexico 1788*. Isleta Pueblo (NM): Historical Society of New Mexico, 1977.

Stanley, F. *The Civil War in New Mexico*. New Edition. Santa Fe: Sunstone Press, 2011.

Steele, T. J. *Santos and Saints: The Religious Folk Art of Hispanic New Mexico*. Santa Fe: Ancient City Press, 1994.

Steele T. J. "The Spanish Passion Play in New Mexico and Colorado." *New Mexico Historical Review*, Albuquerque, 1978, 53(3):239-259.

Steele, T. J., Rhetts, P., Awalt, B., editors. *Seeds of Struggle/Harvest of Faith*. Albuquerque: LPD Press, 1998.

Taylor, L. *New Mexican Furniture 1600–1940*. Albuquerque: Museum of New Mexico Press, 1987.

Tobias, H. J. *A History of the Jews in New Mexico*. Albuquerque: University of New Mexico Press, 1990.

Tórrez, R. *Myth of the Hanging Tree: Stories of Crime and Punishment in Territorial New Mexico*. Albuquerque: University of New Mexico Press, 2008.

Tripp, V. *1824, Josefina, An American Girl*. Middleton (WI): Pleasant Company Publications, 2000.

Twitchell, Ralph Emerson. *The Leading Facts of New Mexico History, Vol. I*. New Edition. Santa Fe: Sunstone Press, 2007.

Twitchell, Ralph Emerson. *The Leading Facts of New Mexico History, Vol. II*. New Edition. Santa Fe: Sunstone Press, 2007.

Twitchell, Ralph Emerson. *The Military Occupation of the Territory of New Mexico, 1846–1851*. New Edition. Santa Fe: Sunstone Press, 2007.

Twitchell, Ralph Emerson. *Old Santa Fe*. New Edition. Santa Fe: Sunstone Press, 2007.

Twitchell, Ralph Emerson. *The Spanish Archives of New Mexico, Volume One*. New Edition. Santa Fe: Sunstone Press, 2008.

Twitchell, Ralph Emerson. *The Spanish Archives of New Mexico, Volume Two*. New Edition. Santa Fe: Sunstone Press, 2008.

Tyler, D. "The Mexican Teacher." *Red River Valley Historical Review*,1974, 1(3):207-219.

Udall, S. *Majestic Journey: Coronado's Inland Empire*. Albuquerque: University of New Mexico Press, 1987.

Vedder, Alan C. *Furniture of Spanish New Mexico*. Santa Fe: Sunstone Press, 1977.

Villagrá, G. P., Espinosa, G. (translator). *History of New Mexico*. Lancaster (PA): Lancaster Press, 1933.

Weatherford, J. *Indian Givers*. New York: Random House Publishing Group, 1988.

Weber, D. J. *Barbaros: Spaniards and Their Savages in the Age of Enlightenment*. New Haven (CT): Yale University Press, 2005.

Weber, D. J. *Foreigners in Their Native Land*. Albuquerque: University of New Mexico Press, 2003.

Weber, D. J. *On the Edge of Empire: The Taos Rancho of Los Martinez*. New Edition, Santa Fe: Sunstone Press, 2013.

Weigle, M. *Brothers of Light, Brothers of Blood: The Penitentes of the Southwest*. New Edition, Santa Fe: Sunstone Press, 2007.

Weigle, M., editor. *Hispanic Arts and Ethnohistory in the Southwest*. Santa Fe: Ancient City Press, 1983.

Weigle, M., White, P. *The Lore of New Mexico*. Albuquerque: University of New Mexico Press, 1988.

Westphal, D. "The Battle of Glorieta Pass: Its Importance to the Civil War." *New Mexico Historical Review*, 1969, 44(2):137-151.

Williams, J. L., editor. *New Mexico in Maps*. Albuquerque: University of New Mexico Press, 1986.

Worcester, D. E. "The Spread of Spanish Horses in the Southwest." *New Mexico Historical Review*, 1944, 19(3):225-232.

Index

A

Abiquiú, New Mexico, 137, 199
Abreú, Ramón, 230
acequias and irrigation, 99-100, *101*, 253
Ácoma Pueblo, 32, 33, 197
    brutal punishment by Oñate, 30-31
adobe construction, 65-66, 80, 247
"Adventures in the Past," 251
Ágreda, María de Jesús de, 127
agriculture, 29, 96, 99-100
    division of labor, 104
    Navajo (Diné), 21-22
    Pueblo Indian, 19
    tools and techniques, 104-105
alabados (songs of praise). *see* music and songs
Alire, Miguel de, 63
Almacen de Vino (winery), 81
Alvarado, Hernando de, 17, 18
Anasazi Indians. *see* Ancestral Puebloans
Anaya, Rudolfo A., 183, 184, 185, 186
Anaya de Almazán, Francisco, 41, 52, 55, 69
Anaya de Almazán, Joachin, 52
Anaya de Almazán II, Francisco, 37
Ancestral Puebloans, 19
Anza, Juan Bautista, 87-90, 228
    and Comanche Indians, 88-90
    as *criollo* governor of New Mexico, 88
    facilitated peace treaty between Pueblos, Hispanics, and Comanches, 89, 90, 155
    as guest at El Rancho de las Golondrinas, 73, 74, 87
    and Hopi Indians, 88
    memorial plaque to, 87
    Memorial Plaza to, 87
Apache Canyon, 213, 223, 224
Apache Indians (Indé), 21, 22, 33, 50, 83, 85, 89
    campaigns against, 34, 55, 59, 93
    compared to Comanches, 89-90
    confinement or relocation of, 38, 226, 227
    conflict with the Pueblos, 43, 56, 89
    different bands of, 22, 85
    obtain horses, 43, 83
    as raiders, 55, 56, 59, 83, 228
Aragon, Francisco Lopez de, 69
Archuleta, Juan de, 51
Armijo, Manuel, 90, 176, 212, 213, 223
Armijo, Salvador Manuel, 90
Army of the West, 178, 212, 213
Atchison, Topeka and Santa Fe Railroad (AT&SF), 235, 237-238
Athabascan languages, 21
Atwater, Ida, 235
Aztec Indians, 197

B

Baca, Ana, 38
Baca, Ana María, 113
Baca, Cristóbal, 52, 60
    inventory of his estate, 79
Baca, Diego Manuel, 52, 58, 59, 60, 69, 92, 215
    will and estate of, 79
Baca, Ignacio, 52
Baca, Jesús María, 230
Baca, José, 52
Baca, Juan Antonio, 94
Baca, Juan Domingo, 113
Baca, Juan Esteban, 61
Baca, Manuel, 52
Baca, Manuel de, 71, 80
Baca, Marina de Jesús, will of, 209
Baca family, 33, 58, 60-61, 63, 71, 80, 99
Baca House, Manuel de, 71-72, 80
    cocina of, 81
Baca surname, variations of, 33
Baca y Delgado, Manuel, 99
Baca y Terrus, José Francisco, 71, 80, 215, 241

Baca y Terrus, María Rita, 225
baptisms and confirmations, 203-204. *see also* pregnancy, birth, and childhood, rites and customs
Baylor, John R., 221
Becknell, William, 170-171
 "father of the Santa Fe Trail," 170
beds (camas) and mattresses, 72-73, 79, 80, 115, 161, 247
Benavides, Alonso de, 21, 42, 120, 127, 167
Bent, Charles, 174, 214-216, 230
Bent, George, 174
Bigotes of Cicuye (Pecos Pueblo), 17
birth, rites and customs. *see* pregnancy, birth, and childhood, rites and customs
bison. *see also* buffalo
 products of as trade goods, 166
blacksmiths (*herreros*), 109-110, *110*
Bonner, Jesse, 242
Bonner Duff, Glenna, 242
Bosque Redondo Reservation, 227
Brotherhood (La Hermandad). *see* Penitentes, Los
Brothers of Blood. *see* Penitentes, Los
Brothers of Light. *see* Penitentes, Los
Brown, Loren, 183
brujas, 188, 189, 191, 192
 repellant for, *150*, *190*
buffalo, 17, 228. *see also* bison
 decimation of, 221
 hunting of, 18, 179-181
 products of as trade goods, 91
bultos, 142-144
Bustamante, Adrian, 202
Bustamante, Miguel, 99
Bustamante family, 69-70
Bustamante y Tagle, Bernardo de, 58, 69
Bustamante y Tagle, Josefa, 69
Bustillo, Catalina Pérez de, 69

C
cabras (goats), 25, 105, 108
Cabrera, Josefa de, 52
Calhoun, John S., 147
Calvario de Morada de la Conquistadora, *133*

Camino Real, El. *see* El Camino Real de Tierra Adentro
Cañada de Guicú. *see* Guicú
Canby, Edward R. S., 221-223, 225, 226
capillas (chapels), 72, 124, 125. *see also* La Capilla
capitals of New Mexico, 29, 35
Cárdenas, Garcia López de, 18
Carlton, James, 226
Carpintero Shop, 109
carretas (carts), 69, 70, 104, 108
Carretería Wheelwright Shop, 108
Carrillo, Charles, 129, 131, 144
Carson, Kit, 221, 226, 226-227
 ordered slaughter of Navajo *churros*, 107
Casa de la Abuelita, *246*, 246
Casa de Manuel de Baca, 71-72, 80
 cocina of, *81*
Casa Mayor, 68, 80
Casas Grandes (Chihuahua, Mexico), 166
Casita Primitiva, 245-246
Castellanos, Joseph, 52
Castillo, Alonso del, 15
Cathedral Basilica of Saint Francis of Assisi, 47, 56, 129, 233
Cather, Willa, 231
Catholics and Catholicism, 204, 211, 230, 231, 232, 240. *see also* Christianity
 American bigotry towards, 177, 240
 conversion of Indians to, 15, 18, 32, 36, 37, 126, 211, 234
 Franciscan Order of, 26, 32, 36, 37, 38, 126, 127
 importance of, 13, 62, 96, 117, 145, 204
 martyred, 18, 41, 51, 146
 and Penitentes, 129, 130, 136, 140
Catiti, Alonzo, 42
Catron, Thomas B., 219
cattle, 19, 55, 108, 167, 227, 238
cautivos (captives), 91-94, 199
C'de Baca, Andres, 237
C'de Baca, George, 252
C'de Baca, Richard, 255
C'de Baca surname, 33
Ceballos, Bernardino de, 34
Chamuscado, Francisco Sánchez, 18
Charles II (king), 49

Charles III (king), 94
Chávez, Fray Angélico, 18, 141
Chávez, Thomas, 35
Chihuahua Trail, 171-172, 238. *see also* El Camino Real de Tierra Adentro
childbirth, rites and customs. *see* pregnancy, birth, and childhood, rites and customs
"Children's Fair," 249
Chimayó Rebellion of 1837, 175-176, 229
Chiricahua Indians, 22, 85, 228. *see also* Apache Indians
Chisholm Trail, 238
Chivington, John M., 223-225
Christianity. *see also* Catholics and Catholicism
  Indian conversion to, 17, 18, 32, 36, 37, 126
churches, construction of, 37, 124
church-state conflict, 36, 37
churro sheep, 75, 75, 105, 106, 106-107, 107
Cibola, Seven Cities of, 16, 17
cibolaros (Hispanic buffalo hunters), 179-181
Cicuye Pueblo, 17. *see also* Pecos Pueblo
Ciénega. *see* La Ciénega
Cieneguilla. *see* La Cieneguilla
Civil War, United States, 220-226
Clark, Meriwether Lewis, 213
clothing, 152-153
Cochiti Pueblo, 17, 59
cocinas. see kitchens
cofradía (confraternity), 129
colcha, 79
Colorado, mines of, 221, 223, 227
Colorado Volunteers, 223-225
Comanche Indians (Numunu), 128, 180, 227, 228
  compared to Apaches, 89-90
  Cuerno Verde, 88-89, 198
  Ecueracapa, 89, 155
  education of, 155
  and Juan Bautista Anza, 88-90
  Los Comanches (the play), 198
  peace treaty with Pueblos and Hispanics, 89, 90, 155, 181
  as raiders, 85, 86, 88, 89, 94, 110, 128

comancheros, 169, 228
Concha, Fernando de la, 155
Connelly, Henry, 223
conversion of Indians to Catholicism. *see* Catholics and Catholicism
conversos, 27, 50
Coronado, Francisco Vásquez de,
  death of, 18
  entrada of, 16-17
  return to New Spain, 18
Cubero, Pedro Rodríguez, 53
Cuerno Verde (Comanche leader). *see* Comanche Indians
curanderas (healers), 159-161, 202, 247
Curtin, Leonora Frances (Mrs. Y. A. Paloheimo), 241, 242, 257-261
Curtin, Leonora Scott Muse, 160, 241, 242, 257, 258
Curtin-Paloheimo House, 258
custos, 38, 127, 167

D
Death Comes for the Archbishop (Cather), 231
death rites and customs, 135, 209-210
Delgado, Francisco, 81
Delgado, Manuel Francisco, 103, 113, 127, 155-156, 158, 244
  library of, 155, 156
  as owner of Las Golondrinas, 155, 156
  will and estate of, 155
Delgado Ranch, 214, 216
  as name for El Rancho de las Golondrinas, 113, 213, 214
Delgado Tin Shop, 81
Denver and Rio Grande (D&RG) railroad, 237-238
dichos, 186-187
Diego, Juan, 140-141
diseases. *see* health care and diseases
Domínguez, Francisco Atanasio, 127, 128
doors, 67
Dorantes, Andrés, 15
droughts, 39, 88
Dunnington, Jacqueline Orsini, 142
Durango, Diocese of, 128, 129
dyes, 75, 76, 161, 164

285

cochineal, 76
indigo, 76

E
Ecueracapa (Comanche leader), 89, 155
El Alamo, 49, 50, 51, 63, 69, 86, 237
El Calvario (Calvary Mount), 132, 139
El Camino Real de Tierra Adentro, 29, 36, 69, 127, 166-169, 171
  "father of El Camino Real," 167
  importance of, 96, 147, 166
  Las Golondrinas as *paraje* on, 64, 73
El Cuarto de Recibo, 73
El Morro National Monument, "Inscription Rock," 34, 48
El Rancho de las Golondrinas,
  as Delgado Ranch, 113, 213, 214
  first buildings of, 61
  first families of, 58-61
  first reference to, 54
  as movie set, 244
  museum rooms described, 71-75
  ownership of, 58, 155, 156, 240-241
  as *paraje*, 64, 73
  patron saint of, 45, *119*, 125, 193-195
  restoration, preservation, and transformation to a museum, 241-249
  special programming, 249-251. *see also* individual events
El Rancho de las Golondrinas Charitable Trust, 42
El Santo Niño de Atocha (Holy Child of Atocha), 122-123, *123*
  and the Bataan Death March, 124-125
El Turco (the Turk), 17
El Viñedo Gallegos, 81
Emancipation Proclamation, 94
encomenderos, 29
encomiendas, 23, 27, 29, 37, 51, 56
Escalante, Sylvestre Velez, 127
Espejo, Antonio de, 18, 24
Espinosa, J. Manuel, 183
Esquivel, Juan José, 175
estancias, 38, 52
Esteban, 16
  murder of, 15
  other names for, 15
Eulate, Juan de, 93

F
"Fall Festival," 193
Farfán, Francisco, 51, 52, 57
farms and farming. *see* agriculture
fashions, 152-153
Fenyes, Eva Scott Muse, 258, 260
Ferdinand and Isabella, 31, 35
"Fiber Arts Festival," 249
"Fiesta de Los Niños," 250
Fiesta de Santa Fé, 56, 69
fiestas, 70, 192-193
floors, 67
fogóns (fireplaces), 67, 72, 73, 74. *see also* La Cocina con Fogón de Pastor
folk dramas, 196-200
folklore, 183-187
foods, 96-98, 108, 132
  of Pueblo Indians, 19
France,
  illegal trade with New Mexico, 169
  rivalry and war with Spain, 83-85
  supplying arms to Indian tribes, 88
  traders from, 83, 84, 91, 92, 230
Franciscans. *see* Catholics and Catholicism
French and Indian War, 85
furniture, 79-80, 115, 247

G
Gadsden Purchase, 218
Gallegos, Bernard P., 158-159
Garcia, Miguel, 52, 54
Garcia, Nasario, 183
genízaros, 92, 94, 113, 137, 176, 199. *see also* Plains Indians.
  as Penitentes, 130
Geronimo (Chiricahua Apache leader), 228
Glorieta Pass, Battle of, 223
  re-enactments, *222, 224, 225*
goats. *see cabras*
Godoy, Francisco Lucero, 47
gold, 16, 18, 24, 29
  fields in California, 218, 221, 223
  fields in Colorado, 221
  mythical kingdom of, 16, 17
Golondrinas, Las. *see* El Rancho de las Golondrinas,

Gonzáles, Andres, 99
Gonzáles, José Andres, 100
Gonzáles, José (of Ranchos de Taos), 176
Gonzáles, María Cleofas, 236
Gonzáles, Nazario, 94, 100, 225, 234
Goodnight-Loving Trail, 227, 238
Gran Quivira, 127
Great Taos Trade Fair, 90, 92
Gregg, Josiah, 156, 158, 159, 170, 176, 177, 178
Griego y Maestas, José, 183, 184, 185, 186
Griffin, William, 95
Grijalva, Josefa López Sambrano de, 42, 47
grist mills, *see molinos*
Guadalupe, Our Lady of. *see* Our Lady of Guadalupe
Guicú, 100, 240. *see also* La Ciénega, village of,
   Cañada de, 59
   San José de, 59, 125
gypsum rock, 66

H

Harrington, John P., 257, 258
"Harvest Festival," 81, 97, 105, 182, 250
Hawikúh (Zuni town), 15, 16, 17
Healing Herbs of the Upper Río Grande (Curtin,L.S.M.), 160, 257
health care and diseases, 39, 159-161. *see also* herbs, healing
"Herb and Lavender Fair," 250
herbs, healing, 161-165, 202
   uses in witchcraft, 191
Hermandad (The Brotherhood). *see* Penitentes, Los
Hermanos de Luz (Brothers of Light). *see* Penitentes, Los
Hermanos de Nuestro Padre Jesús Nazareno (Brotherhood of our Father Jesus of Nazareth). *see* Penitentes, Los
Hermanos de Sangre (Brothers of Blood). *see* Penitentes, Los
Hermanos Penitentes (The Penitent Brothers). *see* Penitentes, Los
herreros. see blacksmiths
hidalgos (minor nobleman), 27, 30
hide-tanning, 181, *181*
Hojalatería (tin workshop), 81

"Hollywood on the Ranch," 251
Holy Child of Atocha, 119, 122
Hopi Indians, 30, 50, 51, 88
hornos, 71, 73, 251
horses and horsemanship
   aided ciboleros (Hispanic buffalo hunters), 179-180
   assisted Indians during Pueblo Revolt, 41
   assisted Plains Indians for raids, 43, 83
   breeding neglected since horses easily stolen, 174
   New Mexicans had good horsemanship, 174
Humaña, Antonio Gutiérrez de, 19

I

iglesias, 124, 207, 210. *see also* churches
Indians, nomadic. *see* nomadic Indians, and individual tribes
Indians, Plains. *see* Plains Indians, and individual tribes
Indians, Pueblo. *see* Pueblo Indians, and individual tribes
Inquisition, Spanish, 36, 37, 38, 42, 127, 189
Isleta Pueblo, 41-42

J

Jaramillo, Alonzo Varela, 69
Jémez Pueblo, 51
jergas (woven wool rugs), 75, 79, 106, 153
   as covering and bedding on the floor, 67, 73, 80, 160
   as trade goods, 172
Jewish ancestry, 112. *see also conversos*
Jicarilla Apache Indians, 22, 85, 88. *see also* Apache Indians
Jorge, António, 52
Jorge, Bernabé, 52, 54, 69
Jornada del Muerto, 167
Josefina, American Girl doll, 171, 172, 251
Jumano Indians, 22, 127

K

kachinas (beneficent spirits), 39
Kearny, Stephen Watts, 178, 212-215
Kearny Code, 214, 219

Keresan Indians, 20, 21, 30, 54
Keresan language, 19
Kessell, John L., 44, 46, 49, 53, 259
Kewa Pueblo, 28, 38, 42, 51, 59
   formerly known as Santo Domingo Pueblo, 17
Kiowa Indians, 180, 227
kitchens (*cocinas*), 72, 76, 81. *see also* La Cocina con Fogón de Pastor
   description of, 72-73

L

La Capilla, 61, 62, 125, *126*, 140
La Ciénega, village of,
   modern changes, 252-254
   other names for, 59
   Spanish settlers of, 59
La Ciénega Pueblo, 42, 54
   aka La Ciénega de Carbajal Pueblo, 20
La Ciénega Valley. *see also* individual subjects
   as art colony, 240, 254
   modern changes, 252-254
   Pueblo Indians living in, 20
La Cieneguilla, hamlet of, 52, 128, 240, 255
   Indian raids on, 55, 59, 86, 128
La Cieneguilla grant, 41, 255
La Cieneguilla Pueblo, 50, 55, 255
   petroglyphs, *21*, 21
La Cocina con Fogón de Pastor, 61, 72-73
La Conquistadora, 42, 50, 120, 122, 233
   aka Nuestra Señora de la Asunción, 42
   aka Nuestra Señora de los Remedios, 42, 47
   aka Nuestra Señora del Rosario, 42
   Confraternity (Cofradía) of, 69, 196
   procession of, 196
   renamed Our Lady of Peace, 47
"La Constancia," 111
La Hermandad. *see* Penitentes, Los
La Llorona, 183-184
Lamy, Jean Baptiste, 142, 227, 230, 233
   conflict with Padre Martínez, 230-232
   established parochial schools, 233-234
Lamy, John, nephew of Jean Baptiste Lamy, 232
Lancastrian System of education, 157, 158

land, allocation of, 99
land grants, 25, 52, 61, 63, 218
   Cerrillos, 55
   La Ciénega Pueblo, 54, 55
   La Cieneguilla, 41, 255
   Maxwell, 230
   Mora, 219
   Santa Cruz, 154
   Tierra Amarilla, 219
Lane, William Carr, 217
La Sala de Fundadores (the Founders' Room), 61, 125
La Salle, Robert Cavelier de, 83
La Salón y Capilla, 61. *see also* La Capilla; La Sala de Fundadores
Las Golondrinas. *see* El Rancho de las Golondrinas,
Las Leyes de las Indias, 58, 147
Las Posadas, 200
Las Vegas, East, New Mexico, 238
latias, 66
La Tiendita, 173
La Villa de Santa Fé. *see* Santa Fe, New Mexico
La Villa Real de Santa Fé de San Francisco de Asis. *see* Santa Fe, New Mexico
law and order,
   for Indians, 147
   Spanish, 58, 147-150
   in Territorial period, 218-220
Leonora Curtin Wetland Preserve, 257
Lincoln, Abraham, 94, 212
Lipan Indians, 22. *see also* Apache Indians
literacy, 153-159
livestock, 104-108, 110. *see also* different animals
Lomas y Colmenares, Juan, 24
"Long Walk," the, 227
looms, 77-79
Lopez, Manuel, 59. *see also* Tenorio de Alba, Manuel
López de Aragon, Francisco, 38
López de Mendizábal, Bernardo, 38
Los Comanches (the play), 198
Los Hermanos de Luz. *see* Penitentes, Los
Los Hermanos de Nuestro Padre Jesús Nazareno. *see* Penitentes, Los

Los Hermanos de Sangre. *see* Penitentes, Los
Los Hermanos Penitentes. *see* Penitentes, Los
Los Matachines, 197, 197-198
Los Moros y Los Cristianos, 28, 29, 196-197
Los Pastores, 199, 201
Louisiana Purchase, 85
Lummis, Charles, 137
Luna, Solomon, 238

M
Magoffin, James, 213
Magoffin, Susan Shelby, 113
Malinche, 198
Manifest Destiny, 176-178, 212
Manrique, José, 90
Manso de Contreras, Juan, 42
Manuel Apodaca Blacksmith Shop, 110
Márquez, Diego, 38, 42
Márquez, Margarita, 42
marriage rites and customs, 111-112, 149, 205-209
Martín, Cristóbal, 63
Martínez, Antonio José, 158, 216, 217, 229
    conflict with Bishop Lamy, 230-232
    excommunication of, 230
    and publishing, 229-230
Martínez, Felix, 59
Martínez, Julian (Mexican sculptor), 87
Martínez y Alire, Jerome, 129
medical care. *see* health care and diseases; herbs, healing
Medina, Alonso de, 52
Medina, Manuela de, 52, 57
Meem, John Gaw, 248, 260
Melasera Vieja, 97
Mendoza, Antonio de, 16
Mescalero Apache Indians, 22, 85, 226, 227. *see also* Apache Indians
mestizos, 27
Mexico,
    independence from Spain, 13, 128, 145
    Mexican-American War, 177-178, 212-219
    relations with Texas, 211
    relations with United States, 211

trade restrictions of, 170
mills, grist. *see molinos*
missionaries, Franciscan, 18, 127, 128, 145
Moctezuma, 198
molinos (grist mills), 100-104, 244, 253
    El Molino Grande de Sapelló, 243, 244
    Molino Barela de Truchas, 101, *102*, 103, *103*, 244
    Molino Viejo de las Golondrinas, 103, 244
    Molino Viejo de Talpa, 104
Mondragon, Roberto, 254
Monterrey, Count of, 26
Montoya, Andres, 52, 69, 79, 93, 98
Montoya, Bartolomé, 61
Montoya, Diego de, 61
Montoya, Juan de, 35
Moors, 112, 122, 197
    defeat of in Spain, 28, 31, 33, 35, 45, 111, 122
    influence on *Los Matachines*, 197
    invasion of Spain, 16, 28
    Los Moros y los Cristianos, 196-197
Moqui Indians, 59. *see also* Hopi Indians
Mora, Antonio José, 86
Morada de la Conquistadora, 137-139, *138*
moradas, 131, 133, 137, 138, 139
Mora House, 161, 165, 247, 249
Mora-Lisano family, 86
morality plays, 192, 199-201
mules *(mulas)*, 25, 59, 69, 108, 110, 174, 188
    Colonel Kearny pastured at Delgado Ranch, 213
    Diego de Vargas pastured in upper La Ciénega, 49
    for Governor Henry Connelly, 223
    how used as pack animals, 174
    mulateros (muleteers), 174
    slaughtered by Major John M. Chivington at Cañoncito, 225
    at Valverde Ford, 222
Munroe, John, 218
music and songs,
    as expression of faith, 117, 134, 194-195, 201
    as tool for converting Indians, 37
    wedding songs, 207-208

N

Nana (Chiricahua Apache leader), 228
Nanillé, 199
Naranjo (Pueblo leader). *see* Pueblo Revolt of 1680
Narváez, Pánfilo de, 15
Native Americans, 13. *see also* Indians, and individual tribes
"Native Market," 258
Navajo Indians (Diné), 21, 22, 33, 50, 56
    campaigns against, 34, 93
    churros ordered slaughtered by "Kit" Carson, 107
    confinement or relocation of, 226
    the "Long Walk," 227
    as raiders, 56, 226
    United States war against, 107, 226-227
Nazareno, Nuestro Padre Jesús, 138
New Mexico,
    under the Confederacy, 223
    as territory of United States, 218
New Spain, 15, 16, 18, 23, 24, 26, 35, 36, 37. *see also* Mexico
Niza, Marcos de, 15, 16, 17
Noel, Delores, 235
nomadic Indians, 19, 21, 22, 43, 181, 229. *see also* Plains Indians
norias (water wells), 71, 73
Nuestra Señora de Guadalupe, 140. *see also* Our Lady of Guadalupe
Nuestra Señora de la Asunción. *see* La Conquistadora
Nuestra Señora de los Remedios, 45, 46. *see also* La Conquistadora
Nuestra Señora del Rosario, 122. *see also* La Conquistadora
Nuestro Padre Jesús Nazareno, 131
Nueva España, 15. *see also* Mexico

O

Ohkay Owingey Pueblo, 29, 35, 88, 198
Oklahoma, 17, 18, 86, 218
    Indian Territory of, 227
Oñate, Cristóbal, 34
Oñate Monument and Visitors Center, 31
Oñate y Salazar, Adelantado Juan de, 19, 126, 129
    as *alcalde mayor* (governor) of San Luis Potosi, 24
    brutal punishment of Ácomans, 30-31
    death of, 34
    entrada of 1598, 19, 23-28, 129
    family of, 23
    "father of El Camino Real," 167
    as governor of New Mexico, 24-34
    at "Inscription Rock," 34
    Los Moros y Los Cristianos, 196
    relations with Pueblo Indians, 28, 29, 30, 32
    resignation of, 33
    trial of, 33, 34
Oratorio de San Ysidro (Saint Isidore Chapel), 193, 248, 248
Ortiz, Toribio, 63
Ortiz family, 59
Ortiz y Pino, Jerry, 255
Otermín, Antonio de. *see* Pueblo Revolt of 1680
Our Lady of Conquest, 47. *see also* La Conquistadora
Our Lady of Guadalupe, 119, 140-142
    "Four Apparitions of" (a morality play), 201
Our Lady of Peace, 47. *see also* La Conquistadora
ox-blood floors, 67

P

Páez Hurtado, Juan, 56, 196
Paloheimo, Leonora Frances Curtin. *see* Curtin, Leonora Frances
Paloheimo, Y. A., 241, 242, 257, 259
parajes, 64, 69, 73, 168
parroquías, 55, 233
Pawnee Indians, 83, 84, 85
peace treaty between Pueblos, Hispanics, and Comanches, 89, 90, 155, 181
Pecos Pueblo, 17
Pecos Pueblo Trade Fair, 90, 92, 169
Peñalosa, Diego Dionisio de,
    as governor of New Mexico, 37

Penitentes, Los, 129-140
    The Brotherhood, 129
    death customs of, 135
    La Hermandad, 129, 132
    Los Hermanos de Luz, 130
    Los Hermanos de Nuestro Padre Jesús Nazareno, 129, 130
    Los Hermanos de Sangre, 129
    Los Hermanos Penitentes, 129
    and Padre Martínez, 229
    privacy of, 136-137
    Semana Santa, 132-134
    and women, 130, 131
Peralta, Pedro de,
    as founder of La Villa de Santa Fé, 34, 35
    as governor of New Mexico, 34, 35
Pérez, Albino, 175-176
petroglyphs, 21, 21, 255
Pierce, Donna, 61
Pigeon's Ranch, 224, 225
Pike, Zebulon Montgomery, 170
Pino, Elfego, 241, 258
Pino, Facundo and María, 242, 253
Pino, Germán, 232, 236
Pino, Pedro Baptista, 89-90, 99, 113, 127, 155, 158, 241
Pino family, 60, 241
Pino House, 242, 253
Piro Pueblo, 42
placita, 70
Placita, Golondrinas, 70, 71, 72
Plains Indians, 83, 88, 226, 227. see also individual tribes
    as raiders, 86, 226
    relations with Anglo Americans, 226, 227, 228
    on reservations, 227
    as slaves, 92, 94, 130. see also *genízaros*
    as traders, 166, 169
Po-he-yemo (of Taos). see Pueblo Revolt of 1680, Naranjo
Polk, James K., 212
Popé (San Juan Pueblo medicine man), 39-41, 43
pregnancy, birth, and childhood, rites and customs, 202-203

pregnancy, birth, and childhood rites and customs
    baptisms and confirmations, 203-204
    Padrinos de pila (baptismal godparents), 203-204
    quinceañera, 204
presidios, 48
Price, Sterling, 214, 215, 216
printing presses, 229-230
Protestantism, 136, 234, 239
Pueblo Indians, 19, 22, 89. see also individual tribes; Pueblo-Spanish relations
    ceremonies of, 19, 20, 39
    education of, 154
    La Ciénega (de Carbajal) Pueblo, 20
    La Cieneguilla Pueblo, 21, 50, 55, 255
    livelihoods of, 19
    populations devasted by European diseases, 39
    religious persecution of, 39
    responses to *reconquista* , 50
    Tziguma Pueblo, 20
    use and abuse of, 29, 30, 37, 38
Pueblo Revolt of 1680, 20, 35, 39-44, 127
    Naranjo's important role in, 40, 43
    Otermín as governor during, 40-43
    Popé as leader of, 39-41, 43
    Spanish colonists flee, 42, 47, 52, 120, 167
Pueblo-Spanish relations. see also Pueblo Revolt of 1680
    allies against raiding tribes, 86, 88
    gradual acculturation occurs, 43
    improvement after Pueblo Revolt, 56
    peace treaty between Pueblos, Hispanics, and Comanches, 89, 90, 155, 181
    Pueblo-Spanish War, 44
    pueblo uprising of 1696, 51
Pyron, Charles, 223

Q
quinceañera, 204
Quiros, Diego Arias, 52
Quivira Pueblo, 17, 18

R
Rael, Alonso, 255-256

Rael de Aguilar, Alonso (a.k.a. Alphonso), 55
raiders, Indian, 22, 33, 35, 68, 69, 85, 86, 129. see also Apache Indians; Comanche Indians; Navajo Indians
railroads, 173, 235, 236-239
ranching, cattle, 227
Rancho de Las Golondrinas. see El Rancho de las Golondrinas
Ratón, New Mexico, 238
Ratón School, 235, *236*
re-conquest *(reconquista)* of 1692. see Vargas, Diego de
"Renaissance Fair," 250
repartimiento (labor system), 30, 37
requerimiento, 17
reredos (altar screens), 121, 125, *126*
resguardos, 66
residencias, 53
retablos, 142-143
Riba, Miguel García de la, 52
Río Arriba Revolt, 175-176
Riva, Juan Garcia de la, 54
Rodríguez, Agustín, 18
Rosario Chapel, 47
Rosas, Luís de, 37-38
Ruiz, Juan, 51

S
saints, 121, 121-123
    patron, of agriculture, 45, 119, 125
    patron, of cooks, 121
    patron, of El Rancho de las Golondrinas, 45, *119*, 125, 193-195
    patron, of Madrid, Spain, 45, 125
    patron, of shepherds, 121
Salazar, Juan de Frías, 26
salt, 38
San Antonio de Padua, 121, 122
Sanchez, Robert, 47
San Felipe Pueblo, 17, 28, 59
San Francisco, *presidio* of, 87
San Gabriel del Yunge Oweenge, 29, 33, 35
San Gerónimo Day, 195-196
San Ignacio de Loyola, 119
San Ildefono Pueblo, 19
San José de Guicú. see Guicú

San Juan Pueblo, 29. see also Ohkay Owingeh Pueblo
San Pascual Bailón
    patron saint of cooks, 121
    patron saint of shepherds, 121
San Santiago, 31, 122, 197
Santa Fe, New Mexico,
    350th anniversary of the founding of, 47
    founding date debate, 35
    as La Villa de Santa Fé, 34-35, 48, 50
    as La Villa Real de Santa Fé de San Francisco de Asis, 35
    officially renamed Santa Fé 1608, 35
Santa Fe Botanical Garden, 257
Santa Fe Ring, 219
Santa Fe Trail, 75, 76, 91, 227, 247
    description of, 170-173, 236
    effects on New Mexico, 147, 152, 173
    "father of the Santa Fe Trail," 170
    and the Mexican-American War, 178, 212
Santa María, Juan de, 18
santeros, art of, 142-144
Santo Domingo Pueblo, 17. see also Kewa Pueblo
Santo Tomás, 198
San Ysidro Labrador (Saint Isidore the Farmer), 45, 119, 121, 151, 248
    bulto of, *119*, 125, 193
    patron saint of agriculture, 45
    patron saint of El Rancho de las Golondrinas, 45, *119*, 125, 193-195
    patron saint of Madrid, Spain, 45
    procession of, 193-195, *194*
schools and education, 153-159, 233-235
Scurry, William, 224
Sebastiana, Doña (allegorical figure of Death), 138-139, 184-185
Segesser Hide paintings, 85
Seven Cities of Cibola, 16, 17
Sheehan, Michael J., 140, 232
sheep. see also *churro* sheep
sheep husbandry, 146-147
Shepherd's Cabin, 244-245
Sibley, Henry H., 221-222, 225
Sierra Village, 161, 193, 244, 245, 245, 246
Sigüenza de Góngora, Carlos, 49

Siler, Kip, 225
Simmons, Marc, 13, 35, 71, 176, 184, 222, 256, 259
slaves and slavery, 15, 220-221
　acceptance and prevalence of, 93
　Black, 27, 53, 55, 211, 212, 220
　Indian, 15, 93, 94, 95, 112, 167. see also cautivos; genizaros
　laws regarding, 94, 95, 145, 211
Slough, John, 223
social life and customs, 96, 111-114, 149-151, 202-210. see also death rites and customs; marriage rites and customs; pregnancy, birth, and childhood rites and customs; women's lives
Sosa, Gaspar Castaño de, 18-19
Southern Pacific Railroad, 238
Spain,
　acquires Louisiana Purchase, 85
　colonization of New Mexico, 13, 15-19, 24-39, 45-56
　lack of funds for New Mexico's churches, 88
　New Mexico's cultural ties to, 256
　prohibitions against trade with foreigners, 83-84, 92, 169
　rivalry and war with France, 83-85
　support of American colonies, 88
"Spanish Colonial Days," 251
Spanish Market, 258
"Spring Festival," 193, 249
stagecoaches, 236, 237
St. Vrain, Céran, 174
"Summer Festival," 250
Sumner, "Bull," 213

T
Taller de Cuero leatherworking shop, 91
Talleres de Tejer (weaving workrooms), 75, 78
Tamarón y Romeral, Pedro, 86
Tanoan Indians, 21
Tanoan language, 19
Taos Pueblo, 17, 195-196
Taos Rebellion of 1847, 214, 227, 229, 230
Tapeste de Teñir (Dye Shed), 76, 77
telegraphs and telephones, 238

Tenorio, Miguel, 63
Tenorio de Alba, Manuel, 59, 92
terrones, 80
Tewan language, 19
Tewa Pueblos, 17
Texas,
　annexation by the U.S.1845, 177, 178, 211
　boundary dispute with New Mexico, 218
　claims on New Mexico, 178
　as Republic, 177, 178, 211
　revolt of 1836, 177, 211
The Brotherhood. see Penitentes, Los
The Exposition on the Province of New Mexico, 1812 (Pino), 89-90
The Land of Poco Tiempo (Lummis), 137
Tiendita (little country store), 81
tierra amarilla (yellow clay), 66
Tigüex villages, 17-18
Tigüex War, 18
tin work, 81
Tiwan language, 19, 41
Tompiro language, 22
torreónes defensivo (watchtowers), 68, 68, 74
Towan language, 19
trade and traders, 93, 147, 168, 170
　cautivos (captives) as trade goods, 90-94
　French, 83, 84, 169
　Indian, 19, 39, 68, 89, 90-92, 166, 169
　Mexican restrictions on, 170
　Spanish prohibitions against, 83-84, 92, 169
　trade fairs, 90-92, 169
　trade goods, 76, 79, 91, 169, 173, 180-181
Traditional Historic Communities designation, 255
trails and roads, 166-173. see also Chihuahua Trail; El Camino Real de Tierra Adentro; Santa Fe Trail
trapping and hunting, 178-181
Treaty of Guadalupe Hidalgo, 217, 219
Treviño, Juan Francisco, 39
Tupatú, Lorenzo, 47, 48
Tupatú, Luis, 43, 47, 48
Turley, Simeon, 215

293

U
United States,
  Civil War, 220-226
  Mexican-American War, 177-178, 212-219
  relations with Mexico, 211, 217
  war against and relocation of Indians, 226, 227
Urrutia, José de, 52
Ute Indians (Nuutsiu), 22, 85, 88, 89

V
Vaca (Baca), Cristóbal, 32
Vaca, Cabeza de, 15, 22, 32
Vaca surname, variations of, 33
Vargas, Diego de,
  arrest, trial, and vindication, 53
  death of, 55–56
  entrada of, 45-47, 142
  family of, 45, 46, 55
  financial claims of, 49
  granted *encomienda*, 54
  at "Inscription Rock," 48
  and La Conquistadora, 120
  Mexican lover, Nicolasa Rincón, 46, 55
  and re-conquest *(reconquista)* of 1692, 46-52
  requests for rewards, 49, 53
  violence after re-conquest 1693, 50
Vargas, Juan Manuel de, 53
Vega, Cristóbal de la, 52
Vega y Coca, María Josefa, 52, 61
Vega y Coca, Miguel, 52, 57-61, 63, 69
  as alcalde, 59, 63
  purchased Las Golondrinas *estancia*, 58
Vega y Coca family, 57-61, 63, 80
  lineage of, 64
Velasco, Cristóbal, 51
Velasco, Luis de, 24, 26, 34, 36
Vélez Cachupín, Tomás, 94
Victorio (Chiricahua Apache leader), 228
Vieira, José, 232
vigas, 66, 73
Villagrá, Gaspar Pérez de, 26, 27, 31, 122, 197
Villasur, Pedro de, 85

Virgen de Guadalupe, 141. *see also* Our Lady of Guadalupe
"Viva México!" celebration, 249

W
wagon trains, 69, 168-169
walls, adobe, 66-67, 247-248
water supply. *see also acequias* and irrigation
  allocation of, 99-100
weaponry, 68, 74
weaving, 75-79, *78*
Weigle, Marta, 183
westerns (literature), 177
Wheelwright Shop. *see* Carretería Wheelwright Shop
windows, 66, 67, 73
"Wine Festival," 249
wine making, 81-82, 108
witchcraft, 159, 187-192
women's lives, 111-112, 114-116, 149-151, 218
  clothing of, 152-153
wool, 76, 77, 79, 161. *see also jergas*
  from buffalos, 180
  from *churro* sheep, 76, 79, 106, 170

Y
yarns, 76, 77, 79
yeso, 66, 67, 142, 143, 144
Yunge Pueblo. *see* San Gabriel del Yunge Oweenge

Z
Zaldivar, Juan de, 24, 30
Zubiría y Escalante, José Antonio Laureano, 129
  forbid Penitente practices, 136
Zumárraga, Juan de, 140-141
Zuni Pueblo, 15, 17, 127
Zutucapán (Ácoman chief), 30

www.ingramcontent.com/pod-product-compliance
Lightning Source LLC
Chambersburg PA
CBHW020832160426
43192CB00007B/621